Y0-BCR-965

2011

THE PRACTICE OF KALACHAKRA

DATE DUE

GAYLORD — PRINTED IN U.S.A.

THE PRACTICE OF KALACHAKRA

by Glenn H. Mullin

Including translations of important texts on the Kalachakra Tantra

Foreword by H. H. the Dalai Lama

Snow Lion Publications
Ithaca, New York

Snow Lion Publications
P.O. Box 6483
Ithaca, New York 14851
USA

Printed in the USA

ISBN 0-937938-95-5

Library of Congress Cataloging-in-Publication Data

Mullin, Glenn H.
    The practice of Kālachakra / by Glenn H. Mullin : with
translations of important texts on the Kālachakra tantra : foreword
by H.H. the Dalai Lama.
        p.   cm.
    Includes bibliographical references.
    ISBN 0-937938-95-5 : $12.95
    1. Kālachakra (Tantric rite)   I. Title.
BQ7699.K34M85   1991
294.3'925—dc20   91-27945
                                                        CIP

Table of Contents

PART TWO: SELECTED TIBETAN READINGS

LIST OF ILLUSTRATIONS

THE DALAI LAMA

FOREWORD

All teachings given by the Buddha have as their essential purpose the taming and transformation of the mind. The Buddhist view is that when we improve the quality of our mind, our wisdom, not only do we benefit ourselves in the most lasting and pervasive sense, but indirectly we also greatly benefit all other sentient beings. Training the mind is the key to achieving lasting inner peace and happiness.

The spiritual path can be likened to building a house. Even though we might like to begin by erecting the walls or roof, in fact we must first put in the foundations.

Similarly, when we approach the task of transforming the mind we have to begin by establishing a firm foundation. We may feel that because the real enemies of sentient beings are our own delusions, we should immediately apply the most powerful antidote in order to totally remove them from their source. However, the transformation of the mind is one undertaking that can only be accomplished in stages. We must begin at the beginning.

The first step is to cultivate the intention to avoid engaging in negative, harmful, self-destructive ways of body, speech and mind. This creates an inner environment wherein we can accomplish the second step, which is the elimination of the delusions. Thirdly, we attempt to extract the very seeds or imprints of delusion.

For this reason the Buddhist path begins with cultivating the three higher trainings of self-discipline, meditative concentration, and the wisdom understanding emptiness. When these three have been made firm one can take up the methods of the bodhisattva path, in which one cultivates the aspiration to achieve highest enlightenment for the benefit of all sentient beings, and on the basis of that aspiration engages in the six perfections of generosity, self-discipline, patience, effort, meditative stabilization, and wisdom. Finally, these methods can be complemented with the tantric practices, which begin with the receiving of the initiations and tantric commitments, and involve the powerful trainings of the generation and completion yogas.

In this way we can gradually build the house of a spiritual practice having the potency to totally uproot the delusions, and to transport the mind to the state of final enlightenment.

Tantric practice is more powerful than the general sutra trainings for a number of reasons. One of these is that it fully integrates the factors of method and wisdom. In the sutra path one meditates on emptiness, or the non-inherent existence of phenomena, within the framework of the compassionate aspiration to highest enlightenment. Meditation on emptiness is the factor of wisdom, and the bodhisattva aspiration is method. However, in the sutra path these two cannot be generated simultaneously within one moment's consciousness by a practitioner on ordinary levels. In the tantric path, as method one generates the mandala and deities, and then focuses on their empty nature. In this way method and wisdom arise simultaneously in the entity of one mind.

In buddhahood, method and wisdom, body and mind, are of one taste. The tantric path utilizes this dynamic from the very beginning, and thus produces a far more rapid enlightenment. The exclusive nature of the tantric path is that it brings an important aspect of the result of practice - ie., the integral character of buddhahood - into the structure of our training right now. The meditation is performed with awareness of emptiness, and it is that consciousness focused on emptiness which is generated in the form of the mandala deities. This is a feature of all four classes of tantras. In highest yoga tantra this principle is taken even further, with the practitioner utilizing the most subtle levels of bodily energies and of consciousness, levels inaccessible to the untrained person.

Here the clear light mahamudra is taken as the exclusive substantial cause of a Buddha's wisdom-truth body. Through bringing clear light mahamudra into the path, sudden enlightenment becomes possible. This most subtle technique is found only in highest yoga tantra.

In general, an understanding of a spiritual method is itself a blessing; but in order to enter the tantric path it is said to be necessary to first receive the blessings of the initiation ceremony from a qualified master holding an unbroken lineage of transmission. This empowers one to enter into the tantric yogas, and plants the seeds for future realization.

Later, when one engages in the generation and completion stage yogas, one must rely upon a qualified teacher in order to apply the powerful tantric methods successfully. The traditional scriptures advise us to choose a teacher carefully, using reason and wisdom as our tools, and not to rely on blind faith. Moreover, even though we are advised to maintain respect and faith in the teacher, this too must be done on the basis of common sense; should an instruction of our teacher contradict what we know of Dharma, we should respectfully and politely voice our qualms, and not just mindlessly acquiesce. As the glorious Indian master Nagarjuna pointed out, faith must always be guided by intelligence and wisdom.

There are several different views as to the exact time when Buddha first gave the Kalachakra teaching. The Second Dalai Lama's guru, Khedrub Norzang Gyatso, and other lamas like Taktsang Lotsawa, conclude that Buddha taught it a month before he passed away. Another view is that it was given the year after his enlightenment. Both of these groups have well-developed theses to support their views on the subject, based on diverse sources.

Nonetheless, both accept that the transmission was carried from India to Shambhala soon after it was taught, and that it remained there until the master Chilupa retrieved it.

The system was brought to Tibet in two separate lines, known as the Dro and Rva Traditions. Later these were united by the omniscient Buton Rinchen Drub. It was from Buton's immediate disciple Chokyi Pel that Je Tsongkhapa received the transmission.

Tsongkhapa in turn extensively practiced and taught the Kalachakra teaching. Eventually it came to the Seventh Dalai Lama, who contributed significantly to its preservation, clarification and transmission. In this way the lineage was passed from generation to generation, coming down to us today in an unbroken stream.

In most tantric traditions initiation is given to small groups of trusted students, the number often being limited to twenty-five. However, Kalachakra is an exception in this regard, and there is a tradition of giving it at large public gatherings.   Certainly, not everyone who attends will have a sufficient inner basis to receive the full benefits of the initiation, but it is believed that anyone attending with a positive attitude will establish and strengthen positive karmic instincts.

The Kalachakra system belongs to the category of highest yoga tantras, and therefore is a secret doctrine.   In ancient days all tantric teachings were practiced and transmitted with extreme discretion.   The open publication of tantric literature was discouraged, and access to it was restricted to initiates. However, over the last century numerous Western scholars and enthusiasts have written extensively on tantric buddhism, often without sufficient grounding in the system as a whole.   As a result, many erroneous ideas concerning the nature of tantric practice have emerged.   There seems to be no other remedy to the situation than to allow scholars trained within the tradition to write and produce translations on the subject.

In addition, today's world seems to be in need of a powerful medicine. And of all teachings given by the Buddha, those of highest yoga tantra are the most powerful.   These methods are said to be especially applicable to the condition in which the human community finds itself today.   When the techniques of highest yoga tantra are applied on the foundations of the three higher trainings, the bodhisattva's compassionate aspiration to highest enlightenment, and the practice of the six perfections, they have the ability to induce enlightenment within this one short lifetime.

Kalachakra represents one of the most extensive of the highest yoga tantras.   I offer my prayers that this volume may contribute to the understanding and appreciation of this sublime teaching of the Buddha, that he delivered to humanity out of his profound sense of compassion two and a half millenniums ago.

10 May 1991

Technical Note

Throughout the text I have written Tibetan names of people and places as they are pronounced rather than as formally transliterated. Tibetan abounds with prefixes, superscripts, subscripts and suffixes, many of which are silent or change the sounds in ways the non-specialist could not possibly guess. For example, *'Phrin-las* is pronounced *Trinley*; *Khedrupjey* is spelled *mKhas-grub-rje*; and so forth. To accommodate the needs of specialists the formal spellings are given in an appended glossary.

My phonetic rendering is quite standard, with the exception that I treat both *pa* and *pha* as the letter *p*; also, *ta* and *tha* are rendered as a simple letter *t*. The result is a pronunciation closer to correct than the alternative. Scholars can recreate the more precise Tibetan spelling from the glossary. *Ba* as a suffix becomes the letter *p*; *ga* as a suffix becomes *k*. Words ending in an open *e* sound are spelled with an *-ey* ending (e.g., *Shigatsey* instead of *Shigatse*).

Concerning the treatment of Sanskrit names and terms, I have reserved the use of diacritics to the Bibliography and Glossary. An exception is made with the mantras and mantric syllables that appear in Part Two, as the absence of diacritics here might cause confusion. In general, the Sanskrit words that I have used throughout the body of the text are those that I feel have been or should be adopted into standard buddhist English diction, much as words like karma, samsara, buddha, buddhahood, Hinayana, Mahayana, and so forth are now accepted as proper English words, being included in both Oxford and Webster dictionaries (without diacritics). In the footnotes I do not put diacritics on words of Indian buddhist origin that I feel are now legitimately established as part of the English language. The sacred (and unfortunately somewhat unsightly) diacritic is reserved for mantric syllables.

Preface

I would like to begin by thanking His Holiness the Dalai Lama for giving his blessings to this small project. As with all of my books, before undertaking the work I approached His Holiness for advice, and sent his secretary a list of the Tibetan texts that I planned to incorporate. In this case the list included *Concerning the Kalachakra Initiation,* that His Holiness had himself written, and I had co-translated (with Ven. Doboom Tulku), a decade earlier. I also requested His Holiness to contribute a Foreword and to recommend a *sadhana* that he felt would be appropriate to include. A week later I received both, the latter in the form of a copy of Buton Rinchen Druppa's *The Best of Jewels,* a wonderful little text ideal for the purposes of this volume. I would like to comment that since winning the Nobel Peace Prize in 1989 the demands on His Holiness' time have increased a hundredfold, and I deeply appreciate his graciousness in this regard. We Westerners refer to him as 'His Holiness'; the Tibetans use the warmer and more poetically descriptive epithet Yishin Norbu, 'the Wishfulfilling Gem.' And indeed, His Holiness is exactly that.

My personal spiritual involvement with the Kalachakra tantric tradition began in 1973, when I joined a crowd of a hundred and fifty thousand Himalayan buddhists attending an initiation being given in Bodh Gaya, India, by His Holiness. At the time I was studying Tibetan language, literature, philosophy and meditation at the Library of Tibetan Works and Archives, Dharamsala. I had previously only heard and read of the Kalachakra legacy; the Dalai Lama's public transmission certainly whetted my appetite, and during the subsequent decade of my studies in Dharamsala I had the pleasure of touching upon Kalachakra materials a number of times.

In 1981 I traveled south to Ganden Shartsey Monastery to study the First Dalai Lama's *Notes on the Two Yogic Stages of Glorious Kalachakra* under the Ven. Lati Rinpochey. Rinpochey's lucid commentary rendered the First Dalai Lama's cryptic work readily accessible and infused it with warmth, presence, and vitality. At the time I prepared a translation of this important work with the assistance of one of Rinpochey's young lama wards, the rather mischievous Thepo Tulku. The following year this was published in *The First Dalai Lama: Bridging the Sutras and Tantras*, (New Delhi: Tushita Books, 1982), a study of the life and writings of that wonderful sage. Shortly thereafter it was released in the US by Snow Lion Publications, where it received three editions before going out of print.

However, given the level of interest in the Kalachakra tradition, my publishers at Snow Lion felt that it would be useful to the reading public to keep the First Dalai Lama's Kalachakra commentary in print as the centerpiece of a book in itself, due to its complex and technical nature, supplementing it with a substantial introduction as well as with contextually relevant Tibetan readings.

For this edition I have considerably revised my earlier translation, prepared a decade ago. My understanding of the system as a whole has grown since then, of course, and so has other Western research. Also, in its earlier form it was but one of sixteen items illustrative of the First Dalai Lama's writings, whereas here I have rendered it with more emphasis on a technical approach to terminology. To the best of my knowledge my 1981 rendition of the First Dalai Lama's *Notes* was the

first translation into the English language of a major work dealing with the Kalachakra six yogas. Earlier studies had cen-
tered mainly on historical or mythological elements of
Kalachakra, or on its sciences of astronomy, astrology, alchemy,
its links to Tibetan medicine, and so forth.

I have not attempted to present here a summary of these
various branches of the Kalachakra tradition. Nor have I focused on a formal study of the Kalachakra six yogas as such.
Rather, my aim has been to provide the reader with an overview of the Kalachakra spiritual legacy as a living tradition,
based mainly on the ideas expressed by the First Dalai Lama
in his *Notes.* I have attempted to expand upon these ideas by
drawing from the writings of other great lineage masters, especially the Second, Seventh, Thirteenth and Fourteenth Dalai
Lamas, various of their tutors, and some of the Panchen Lama
incarnations.

This volume is arranged in two parts: the first is my own
overview of the Kalachakra system, and the second presents
a collection of seven translated Tibetan texts relevant to the
Kalachakra yogic tradition.

In Part One, which is in twelve chapters, I have attempted
to portray the perspective of the Tibetan attitudes toward the
Kalachakra yogas. My placement of Kalachakra within the
overall structure of buddhist doctrine, as detailed in chapters
six through ten, is largely directed by the Thirteenth Dalai
Lama's *Guide to the Buddhist Tantras,* which I quote extensively. In general the Great Thirteenth follows the blueprint
advocated by Lama Tsongkhapa, founder of the Gelukpa school
of Tibetan buddhism. This is particularly relevant to my purposes because Lama Tsongkhapa was one of the First Dalai
Lama's most important spiritual masters.

I must apologize to the casual reader if occasionally some
of the material I have incorporated into Part One seems difficult. All I can suggest is that the easier sections be studied
first, and the more difficult be given several readings. I have
done my best to express the complex tantric concepts in as
straightforward a manner as possible; however, the tantras are

the highest and most esoteric doctrines taught by the Buddha, so we should expect to have to make some effort to gain an understanding of them.

The materials translated in Part Two were studied and translated with a number of Tibetan lama friends over the years.

As mentioned above, the First Dalai Lama's *Notes* (Chapter Seventeen of the present volume) was prepared under the supervision of Ven. Lati Rinpochey of Ganden Shartsey. In the previous rendition of this work I blended important points from Rinpochey's commentary into the translation, separating them from the First Dalai Lama's texts in parentheses. In this edition they have been taken out of the text and placed in the footnotes.

In 1980 in coordination with Ven. Doboom Tulku, then a personal secretary to His Holiness the Dalai Lama and presently the director of Tibet House, New Delhi, I translated a second text related to the Kalachakra tradition. This was the present Dalai Lama's *Concerning the Kalachakra Initiation*, originally written as a guideline to people contemplating attending the Kalachakra initiation that he was scheduled to give a year later in Madison, Wisconsin. Our translation was first published as an article in *The Tibetan Review* (April, 1981). I would like to express my thanks to His Holiness for his permission to include the text here. With Doboom Tulku I also read and translated the Kalachakra *guruyoga* method included here as Chapter Eighteen.

The Seventh Dalai Lama's *Prerequisites of Receiving Tantric Initiation*, included as Chapter Fifteen, was translated in 1981 under the guidance of Ven. Amchok Tulku, also of Ganden Shartsey Monastery. At the time I was teaching English to Amchok Tulku, and he was teaching me Tibetan. I first published an abridgement of our rendition in a collection of tantric liturgical practices, intended for limited circulation to initiates only, entitled *Concerning Yamantaka, Volume One* (New Delhi: Tushita Books, 1981).

I also read and translated the First Panchen Lama's *An Aspiration to Fulfill the Stages of the Glorious Kalachakra Path* with

Ven. Amchok Tulku. I felt that this was particularly auspicious, as there is an intimate link between the Panchen and Amchok incarnations. The present Amchok Tulku was discovered by the (recently deceased) Seventh Panchen Lama when the latter was only ten years of age. That Panchen had himself been identified as an infant by the previous Amchok Tulku. Thus these two had close spiritual connections. This continued throughout the years, and as fate would have it I became personally affected by their bond. In 1986 I had organized an international teaching tour for Amchok Tulku; but then a month before he was to leave he received a message from the Panchen Lama asking him to meet him in Nepal and to travel with him back to Lhasa and Peking.

Amchok Tulku disappeared for a year, and the tour was hastily cancelled. When I arrived in Dharamsala to collect him I was greeted by a photograph of a little nomadic boy with his thumb in his mouth, dressed in sheepskin boots and coat, with a single paragraph written on the back: "Glenn, I'm sorry for any inconvenience, but this little boy has called me back to Tibet for awhile." Thus instead of traveling the world Amchok spent the winter teaching in the Panchen Lama's newly established 'Incarnate Lama' school in Peking. At the time of writing, his monastery in Amdo, Eastern Tibet, which he re-established on his first visit back to Tibet in 1983, is one of the largest monasteries in the world, with more than a thousand monks. During that second visit Ven. Amchok Tulku also translated for the meeting between the Panchen Lama and former president Jimmy Carter.

The Thirteenth Dalai Lama's *Summary of the Kalachakra Tradition* is extracted from his *Guide to the Buddhist Tantras*, which was included in my study of the Great Thirteenth's life and works, *Path of the Bodhisattva Warrior* (Snow Lion Publications, 1988). I have here reworked the text slightly, to accord with the terminology used in the other chapters.

Finally, the brief prayer by the Sixth Panchen Lama included as Chapter Thirteen was translated with my lama friend Chomdzey Tashi Wangyal of Drepung Loseling Monastery, who has been working wonders in the manuscript room of the Library of Tibetan Works and Archives since the mid-seventies. Over the years I have read and translated numerous Tibetan texts with this wonderfully humble monk; it gives me sadness to think that I may see much less of him in the future if his plan to return to Kham this year and dedicate the remainder of his life to rebuilding the Dharma in his homeland, where it was destroyed by the Chinese during the years of the Cultural Revolution, is not obstructed by Chinese officialdom.

Central Asian literature is extremely rich in Kalachakra materials. Some thousands (if not tens of thousands) of titles exist in the Tibetan language. I have not attempted to provide here a survey of this vast repository. My focus instead has been the sentiment and character of the tradition as a whole. In addition to those writers whom I have quoted or referred to in other ways throughout the text, I am also particularly fond of the writings of the First Dalai Lama's guru Bodong Chokley Namgyal, the Second Dalai Lama's guru Khedrup Norzang Gyatso, and the Seventh Dalai Lama's guru Trichen Ngawang Chokden. Although in all three of these cases the disciple became more famous than the teacher, the contribution of these three tutors to the preservation and dissemination of the Kalachakra tradition was truly colossal. The First Dalai Lama also studied Kalachakra with four other renowned masters—namely, Lama Tsongkhapa, Khedrupjey, Gyaltsepjey, and Pakpa Yonten Gyatso, each of whose collected works is rich in Kalachakra writings. The Fifth Dalai Lama's guru Panchen Chokyi Gyaltsen was also an inspired writer on the subject, as was the Thirteenth Dalai Lama's (somewhat errant) disciple Panchen Chokyi Nyima. In preparing this volume I have tried to draw mainly from the writings of the Dalai Lamas themselves.

This volume focuses mainly on spiritual aspects of the Kalachakra tradition, rather than on what the Second Dalai Lama calls "the branches of Kalachakra" in the poem that I quote in Chapter Ten. The word 'branches' here refers to the metaphysical or 'scientific' aspects such as alchemy, astronomy, and so forth. A considerable amount has been done on some of these aspects by other scholars. My own interest is the yogic tradition, into which less Western research has been made.

I apologize for any errors that have crept into my treatment in Part One or into the translations in Part Two. I have done my best to avoid mistakes by checking points of doubt with qualified lamas as well as by referring to the traditional scriptural commentaries. But as His Holiness the Dalai Lama once commented when I expressed concern over achieving accuracy in English translation, "A few little errors here and there are merely the stamp of a pioneer effort covering new and uncharted territory. Someone has to begin the process." No doubt a hundred years from now much of what is being done today by tibetologists around the world will take on something of a rustic air, if we can judge by how translations made even fifty years ago read to us now. Our knowledge of the buddhist tantric tradition is constantly developing, and English terminology for buddhist ideas is becoming more precise. May those of a spiritual interest in the Kalachakra teaching learn from what I have gotten right; and may future scholars learn from (and correct) any mistakes I have incurred.

For those looking to take up the actual Kalachakra methods of the generation and completion stage yogas, this volume should not be regarded as a practice manual in and of itself. The Vajrayana can only be successfully attempted under qualified tutorage. Some of the pieces, however, such as the guruyoga method or the sadhana (found in Chapters Eighteen and Nineteen) can be used for daily practice, although anyone interested in doing so should first search out a qualified lama with whom to read the texts and discuss the process. As a result of the Tibetan diaspora, most large cities in North America and Europe now have at least one qualified Tibetan lama in the vicinity.

In conclusion I would like to thank my publishers, Jeff Cox and Sidney Piburn of Snow Lion Publications, Ithaca, New

York, for their continuing efforts in making the rich spiritual, cultural and literary heritage of Tibet available to the international reading public. Thanks also go to Susan Kyser, my editor at Snow Lion; to David Reigle of Eastern School Press for assistance with Sanskrit diacritics, for kindly reading portions of the text and for typesetting *The Best of Jewels*; to Richard B. Martin, South Asian Bibliographer at Alderman Library, University of Virginia, for critical bibliographic assistance; and to Alexander Kocharov and Robert Beer for generously supplying illustrations for this volume.

Glenn H. Mullin
The Library of Tibetan Works and Archives
Dharamsala, H.P., India
March 10th, 1991

**PART ONE:
THE KALACHAKRA LEGACY**

1 The Contemporary Kalachakra Ambience

I had my first real encounter with the Kalachakra tantric tradition in the winter of late 1973. His Holiness the Dalai Lama was to give a public Kalachakra initiation, and I planned to attend.

At the time the initiation was announced I was living and studying in Dharamsala, India. The wave of excitement that ran through the Tibetan community was almost tangible.

The site of the initiation was to be Bodh Gaya, a sleepy little temple village a few miles south of the city of Gaya, Bihar.

Bodh Gaya also has the distinction of being the spiritual center of the buddhist world, at least in the sense of its early history. It is here that Gautama the monk sat under the bodhi tree and manifested the state of enlightenment, here that he became the Buddha. Of the eight great places of buddhist pilgrimage in India, it is accorded the position of the most sacred of all. In fact, some buddhist traditions even state that all one thousand buddhas of this era who perform the role of universal teachers manifest their earthly enlightenment in Bodh Gaya.

It might also be added that Bodh Gaya in the twentieth century is not exactly a model spiritual center. The Turkic Muslim invasions of the thirteenth and fourteenth centuries had laid much of the area waste. The Muslims were especially harsh on buddhism in India. It is said that the nearby monastery of Nalanda was surrounded, and all the monks beheaded on the spot. The walls of every room are said to have been covered in blood. The temples and libraries were burned, and the hands and faces broken off any stone images that were discovered.

To put it bluntly, Bodh Gaya had seen better days; or at least that is how it seemed in 1973. It had never really recovered from the Muslim onslaught. It seemed to have become a smattering of grotty tea shops and grottier restaurants. The buildings that constituted the village, as well as the designated "slum dwellings" behind the stupa, could at best be called the most meager of human habitations.

The principal stupa and the sunken gardens around this wonderful monument, however, are marvelous, and contain a descendent of the original tree under which the Buddha had achieved his illumination. They also house numerous stone images and temple artifacts that had escaped destruction during the Muslim period, largely due to having been buried before the final attacks.

After the Muslim purges Bodh Gaya fell out of use as an international pilgrimage center. Buddhists around the world began to develop alternate pilgrimage sites in more congenial and accessible locations. The result was that the Central Asians began to look to Lhasa as the replacement; the Chinese to Wutai-shan, the Five Mountain Peaks; the Japanese to Kyoto; and so forth.

Bodh Gaya saw a small flurry of activity in the 1950s, when Prime Minister Nehru invited the governments of numerous buddhist countries around the world to each build a temple in the area, offering to donate land for the project. As a consequence, over the years since then a dozen or so temples have appeared.[1]

By 1973 the flood of Tibetan refugees to India in the late

fifties and early sixties had sparked fresh buddhist activities in Bodh Gaya. The presence of great Tibetan lamas at Bodh Gaya every winter, as well as of throngs of Tibetan pilgrims, in turn intensified the interest of the buddhist peoples of the various Himalayan kingdoms: from Ladakh, Lahoul, Spiti and Kinnaur on the west, to Sikkim, Bhutan and upper Arunachal Pradesh on the east, all of whom practice Tibetan buddhism. During the winter months, when the Bihar weather becomes survivable, thousands of people would make the journey to the Place of Enlightenment, the Diamond Seat.

The fact that the Dalai Lama himself was to give the Kalachakra initiation in such a holy place for the first time had the Himalayan buddhist world buzzing.

Two months before the initiation was to begin the crowd of pilgrims began to gather. Most of them wanted to do some hundreds of thousands of repetitions of their principal mantra practice during the pilgrimage; or perhaps a hundred thousand full length bodily prostrations. Others would set as their objective circumambulating the great stupa several thousand times. The Dalai Lama's initiation would be the crescendo, the grand finale, to their devotions.

The Kalachakra initiation is, for the Central Asians, something of a buddhist festival. Entire villages and tribes come, with babies, adolescents, middle-aged people and grandparents. Those too young, old or weak to walk are carried.

Businesses spring up everywhere, to buy from and sell to the crowd. Most pilgrims bring a few items to sell in order to pay their way back home, small articles of antiquity being the most usual. Roadside shops-on-a-blanket are everywhere. In the Bodh Gaya initiation of 1985 some entrepreneur even brought in a circus, with ferris wheels and merry-go-rounds. The atmosphere is one of revelry and celebration. The only Western equivalent I can think of is Ferlinghetti's "A Coney Island of the Mind."

Having a strong nomadic sense, the Tibetans seemed little concerned by the lack of facilities at Bodh Gaya. Some stayed at the scant accommodations to be had at the local temples;

others rented balconies or huts in nearby villages; but the vast majority simply put up tents by the river, wherever they could find an empty spot. The Indian army moved in and installed a vast network of water taps and portable toilets, and before long a tent city of more than a hundred thousand had sprung up. In the 1985 Kalachakra initiation in Bodh Gaya twelve years later, more than three hundred thousand people descended upon the area.

It should be noted here that very few of those attending an initiation of this nature would plan on ever seriously undertaking the yogic practices found in the Kalachakra tradition and discussed in this book. Perhaps one in a hundred would even adopt a simple daily recitation practice, such as the *guruyoga* text found here in Chapter Eighteen. Maybe one in a thousand would aspire to ever actually practice the six yogas; and of those, only a dedicated handful would ever actually get around to performing the meditation retreat that constitutes the essential training.

For most attenders, the purpose of sitting through the initiation ceremony would not be to receive empowerment as a permission to enter into the yogic endeavors, but rather to have the opportunity to bask in the bright rays of spiritual communion with the initiating lama, in this case His Holiness the Dalai Lama, and hopefully to absorb a sprinkling of spiritual energy from the occasion. As well, the hope would be to generate karmic seeds that establish a link with the lama and also with Shambala, the mythological pure land of the Kalachakra doctrine.

Most public Kalachakra initiation ceremonies are preceded by five or six days of essential buddhist teachings. These usually begin at about noon and continue until dusk, with everyone sitting on blankets in the sun, the children playing games between the islands of adults. Mothers breast feed their babies while the older people snooze discreetly in the shade, the steady melody of the Dalai Lama's rich voice flowing over them in waves from a network of loudspeakers. The subject of discussion during these preliminary days is much along the lines of the ideas presented by the Seventh Dalai Lama in *The Prereq-uisites of Receiving Tantric Initiation,* included here as Chapter Fifteen. After these fundamental teachings have been given the actual initiation process commences, beginning with a day of lama dances, in which the place of initiation is claimed and consecrated. This is then followed by either two or three days of initiations, and generally a day of spiritual celebration in the form of a *gurupuja* ceremony, in which the lama gives his parting advice to the crowd. Finally the entire group of how-ever many tens of thousands of initiates lines up and files in single column through the temporary chapel in which the Kalachakra sand mandala has been constructed, and then past His Holiness in order to receive an individual hand blessing.[2]

Thus the entire event traditionally takes place over a period of ten or twelve days, with the crowd gathering each day at noon and sitting until early evening, before and after each ses-sion scurrying hurriedly to accomplish the mundane tasks of the day, like finding food, relocating lost children, washing off some of the dust that now hangs in clumps from one's body, avoiding being trampled by the frantic mobs in motion, and so forth. Meanwhile the businessmen continue to ply the crowds in an effort to profit from the spiritual intensity of the moment; and there is also the occasional conflict, such as the time when, during one of the Dalai Lama's afternoon talks, a Bhutanese farmer stepped over a Khampa nomad's coat and received a serious knife wound for his indiscretion.

Such was my initial contact with the Kalachakra tradition. It was more like a fantastic, mystical, tantric party that con-tinued day and night for two weeks, than a solemn religious event. Babies were born; old people died; lamas and medita-tors sat practicing their devotions under every tree and in ev-ery nook and cranny; and lovers slipped off to the riverbanks at night to share the joys of the heart. All of them were equal in their temporary orbit around the Kalachakra sand mandala that stood at the middle of the village and now served as the center of our universe. The spiritual energy rose from the earth in waves, like heat on a distant horizon. Sleep became pervaded by dreams so vivid it became difficult to separate waking from dream experiences. Then suddenly it was over, like the culmination of a marathon race, with only a few stragglers left as evidence.

The crowd dispersed slowly, as though reluctant to leave a gathering that holds promise of further adventure. Many eventually continued on pilgrimage through the holy places for a month or two, before returning home to their Himalayan mountains and valleys; to their farms or herds; to their monasteries, nunneries and hermitages; or to the refugee settlements scattered across India, from Ladakh in the north to Mysore in the south.

Since that time His Holiness has given the Kalachakra initiation on numerous occasions, several of which I had the fortune to attend. As I write, there is talk that he will give it three times in the following year: one in Mongolia, another in Dharamsala, and the third in New York.

2   Buddha's Outer, Inner and Secret Teachings

Shakyamuni Buddha, who lived and taught in India approximately twenty-five centuries ago, is said to be the fourth buddha of this world era to turn the wheel of the enlightenment tradition. He collected together the fragments of the teachings of the earlier three, and updated them with a number of techniques appropriate specifically to the needs of humanity in this period. It was prophesied that the teachings he delivered would thrive for five thousand years.

There are different ways to categorize the doctrines that he transmitted. One such division is into the threefold path of Hinayana, Mahayana and Vajrayana, or Small Vehicle, Great Vehicle and Diamond Vehicle.

The basis for and context of this threefold division of the teachings is given in a Tibetan verse,[1]

> Practiced externally is the way of moderation;
> Practiced internally is the bodhisattva spirit;
> And practiced in secret are the esoteric mantric
>   methods.

Each of these lines refers to one of the three vehicles: Small, Great and Diamond. In this verse the three are characterized respectively as the outer, inner and secret spiritual methods taught by the Buddha.

In India these three phases of buddhism publicly surfaced in succession, the lower preparing the way for the advent of the higher.

The first to become widespread was the outer teaching, the Small Vehicle. This consisted of Buddha's most fundamental and universal instructions, based on discourses given openly to mixed audiences, beginning with those in Deer Park near Varanasi. Central themes included the four noble truths, the noble eightfold path, the twelve links of interdependent origination, and the three higher trainings of discipline, meditative concentration and wisdom. The emphasis was upon an informal simplicity in meditative application, with strong discipline as the basis.

Historically, this was the aspect of buddhism patronized by King Ashoka in the third century B.C. and propagated by the missionaries that he sent throughout his empire, from Afghanistan in the northwest to Bengal in the northeast. Therefore it has occasionally been called 'early buddhism' by some Western scholars. It should be pointed out that according to the classical Indian and Tibetan records this buddhism was not taught earlier than the other two aspects; rather, it was the form most widely propagated during buddhism's infancy.

In the fifth century after Buddha's passing (the second century of the Christian era) there appeared in India a buddhist sage by the name of Nagarjuna. As prophesied by the Buddha himself, Nagarjuna brought forth the inner teachings, or Mahayana, the Great Vehicle, that had been given to groups of select disciples and transmitted quietly over the centuries, awaiting the maturation of the Indian buddhist civilization. It is said that when this maturation had been achieved Nagarjuna incarnated, retrieved the inner teachings from the *nagas*, or mystical keepers of the doctrine, and widely disseminated them. The more than three dozen *Prajnaparamita sutras*, or

"Discourses on the Perfection of Wisdom," that he received from the nagas quickly met with a wide Indian following. As well, his own "Six Treatises on the Reasoning of the Middle Way" achieved almost instant prominence. In brief, Nagarjuna's vision of buddhism swept the Indian imagination, and thereafter most Indian buddhist thinkers took their principal inspiration from his works.[2]

A second important figure in the pioneer Mahayana movement was the master Asanga, who practiced meditation for twelve years and brought forth the transcripts known as "The Five Treatises of Maitreya." These five, as well as several of Asanga's own writings, soon became established classics.

Both Nagarjuna and Asanga essentially were interpreters of the Prajnaparamita sutras, with Nagarjuna concentrating on the 'wisdom of emptiness' doctrine and Asanga concentrating on the more conventional bodhisattva practices, these being known to the Tibetans as 'the vast bodhisattva ways.' Together these two Indian masters are known as 'the Mahayana forefathers.'

In *A Raft to Cross the Ocean of Indian Buddhist Thought* the Second Dalai Lama writes,

> The two Mahayana forefathers were Nagarjuna and Asanga, both of whom were very controversial in their own times for certain of their works that commented upon Buddha's thought directly, that is to say, from personal visionary experiences rather than by relying upon any specific scriptures. These two masters were instrumental in the formulation of the two Mahayana schools.

The essential substance of the inner or Great Vehicle doctrine was the emulation and cultivation of the bodhisattva spirit and ways; in other words, the cultivation of the aspiration to highest enlightenment as a means of fulfilling compassion and love for other living beings, and the practice of the bodhisattva trainings, such as the six perfections of generosity, self-discipline, patience, enthusiastic energy, meditation and wisdom.

The third trend in Indian buddhism, that of the Vajrayana, the tantric path to enlightenment, began to publicly manifest sometime after the fifth or sixth century A.D. From this time onward until the destruction of buddhism in India, new tantric systems continued to emerge from time to time. The list of important early Vajrayana propagators includes illustrious names such as Indrabhuti, Saraha, Lalitavajra and so forth. Although it is not possible at present accurately to date these masters due to the scarcity of existing records,[3] it nonetheless is well known that they claimed to be transmitting direct lineages of buddhist doctrine, as taught mystically by Buddha to the most mature of his trainees. These tantric doctrines were then transmitted in utter secrecy until the time for their wider propagation ripened. It is relevant to note that the *Kalachakra Tantra* was one of the last highest yoga tantra systems to emerge in India, not making its appearance until the tenth century A.D.

All three of these aspects of the Buddha's teachings—outer, inner and secret—found their way to Tibet; but it was the third aspect, the secret tantric path, that encountered the most enthusiastic reception in the snowy lands to India's north.

It could be pointed out that in India these three trends of buddhist thought and practice did not always co-exist with the same harmony they enjoyed in Tibet. Adherents of the outer schools often refused to accept the validity of later arrivals and developments. For instance, when Vasubandhu saw the Mahayana writings of his brother Asanga he is said to have commented, "My brother performed a meditation retreat for twelve years, but unable to achieve even a good dream, let alone achieve realization of the true teachings, he has fabricated a number of his own traditions."[4]

Nor did the emergence of the tantric doctrines meet with instant approval by all Indian buddhists of the day. Many expressed their reservations.

Gradually, however, the Indians seem to have accepted all

three forms of buddhism. The portrait drawn by eleventh-century Tibetan pilgrims to the monasteries of Northern India, including Nalanda, Vikramashila and Odantapuri, is one of integration, with the three buddhist trends being almost universally regarded as aspects of a greater whole. This is also very much reflected in the Tibetan biographies of important Indian masters of the day, such as those of Atisha, Naropa and so forth.[5]

It was in this shape that buddhism was translated into Tibetan in two great waves of royal patronage: first in the eighth and ninth centuries A.D. under the sponsorship of the Lhasa kings, and then in the mid-eleventh century, principally under the sponsorship of the kings of Guge, Western Tibet.

In *A Raft to Cross the Ocean of Indian Buddhist Thought,* the Second Dalai Lama summarizes these three vehicles as follows:

> Fundamentally the Buddha taught three circles of doctrine. For disciples with inclinations toward a simple path he taught the Hinayana, the Small Vehicle. For those with inclinations toward a more complex approach he taught the Mahayana, the Great Vehicle, the Vehicle of the Perfections. Finally, for those wishing to follow an extremely profound way he taught the esoteric Vajrayana, the Diamond Vehicle, the path incorporating the tantric use of sensuality and passion in its methods.

Here the Second Dalai Lama is speaking in the sense of the trainees who would serve as the main recipients of the specific teachings and would use that aspect as their principal spiritual undertaking.

From the viewpoint of practice, however, the verse quoted earlier suggests the approach to be taken, for it reveals how the outer, inner and secret teachings are to be integrated into an individual's training as successive levels in spiritual endeavor.

In brief, the Tibetan attitude is that one first develops inner stability through the Small Vehicle methods of the three higher trainings (i.e., discipline, meditation and the cultivation of wisdom), and then expands the scope of the undertaking by augmenting one's practice with the bodhisattva aspiration and the trainings of the six perfections. Finally, when by means of the above two applications one has generated the three qualities of the free spirit of detachment, the compassionate bodhisattva attitude, and the wisdom of emptiness, one takes tantric initiation and ventures into the trainings of the Diamond Vehicle.

The Third Dalai Lama describes the benefits of the correct attitude in *Essence of Refined Gold:*

> All the profound teachings taught in the sutras and tantras, as well as in the treatises and elucidations written by the successive generations of buddhist masters, will be seen as methods for oneself to apply, beginning with the more basic practices and building up to the more advanced, in order to overcome the negative aspects and limitations of the unenlightened mind. The significance of all the teachings of Buddha and the lineage masters—from the advice on how to cultivate an effective working relationship with a spiritual teacher up to the highest methods for perceiving the final nature of being—will come into one's own hand.... All the teachings will be seen in perspective to one's own life and training.

3 Exoteric Sutrayana and Esoteric Vajrayana

The above manner of speaking of the three vehicles as outer, inner and secret is made from the perspective of how the three aspects of the teachings spread in India, and how all three are to be integrated into a personal practice.

There are several other classical ways in which the Buddha's teachings are discussed as 'vehicles.'

Nagarjuna's retrieved Prajnaparamita sutras, for example, speak of two basic vehicles, these being the Small and Great, or Hinayana and Mahayana, wherein the former leads to liberation from cyclic existence and the latter to complete enlightenment.

The first of these two is in turn twofold: the Vehicle of Hearers (who mainly live in communities), and the Vehicle of Solitary Practitioners (who mainly live alone). Both of these paths lead to nirvana, or complete liberation from samsara. They differ only in the strength of their merit.

Probably historically these two represent the early monkhood—the Hearers being those who lived with Buddha and his community, and who recorded the teachings; the Solitary Practitioners were probably those monks who took a central contemplative technique, such as insight meditation, and cultivated it in solitude.

Later Indian buddhist writings (specifically, those appearing after the introduction of the buddhist tantras in the sixth century A.D.), and the tradition that was endorsed in Tibet, accepts the above twofold classification, as well as the subdivision of the Small Vehicle into the two styles of practice given above. In addition, they further sub-divide the Great Vehicle into two: the Bodhisattva Vehicle, or path wherein one trains according to the Enlightenment Hero ideal as outlined in the Prajnaparamita sutras retrieved by Nagarjuna; and the Secret Mantra Vehicle, the esoteric tantric path, wherein the ideal is that of the Indian mahasiddhas, who transcended convention. Both of these are of the Great Vehicle, for both take as their basis the bodhisattva aspiration to highest enlightenment and as their goal the attainment of complete buddhahood (and not mere nirvana).

The Second Dalai Lama makes this observation in *A Raft to Cross the Ocean of Indian Buddhist Thought:*

> The transmissions given by the Buddha were of two types: scriptural and realization. The former of these includes the collections (of the teachings of the Buddha) upon which both the Small and Great Vehicle traditions are founded.
>
> As for these two vehicles, the former can be subdivided into the Vehicle of Hearers and the Vehicle of Solitary Practitioners. The latter can be sub-divided into the exoteric Great Vehicle of the Bodhisattva Perfections, and the esoteric Diamond Vehicle, the tantric path of secret mantras.
>
> The former of these two aspects of the Great Vehicle is also called 'the causal Great Vehicle,' and the latter 'the resultant Great Vehicle.'

Here we see the exoteric Bodhisattva Vehicle being referred to as 'the causal vehicle' and the esoteric Secret Mantra Vehicle as 'the resultant vehicle.' The idea is simply that in the former style of practice when one meditates on, for example, love, one views it as a force that acts as a cause of enlightenment; in the latter style, one meditates that one is driven by the full power of love this very moment, just as at the time of the resultant state of complete buddhahood. Thus one style of practice is closer in nature to the causes of enlightenment; the other is closer in nature to the resultant enlightenment itself.[1]

Another manner of classification is into the Sutrayana and Tantrayana. Sometimes these are also called 'shared' and 'exclusive' aspects of doctrine. In this context, 'sutra' refers to the scriptures that contain the exoteric teachings of the Buddha, and 'tantra' refers to the scriptures that contain his esoteric doctrines. All teachings of the Buddha can be subsumed into these two categories.

Here the Sutrayana includes all the teachings of the Small Vehicle, as well as the general Great Vehicle teachings (that is, everything excluding the tantric doctrines). The Tantrayana, which is synonymous with the terms Vajrayana and Mantrayana, contains those Great Vehicle teachings that deal with the tantric path to enlightenment. Hence the Kalachakra tantric tradition is placed within this last doctrinal category.

The essential relationship between the Sutrayana and the Tantrayana in both Indian and Tibetan buddhism is one of preliminary and actual practice, where the Sutrayana methods prepare the foundations for the actual training, which is the tantric methodology.

For this reason the former is sometimes called 'the shared path' and the latter 'the exclusive path.' The former is 'shared' in the sense of providing indispensable foundations to the latter. Being the very substance of the Sutrayana it is obviously present in that category of doctrine; and being the foundations of the Tantrayana, it is also present there. Thus it is shared by both. The Tantrayana, at least in most cases, cannot be successfully practiced without the preliminary trainings in the Sutrayana methods.

The Second Dalai Lama comments in *The Tantric Yogas of Sister Niguma,*

> One should first accomplish the general preliminaries. This refers to those methods that are common to both the Sutrayana and Vajrayana.

In *The Prerequisites of Receiving Tantric Initiation,* presented in this volume as Chapter Fifteen, the Seventh Dalai Lama comments,

> ...the Mahayana is comprised of two distinct vehicles: the *Paramitayana,* or Vehicle (which provides meditation) on the causes (of enlightenment), also called the Vehicle of Symbols; and the *Guhyamantrayana,* or Vajrayana, the Vehicle (which provides meditations) on the results (of enlightenment).
>
> Yet practice of solely the former of these produces enlightenment only after three countless aeons of difficult austerities such as sacrificing limbs of one's body and so forth. In short, it is a long and arduous journey.
>
> But if in our training we couple the Vajrayana with the Paramitayana then after a short comfortable effort we can go to the end of cultivating goodness and overcoming negativity, and can quickly and easily gain the state of all-pervading Vajradhara within one lifetime.
>
> The Vajrayana is a very quick path; but in order to embark upon it we must first train our mindstream through the disciplines of the common path, the Paramitayana, until a degree of stability has been gained. Only then should we enter into the path of secret mantras.

Quoting a passage from *The Root Tantra of Glorious Chakrasamvara,* the Seventh Dalai Lama points out,[2]

When the practices of the sutras (are strong), the horizon of the secret yogas is (in sight).

That is to say, only when the Sutrayana practices have been firmly established as an inner spiritual basis should the Vajrayana teachings be given.[3]

What is it that constitutes the exoteric Sutrayana practices that act as the preliminaries?

In *The Tantric Yogas of Sister Niguma* the Second Dalai Lama describes the nature of 'the shared path' of the Sutrayana by quoting a passage from *The Vajra Verses,*

Those whose minds are ripened by the four initiations,
Who possess confidence and enthusiasm in practice
And whose minds are prepared by the preliminary
    practices
Of meditation upon impermanence and death,
Detachment and the shortcomings of cyclic existence,
They gain buddhahood in as short a time
As six months, a year, or at least in this lifetime
By means of this supreme tantric path.

He then proceeds to unpack the verse by setting it in the context of the threefold development of spiritual perspective presented by Atisha in *A Lamp for the Path to Enlightenment* and propagated throughout Tibet and Central Asia in the form of the *Lam Rim*[4] tradition:

As stated above [in *The Vajra Verses*], the preliminary trainings to be accomplished before entering into this profound (tantric) path are those subsumed under the threefold category of methods for engendering the three scopes of spiritual motivation: (i) the initial scope, which includes trainings such as meditation upon the certainty of death and the uncertainty of the time of death; (ii) the intermediate scope, which involves trainings such as meditation upon the frustrating and painful nature of cyclic existence, methods that generate a sense of detachment from and disillusionment with samsaric indulgence, and give birth to the wish for liberation from samsara; and (iii) the highest scope of motivation, which, based on the above two preliminaries, aspires to highest enlightenment as a means of benefiting all sentient beings and, in order to accomplish this, enters into the altruistic bodhisattva ways, such as the six perfections. To enter the Vajrayana one must firstly accomplish these common (Hinayana and general Mahayana) trainings.

4 Sutrayana as a Preliminary Path

The First Dalai Lama begins his *Notes on the Two Yogic Stages of Glorious Kalachakra* with the advice,

> One should first refine the mind by means of the ordinary Sutrayana methods. In particular, cultivate a definite understanding of the pure view of emptiness.

All the traditional writings assert that before entering into tantric practice one should first develop spiritual stability by means of the general trainings that constitute the foundations of the buddhist life.

Three of the Tibetan texts translated in Part Two—those included as Chapters Thirteen, Fourteen and Fifteen—deal mainly with the Sutrayana preliminaries. The remaining four chapters mainly treat the resultant Tantrayana methods.

In Chapter Thirteen, for example, the Sixth Panchen Lama's brief Kalachakra poem focuses primarily on impermanence, karmic law, love and compassion, and so forth, all of which are Sutrayana teachings. Only two verses are given to the Tantrayana.

In Chapter Fourteen the present Dalai Lama examines the general buddhist perspective on the nature of the human spiritual situation, and goes on to place this in the context of attending a Kalachakra initiation ceremony. He discusses the four noble truths that form the essential structure of the buddhist outlook, and then examines the root of human confusion, which is a misunderstanding of the nature of the self, the I, of both ourselves and other phenomena. He then points out the remedy suggested in the Sutrayana,

> In the Bodhisattva Vehicle methods one meditates that everything one does is for the benefit of living beings. Once it has been understood that all living beings, just like oneself, want happiness and dislike suffering, the attitude which assumes responsibility for their well-being arises. This attitude is an amazing, wonderful and most courageous force, more precious than anything else in existence.
>
> When one uses it as a basis for one's meditation upon the ultimate mode of things, the forces that destroy delusion and distortion are easily cultivated.

Perhaps the most thorough examination of the Sutrayana preliminaries comes in Chapter Fifteen, which is the Seventh Dalai Lama's *The Prerequisites of Receiving Tantric Initiation.* Here the esteemed author places these in the context of preparing the mind for receiving the tantric initiations. His aim is to project an image of the spiritual principles underlying a mind that has been 'tamed' by the Sutrayana practice. This is the inner basis required in order to enter the tantric path and to receive the according initiations.

The Seventh Dalai Lama opens his essay by introducing the four 'pure perceptions' that one should bring with one to the place of initiation—a pure motivation, a pure sense of the environment, a pure sense of other sentient beings, and a pure sense of activity.

He then quickly changes the drift of his thought, and turns to the Sutrayana trainings that act as preparatory practices to the Vajrayana: cultivating an awareness of the precious nature of human life endowed with the freedoms and opportunities that render enlightenment possible; cultivating an awareness of death and impermanence; generating an appreciation of reincarnation and the nature of karmic law; cultivating an awareness of the unsatisfactory nature of unenlightened existence; generating a sense of refuge in the Three Jewels: the Buddhas, the Dharma and the Sangha; generating the altruistic bodhisattva attitude, the compassionate aspiration to achieve highest enlightenment to benefit all living beings; and the cultivation of the wisdom of emptiness, the awareness of the void nature of things.

As is the custom with most Tibetan writers, especially those of the Gelukpa school, the Seventh Dalai Lama largely quotes Indian buddhist masters to illustrate his points. His favorite source works[1] are Nagarjuna's *A Letter to a Friend;* Aryadeva's *Removing the Veils of the Mind;* Shantideva's monumentally important *A Guide to the Bodhisattva Ways;* Chandragomin's *A Letter to a Disciple;* and that classic Indian Mahayana compendium, *Selected Sayings of the Buddha,* which is a collection and arrangement of quintessential teachings of the Buddha on all important aspects of spiritual life, set in verse form.

Two other Indian masters whom the Seventh Dalai Lama quotes liberally by name (usually without stating an exact textual source) are Acharya Vira and Atisha.

The former of these, Acharya Vira, who is also known by the name Ashvaghosha, was one of classical India's greatest buddhist poets. Originally an outspoken anti-buddhist, he challenged Nagarjuna's principal disciple Aryadeva to a debate. Aryadeva defeated him, and Ashvaghosha embraced buddhism. He dedicated the remainder of his life to meditation and to the composition of devotional poetry.[2]

As for Atisha, this refers to the monk Dipamkara Shrijnana, who came to Tibet in 1042 and taught there until his death some thirteen years later, and whose principal disciple, Lama Drom Tonpa, is regarded as being an early predecessor in the string of reincarnations of the Dalai Lamas. The Kadampa school that grew up under Atisha came to influence and inspire all major Tibetan buddhist traditions. Eventually it was adopted as the basic spiritual structure of the Gelukpa school, to which all the Dalai and Panchen Lama incarnations have belonged. Atisha is also an important name in the propagation of the Kalachakra doctrine in Tibet, as we will see later.

The only Tibetan lineage master whom the Seventh Dalai Lama quotes to any degree is Lama Tsongkhapa, founder of the Gelukpa school. This indicates the respect in which he held this illustrious lama.

Each of the Tibetan buddhist orders provides something of its own approach to the Sutrayana trainings. For example, the Sakya school speaks of 'The Methods of Separating from the Four Attachments.' The Kargyupas use the approach known as 'Four Ways to Turn the Mind.' The Gelukpas speak of 'Training the Mind on the Stages of Enlightenment.' The Nyingmapas classify the Sutrayana trainings as 'The Dzogchen Preliminaries,' and also as the 'Dzogchen Lam Rim.'

A threefold arrangement of the Sutrayana trainings was taught by Lama Tsongkhapa. Famed in Tibet as the *lam-tso-nam-sum*, or 'three principal paths,' this tradition condensed all the 'shared vehicle' practices into three themes: those for cultivating the free spirit of detachment; those for cultivating the altruistic bodhisattva spirit, or bodhimind (literally, 'mind of enlightenment') that is based on love and compassion, and that aspires to achieve enlightenment as a means of benefiting the world; and those practices for cultivating the wisdom of emptiness, the non-inherent existence of things.[3]

It is said that all of Buddha's sutra teachings of both Small and Great Vehicles collect into these three themes.

When this system is followed, the meditations upon the preciousness of human life and upon cultivating an effective relationship with a spiritual teacher are taught as foundations for all three categories.

Under the methods for cultivating the free spirit of detachment are the meditations on death and impermanence, the wheel of reincarnation, the unsatisfactory nature of life in the six realms of samsara, the meditations upon taking refuge in the Three Jewels, the four noble truths, and so forth.

The second of the three principal paths, that of cultivating the bodhimind, includes all the meditations that contribute to the growth of the bodhisattva attitude, such as the meditations on equanimity, love, compassion, patience, the sense of universal responsibility, and so forth. It also incorporates cultivation of the six perfections.

The Seventh Dalai Lama lays great emphasis upon this aspect of the Sutrayana trainings. Quoting a passage from Lama Tsongkhapa he says,

> It is not enough to have a Mahayana practice. The practitioner must have the Mahayana perspective. Furthermore, the quality that gives one this is nothing other than the bodhimind: if one has the bodhimind one is a Mahayanist; if one doesn't have it one is not on the Great Way. Therefore dedicate yourself to cultivating the bodhimind....
>
> In order to develop this state of consciousness one must develop two qualities: the thought concerned with sentient beings; and the thought concerned with enlightenment.

He explains what is meant by cultivating the thought concerned with enlightenment:

> Yet although the happiness and welfare of sentient beings are to be fulfilled, a person himself bound in the chains of worldly existence can forget about being able to do anything substantial to help others....
>
> The most powerful worldly god, being himself limited by the fetters of cyclic existence, has no ability to fully benefit other sentient beings. Nor do *Shravaka Arhants* nor *Pratyekabuddhas*, who are free from all chains....
>
> If one could attain the state of perfect buddhahood, that is free from all faults, that sees directly all aspects

of the qualities to be cultivated and faults to be overcome in the quest for enlightenment, and that is physically adorned with the marks and signs of perfection,
the mere perception of which is beneficial, then one
would be beyond the distinction of feeling attraction
or aversion toward the infinite sentient beings. One
would regard all beings with an equal compassion, and
would have the ability to really benefit them. . . .

In brief, the motivation should be, 'For the ultimate
benefit of the sentient beings, who are as infinite as
the sky is vast, I must attain the state of a peerless,
perfect, pure buddha.'

The Seventh Dalai Lama then concludes by describing the
universal compassion of the Mahayana practitioner:

. . .the quality of a supreme being's mind is that it
has turned its back on self-interests and thinks only
of ways to benefit others.

Thus it is like a sun untiringly illuminating the lives
of sentient beings dwelling on the four continents, and
like the great earth which carries the weight of all that
lives upon its surface. The bodhisattvas who possess
it no longer have any liking for self-centered works.
They concern themselves solely with methods to produce benefits and happiness for the limitless sentient
beings.

One might think it somewhat unusual that *The Preliminaries of Receiving Tantric Initiation* does not pay more attention
to the methods for cultivating the wisdom of emptiness, the
third of Lama Tsongkhapa's 'three principal paths.' This perhaps is because he endorses the view that the analytical methods
for approaching emptiness as found in the Sutrayana are not
indispensable requisites of tantric practice; that the methods
for cultivating the wisdom of emptiness as found in the tantric practices themselves are sufficient.

This attitude was once voiced to me by His Holiness the present Dalai Lama, in an audience I had with him in the mid-1970s. I asked him to define the line of demarcation in each of Lama Tsongkhapa's three principal paths that signifies a spiritual maturity sufficiently ripe to enter the tantric yogas. His Holiness replied,

> By meditating on impermanence, the nature of karma, samsara, and so forth, one should have experienced the free spirit of detachment to the degree that, if one sees a particular course of action to be clearly erroneous and spiritually unhealthy, one has the inner strength to remain still and not be carried into it. As regards the cultivation of the bodhisattva spirit, one's aspiration to achieve enlightenment should have become a priority, and one's attitude toward others should be one of caring, a sense that we are all one family. There should be a strong commitment to cultivating the bodhisattva's ways. As for the degree of experience of the wisdom of emptiness, here there is no specific prerequisite, for there are a large variety of very powerful methods for discerning the meaning of emptiness in the tantric vehicle itself. The majority of practitioners should have a basic training in the Sutrayana means; certain trainees, however, can enter the tantric vehicle without that preliminary. They can rely exclusively upon the tantric methods for inducing the wisdom of emptiness.

Whether one is in the category of practitioners who should study the emptiness doctrine from the Sutrayana perspective before entering into tantric training, or is able to enter tantric practice without this as a preliminary, in either case an understanding of the basic sentiment of emptiness becomes necessary from the onset of tantric meditation. For example, it is a principal topic of contemplation during the initiation ceremony itself; and then later, when one takes up sadhana practice, the mantra of emptiness marks the opening section of the liturgy.[4]

In *Concerning the Kalachakra Initiation* His Holiness the Dalai Lama mentions three fundamental qualities that anyone wishing to attend a Kalachakra initiation should consider.

> The first qualification is that of the *bodhichitta*, the altruistic aspiration to highest enlightenment, which cherishes others more than oneself. Here it is said that the best disciple dwells in an unfeigned experience of this sublime mind; the medium disciple has had a small glimpse of it in his or her meditations; the lowest should have at least an appreciation for and interest in developing it.
>
> The second qualification is given in terms of wisdom or special insight training, one's experience of emptiness. Here it is said that the best disciple has an undistorted experience of the nature of ultimate reality as explained in the Madhyamaka or Yogachara schools of Mahayana thought; the medium disciple has a correct understanding based on study and reason in general; and the lowest disciple should at least have a strong appreciation for and interest in learning the philosophical views of emptiness in either of the two above-mentioned schools.
>
> In addition, a disciple seeking the Kalachakra initiation should have a feeling for and interest in this particular tantric tradition. The purpose of initiation is to plant special karmic seeds in the mind of the recipient; but if he or she does not possess the openness born from a basic degree of spiritual interest, it will be very difficult for the seeds to have any impact.

Readers interested in a more detailed explanation of the basic Sutrayana practices that prepare the mind for tantric endeavor are referred to one of my earlier books with Snow Lion Publications, *Essence of Refined Gold*, by the Third Dalai

Lama, a work in the Lam Rim cycle that is supplemented with an oral commentary given by His Holiness in the main temple at Dharamsala in 1976.

In *Mystical Verses of a Mad Dalai Lama* the Second Dalai Lama expresses the Sutrayana focus in song, linking it as a preliminary to the Vajrayana,

> To be constantly aware of death and impermanence,
> To become skilled in living by karmic law,
> To always wear Buddha, Dharma and Sangha as one's
>   crown
> And thus close the door to lower rebirth:
> Turning the mind toward Dharma like this,
> It is not so bad, really, as a way to go.

> To see cyclic existence as a mountain of frustration,
> To identify the root of suffering as ego-grasping,
> To behold the gateway leading to final liberation
> And, in order to gain that sublime state of freedom,
> To intensely practice the three higher trainings of dis-
>   cipline, meditation and wisdom:
> Walking this path leading to knowledge,
> It is not so bad, really, as a way to go.

> To view all beings as having once been one's parents,
> To continually abide in love and compassion for all,
> To achieve maturity in cultivating the two
>   bodhiminds—
> The conventional bodhimind of the bodhisattva at-
>   titude
> And the ultimate bodhimind of wisdom of emptiness—
> And thus become skilled in method and wisdom
>   combined:
> This path for cultivating peerless enlightenment,
> It is not so bad, really, as a way to go.

> To know the faults of grasping at true existence,

To perceive the nature of relativity in causation,
To see the emptiness level of all that occurs
And to experience the highest vision of being:
This is what it means to follow
The sublime path elucidated by Arya Nagarjuna.
It is not so bad, really, as a way to go.

To be ripened by the waters of the tantric initiations,
To understand the vast and profound tantric teachings
And then to cultivate the yogas of the two tantric stages
Whereby enlightenment is quickly and easily attained:
Holding buddhahood in the palm of one's hand like
    this,
It is not so bad, really, as a way to go.

5 The Tantric Path to Enlightenment

Lama Tsongkhapa once wrote,[1]

> For traveling to complete buddhahood
> There are two Mahayana vehicles:
> The Prajnaparamita and the profound Vajrayana.
> Of these, the latter greatly surpasses the former;
> This is as well known as the sun and moon.
>
> There are many people who know this fact
> And pretend to carry the tradition of the sages
> Yet who don't search for an understanding of the
>   profound Vajrayana.
> If they are wise, who is more foolish?
> To meet with this rare and peerless legacy
> And yet still to ignore it:
> How absolutely astounding!

The Thirteenth Dalai Lama's *A Guide to the Buddhist Tantras* makes the following observation concerning tantric practice:

> The Vajrayana is to be practiced in secrecy and is not
> to be revealed to the spiritually immature. Therefore

it is known as 'the secret path.'

It is a special method for protecting the mind from the subtle instincts of the three appearances, in which one meditates in the mode of the resultant stage.

This means that in the Vajrayana one conceives of oneself and all others as sharing in the four pure qualities of a fully accomplished buddha: perfect body, speech, mind, and activities. Therefore it is also called 'the resultant vehicle.'

On this path one applies the yogas of non-dual method and wisdom in order to achieve the transcendental results of the secret mantra. Thus it is known as 'the path of secret mantra.'

Such is the nature of the esoteric Vajrayana, the Diamond Vehicle that brings quick and easy enlightenment.

The importance of complementing one's Sutrayana meditations with the tantric techniques is strongly pointed out by the Third Dalai Lama at the conclusion of his Lam Rim treatise *Essence of Refined Gold:*

These are the practices shared by the sutra and tantra vehicles. Once you have gained solid experiences in them, you should cast aside all hesitation and enter into the way of secret mantra, the great Vajrayana. The gateway to this secret path is an appropriate initiation gained from a fully qualified tantric master in order to ripen the mindstream. At the time of the initiation one pledges to carry out certain practices and to avoid certain modes of conduct that contradict tantric attainment, and these should be honored. If you gain initiation into any of the three lower divisions of tantra— *kriya, charya* or *yoga*—you should go on to practice their systems of 'yoga with symbols' and the 'yoga without symbols.' If you are initiated into the highest division of tantra—*maha anuttara yoga tantra*—you should first master the generation stage practices and then those of the completion stage.

Most Tibetan commentaries on the stages of tantric practice agree that there is no difference between the exoteric Sutra Vehicle and esoteric Vajra Vehicle in terms of the buddhahood that is the result to be attained, the bodhisattva attitude used as the basic motivating factor, or the nature of the view of emptiness, the final reality, that is experienced. In these respects the terms superior and inferior do not apply.

Yet the Vajrayana nonetheless is considered to be the highest teaching given by the Buddha.

The Thirteenth Dalai Lama's *A Guide to the Buddhist Tantras* lists four ways in which the Vajrayana excels the Sutrayana:

(a) Its manner of generating the experience of emptiness is implemented by the peerless means of inducing the wisdom of semblant mind isolation which arises through working with the coarse and subtle energies of the body and causing them to enter into, abide and dissolve within the central channel. Thus the Vajrayana method of cultivating insight into emptiness is uncontrived.

(b) It has a more immense reservoir of methods, such as the meditation on a causal form that is in accord with the nature of the *rupakaya* to be attained.

(c) Its path is quickly accomplished without hardship. In the Perfection Vehicle many lifetimes of intense effort are required in order to attain the state of enlightenment, whereas on the Vajrayana full enlightenment can easily be achieved within this one short life.

(d) Finally, it is fashioned especially for those of sharpest capacity, who are able to make quick progress along the path.

Thus here the four great qualities of tantric practice are listed:

it contains superior techniques for generating insight into emptiness; it has more expansive methods, such as that working with enhancing production of a form body of a buddha; it produces quicker accomplishment; and it is to be practiced by those of highest capacity.

Of these four the most important from the standpoint of yogic practice is probably the first, for it is these special yogas for refining the bodily energies supporting consciousness that provide the speed of the Vajrayana. Through refining the bodily energies, the meditator is able to give birth to a more subtle consciousness. This consciousness is then used to meditate on emptiness.

It should be pointed out that the interpretation the Thirteenth Dalai Lama gives above to the four classes of tantric practice are primarily slanted for highest yoga tantra. These four qualities are interpreted differently in each of the four tantra classes. The term 'semblant mind isolation' mentioned by the Great Thirteenth is exclusive to highest yoga tantra literature.

In the philosophical and religious senses the second of the above four qualities is perhaps the most important of all: the idea of creating a simulated *rupakaya*, or form body of a buddha, primarily through the powers of meditation.

I do not want to go into the intricacies of the Mahayana doctrine of *kayas*, or bodies of a buddha. The basic idea in the Sutrayana is that at the time of enlightenment our collection of meritorious energy transforms into rupakaya, the form of a buddha, and the collection of wisdom transforms into *dharmakaya*, the truth body of a buddha. The latter is a wisdom body essentially benefiting oneself; the former is the aspect used to manifest throughout the universe in accordance with the needs of living beings.

Here the collection of wisdom refers to that force generated by meditation upon the wisdom of emptiness. The collection of merit refers to the special energy generated by all other spiritual practices, such as observance of the discipline of restraining oneself from entering the ten negative courses of action (killing, stealing, speaking cruelly, etc.) and instead cultivating the ten positive courses (saving lives, generosity, speaking lovingly, etc.); meditation upon karmic law, love and compassion, the bodhisattva spirit, and so forth. All positive, spiritual and yogic endeavors, with the exception of those included in the practice of wisdom, contribute to the accumulation of merit.

The Vajrayana has methods to amplify and accelerate both processes of accumulation; but its techniques of fabricating a form body are most unique.[2]

His Holiness the present Dalai Lama informally discusses this topic in *Cultivating a Daily Meditation.* When asked a question related to the benefits of tantric meditation he replied,

> The main reason we want to achieve buddhahood is to help other sentient beings. The actual buddha quality which helps and serves all sentient beings is the form body, not the truth body. So when bodhisattvas cultivate the genuine aspiration to achieve enlightenment, they concentrate mainly on achieving the form body.
>
> In order to achieve the resultant form body, one has to accumulate the necessary causes and conditions according to the laws of cause and effect which pervade all impermanent phenomena, including the buddhahood state. One has to gather a substantial cause for this form body, which the practice of wisdom cannot become. Achievement of the form body is like the resultant imprint of accumulated merit.
>
> Although according to the sutras the practices of giving, discipline and so forth can also be causes for the form body, they cannot be its substantial cause. The factor which serves as the complete, substantial cause for the form body is the one practiced in tantra, the special energy, the winds.
>
> On the other hand, wisdom realizing emptiness is a substantial cause for the achievement of the truth body.

Since there are two types of resultant bodies, there are also two different causes. If the subtle bodily energies are not generated together with wisdom, then there cannot be the combination of method and wisdom.

Therefore one should develop a type of mind which, although of one entity, also has the part of method and the part of wisdom for the actualization of the form body and the actualization of the truth body, complete within the entity of one mind.

As stated earlier by the Third Dalai Lama, the Vajrayana is divided into four divisions in accordance with the four classes of tantras: kriya, charya, yoga, and highest yoga tantra. The first three of these are known as the 'lower tantras,' and are practiced in two stages: the yoga with signs; and the yoga beyond signs. Highest yoga tantra is also practiced in two stages, although these are called the generation and completion stages.

As we will see later, in both lower and highest tantra systems the first of the two stages mostly deals with the invocation of oneself as the mandala deity, the recitation of mantras, and the performance of certain ritual activities (many of a magical nature). The second stage, called 'the yoga beyond signs' and 'the completion stage,' uses less cosmic symbolism, focusing instead on more inner elements.

The four categories of tantras mentioned above are described by the Thirteenth Dalai Lama in *A Guide to the Buddhist Tantras:*

The nature of the Vajrayana path is fourfold, the division being made according to the four classes of the tantras. This fourfold classification is symbolized by the four levels of engaging in passionate communication with the mystical Knowledge Woman as methods of achieving the path to enlightenment (i.e., exchanging glances, laughing and touching, kissing and hugging, and entering into sexual union).

The four tantra classes are named kriya, charya,

yoga, and highest yoga tantra. In the first of these, great emphasis is placed on external rituals, such as washing and physical purification. In the second tantra division there is an equal balance of external activity and inner yoga. In the third division the inner yogas take precedence over the outer activities. Finally, in the fourth tantra division the emphasis is always on the inner yogas.

The principal difference between the three lower tantra classes and highest yoga tantra is stated as follows by His Holiness the present Dalai Lama in *Concerning the Kalachakra Initiation:*

> In the three lower tantra classes one generates a coarse consciousness combining method and wisdom, and then meditates on emptiness.
>
> The yogic techniques for engaging the powerful, subtle levels of consciousness focused in meditation born from the inseparability of method and wisdom are found only in the texts of highest yoga tantra.[3]

6 The Three Lower Classes of Tantra

As we will see in the following chapter, each of the three lower tantra divisions—kriya, charya and yoga—has a number of systems within it. These are symbolized by an individual mandala, with a deity at the center symbolizing the entire yogic tradition entailed by that tantra. The process begins with initiation, and the initiation ritual itself varies with each of the three tantra classes.

The first level of training is called 'the yoga of symbols,' a meditation involving the visualization of oneself and others as enlightened mandala deities. All forms become the mandala and its deities; all sound is heard as mantra; and all thoughts arise as the joyous interplay of divine awareness with the objects of knowledge. The exact terms used to characterize this ecstatic union of consciousness and its objects varies with each of the four tantra classes, and sometimes even within different tantra systems of the same class. The nature of the deities being visualized are described somewhat differently in each tantra class, although there is a similar theme of the deities being symbols of the aspect of one's consciousness to be utilized in accomplishing enlightenment, the actual methods by which enlightenment is attained, and the enlightenment state itself as an existential norm. These three in Tibetan are known as *zhi lam drebu,* or the basis, the path and the result.[1]

The Seventh Dalai Lama expresses the essence of the practice of the 'yoga of symbols' this way in *Songs of Spiritual Change,*

> Wherever you go, whatever you do,
> See yourself in the form of a tantric divinity
> With a phantom body that is manifest yet empty;
> Abiding thus in the inconceivable mansion of wisdom,
> Take sounds as mantra and thoughts as divine
>   inspiration.

The second level of training is called 'the yoga beyond symbols.' Here the style of meditation becomes more formless and internal. In a verse describing the stages in his own tantric training Lama Tsongkhapa writes,

> One may say that the highest yoga tantras
> Are supreme amongst the four tantra classes;
> But if when saying this one does not know
> The paths of the three lower tantra divisions,
> One's words fade into meaninglessness.
>
> Understanding this to be the case,
> I first familiarized myself with the kriya tantras,
> Both general and specific, of the three kriya
>   families. . . .

The first of the four tantric classes is that known as kriya. Here the 'three families' of the kriya division to which Lama Tsongkhapa is referring are the supreme family of Vairochana, also called the Tathagata Family, which includes mandala deities such as Manjushri, Ushnishavijaya and Sitatapatra, etc.; the intermediate Padma Family, which includes Avalokiteshvara, Tara, etc.; and the fundamental Vajra Family, including Vajrapani, Vajravidarana, etc. All kriya systems fall within one of these three 'families.'

As with all tantric paths, the process begins with receiving the initiations. The rite through which initiation is bestowed opens with the claiming of the place of the empowerment ceremony. The mandala deities are then invoked, the initiation vase is empowered, the disciples are enhanced, and so forth. Next follows the initiations of the flower garland, water, and crown. The disciples are thus ripened and matured by these processes, and are authorized to enter into practice of the kriya yogas.

The principal yogic technique employed in the practice of the kriya tantras is that known as 'the *dhyana*[2] of four branches of recitation.' The Thirteenth Dalai Lama's *A Guide to the Buddhist Tantras* describes these as follows:

> First there is the self-basis, or generation of oneself as a mandala deity. This involves meditation upon the six deities [or stages of arisal as a deity]: suchness, mantric sound, mantric letters, emanated forms, mudras, and symbols.
>
> Next is the alternate basis, which means generating the supporting and supported mandala and deities in front, sending forth praises and offerings, etc.
>
> Thirdly there is the mental basis, in which one meditates that one's mind rests on a moon disc at one's heart.
>
> Then finally there is the audial basis, wherein one concentrates upon the seed mantric syllable and mantra rosary on that moon disc, and then does the mantra recitation.

In addition to these yogic methods, the kriya methods speak of the dhyana of abiding within fire. Here one visualizes oneself as the chief mandala divinity, envisioning that at one's heart is a radiant, blazing fire in the nature of emptiness. One fixes the mind upon this fire. The sound of the mantra emanates from within the fire. Focusing the mind upon this is the dhyana of sound.

These are the practices known as 'the yoga of symbols,' the first stage of the kriya yogas.[3] Once one has developed proficiency in them one goes on to the 'yoga beyond symbols,' in which one engages in *shamatha* (meditative tranquility) and *vipashyana* (higher insight) meditation propelled by physical and mental ecstasy. This is the practice known as the 'dhyana bestowing liberation at the end of sound.'

The Great Thirteenth concludes his survey of the kriya tantras by saying,

> Through relying on these various dhyanas in conjunction with the yoga of symbols and yoga beyond symbols, one gains highest, intermediate or basic attainments, and by becoming a knowledge holder of life achieves supreme accomplishment.

The second class of tantras is that known as charya, or 'action.' Lama Tsongkhapa gives his assessment of them,

> The second tantra class is called charya.
> The principal charya tantra system
> Is the *Vairochana Abhisambodhi Tantra.*
> By training in that system I gained definite experience
> In the supreme points of the charya tantras.

As in the kriya division the actual practice of the charya tantras is twofold, consisting of the yoga of symbols and yoga beyond symbols.

Again, application to the charya tantras must be preceded by initiation. Here four vase initiations are given. These, as well as the bases of purification associated with this process, have several different names in the different charya traditions. The most common names for these four are the initiations of water, head-dress, vajra and bell, and name initiations.

The Great Thirteenth's *A Guide* summarizes the nature of the charya path:

The body of the charya training, path, together with
the results attained, are much the same as in the kriya
systems. However, here in the practice of the generation of the mandala of oneself as the divinity it is not
necessary to have the complete six deity stages [as was
the case in the kriya yogas explained above]. Also, here
the dhyana of four branches of recitation is applied in
both inner and outer aspects [which was not the case
in the kriya tantras].[4]

The third of the tantric divisions is known as yoga tantra.
A verse from Lama Tsongkhapa reveals his approach to them.

Foremost amongst the principal traditions of
The third tantric division, known as the yoga tantras,
Are the *Tattvasamgraha* and *Vajra Shekhara Tantra*.
By training in systems such as these,
I experienced a yoga tantra feast.

In the yoga tantras it is said that the four elements arise with
the strength of the four basic delusions—the three root delusions of attachment, aversion and ignorance, together with self-
ishness. These are to be transformed into the resultant four
primordial wisdoms[5]—distinguishing wisdom, the wisdom of
equanimity, the accomplishing wisdom, and the mirror-like
wisdom. The means is the yoga of non-dual profundity and
radiance in union, together with the Mahayana attitude (i.e.,
the bodhimind) and a special application of the perfections
of generosity, wisdom, and enthusiastic perseverance.

These four primordial wisdoms manifest in the four Tathagata
Family aspects: Tathagata 'Diamond Sphere'; Vajra 'Victory
over the Three Worlds'; Padma 'Tamer of the Living'; and
the Karma Family of 'Accomplishing Feats,' that unites both
Ratna and Karma natures.

As a preliminary to practice of the yoga tantras one must
receive initiation into whichever of these Tathagata Families
is appropriate to one's individual character. The basis of the

initiation ceremony can be a chalk, cloth or meditation mandala.

The actual initiation entails taking the bodhisattva vow, the pledges of the five Tathagata Families,[6] the pledge of secrecy, the five knowledge initiations and also the master's initiation, and then concludes with the verses of appreciation, etc. When the disciples are thus ripened and matured by means of receiving initiation, they become authorized to enter into the yogas of the two stages—those of symbols and those beyond symbols.

The Great Thirteenth's *A Guide to the Buddhist Tantras* describes the path of the yoga tantras,

> By means of the mandala and the supremely victorious activities being performed in either extensive, medium or abbreviated forms one cultivates the coarse yoga of symbols. Firstly one visualizes oneself as the mandala divinity and then generates the divinity in front, incorporating both supporting and supported mandalas in the meditation. After this has been accomplished the subtle mandala is generated at the tip of the nose of oneself envisioned as the divinity. The signs and symbols of the family with which the mandala is linked are similarly visualized. The mind is then held on this subtle image, and by forcefully engaging the methods common to all three lower tantra classes one accomplishes the subtle yoga of symbols.
>
> Next one engages in the yoga beyond symbols by absorbing the mind in the sphere of purification in emptiness, the objects purified including the self-generation and frontal generation mandalas, deities, mantras and so forth. In this way the ordinary aspects of body, speech, mind and activities gradually acquire the visible and tangible characteristics of the supported and supporting divinity forms. This is 'the body *mahamudra*.' The sound of the mantra is spontaneously heard. This is 'the speech *dharmamudra*.' The wisdom of non-dual profundity and radiance, which is main-

tained by shamatha and vipashyana combined, is 'the
mind *samayamudra*.' The appearance of impure activities automatically ceases and the four tantric activities
of pacification, increase, power and wrath are accomplished merely by means of meditative absorption. This
is 'the activity *karmamudra*.'

In this tradition it is said that when the seal of these
four *mudras* is applied by a bodhisattva holding the
form of a buddha and who is a knowledge holder on
the tenth stage abiding near the end of cyclic existence,
the all-pervading buddhas are inspired to arise from
their *samadhi*. They then reveal the empowerments and
knowledge mantras, by means of which the bodhisattva
experiences the five clear purifications (or five enlightenments) and achieves final enlightenment.[7]

A number of important technical terms have been used here
that we will see later in different contexts. Included in these
is *dhyana*, a term found in abundance throughout the literature of the lower tantras; as we will see later, this word is also
integral to the Kalachakra yogas, although there it is given quite
a different application. The four mudras mentioned above are
also discussed at length in the Kalachakra system; although
again within a considerably different context.

It is said that one of the reasons a study of the lower tantras
is a useful preliminary to a study of the higher is because very
often the way a term (and the yogic technique that it represents)
is used in the simpler systems provides the background for
appreciating it in the more sophisticated environment of the
highest yoga tantras.

The Second Dalai Lama describes the basic sentiment of
tantric practice in his *Mystical Verses of a Mad Dalai Lama:*

The experience of the yogi is then this:
The world is seen as the mystical mandala
And all living beings as tantric deities;
Everything that one eats and drinks

Becomes transformed into blissful ambrosia;
All of one's activities become spiritual,
Regardless of how they conventionally appear;
And every sound that one makes
Becomes part of a great vajra song.

I, a tantric yogin, have a blissful mind;
I, a tantric yogin, spontaneously generate goodness
In everything that I do.
All male divinities dance within me
And all female divinities channel
Their sacred vajra songs through me.

7 *Entering into the Highest Yoga Tantras*

The incomparable Lama Tsongkhapa says this of the highest yoga tantras:

> With the sages of holy India,
> The two systems of highest yoga tantra
> Famous as the sun and moon
> Were the male tantra of Guhyasamaja and
> The female yogini tantra of Heruka Chakrasamvara,
> Both of which have root and explanatory tantras.
>
> From amongst the highest yoga tantras,
> The supreme teachings given by Buddha,
> The most extensive is that of glorious Guhyasamaja,
>   king of the tantras.
> Understanding the sublime path of Guhyasamaja
> Bestows fearless, confident understanding
> Of all the teachings of the Buddha.
>
> It is said that the female highest yoga tantras
> Are inconceivably numerous;
> But of all these the central and supreme

Is that of Heruka Chakrasamvara,
A tantric tradition that stands as an ornament
On the very tip of the victory banner.

Another important highest yoga tantra system,
And one with a unique manner of presenting the path
Is that of Kalachakra, 'the Wheel of Time,'
Which is based upon *The Kalachakra Abbreviated
    Tantra*
Together with its commentary *A Stainless Light*.

Three major traditions of highest yoga tantra are listed here by Lama Tsongkhapa: those of Guhyasamaja, Heruka Chakrasamvara, and Kalachakra.

Often to this is added a fourth, that of Vajrabhairava, otherwise known as Yamantaka, 'the Destroyer of Death.' This lineage is not mentioned separately by Tsongkhapa, due to its similarity to the Guhyasamaja tradition.

The highest yoga tantras are placed in three classes, known as male, female, and non-dual (i.e., both male and female elements in balance). Sometimes in addition to this the male tantras are again sub-divided into three basic types: those mainly using desire as the path; those mainly using aggression; and those mainly using mental lethargy as a force for the path to enlightenment.

When spoken of in these terms, Guhyasamaja is said to be the principal male highest yoga tantra using desire and passion as the path to enlightenment. Yamantaka is the principal male highest yoga tantra using aggression and anger as the path. Heruka Chakrasamvara is a female tantra, and thus mostly uses desire as the path.

As for Kalachakra, the early Tibetan masters classed this as a non-dual tantra on the basis that it combines both male and female techniques in equal balance. In the Gelukpa school, however, it is classified as a female tantra, because of its focus on the doctrine of emptiness.

In explaining the above verse by Lama Tsongkhapa the Thirteenth Dalai Lama discusses the tantric doctrine of the substantial cause that accords with the nature of a buddha's form body, or rupakaya. This is the subtle level of energy upon which consciousness rides from lifetime to lifetime, like a rider on a horse. These subtle energies are to be shaped into the impure and then pure illusory bodies. It is said that the principal sources explaining the methods for attaining this illusory body are the male tantras, the most extensive of these being the Guhyasamaja tradition.

He then speaks of how the cause that accords with the nature of a buddha's truth body, or dharmakaya, is the most subtle level of consciousness; this is to be generated as the semblant and actual clear light consciousnesses. The principal sources explaining the methods for realizing this clear light are the female tantras. The most extensive of the mainstream female tantras is the Heruka Chakrasamvara cycle. (Kalachakra is also a female highest yoga tantra, although, as we will see later, it does not use terminology such as 'illusory body' and 'clear light.')

The initiation process of highest yoga tantra differs considerably from those of the three lower tantras. Most highest yoga tantra initiations begin with the standard procedures of the master analyzing, claiming and purifying the place of the rite. He then establishes protection and consecration. This is followed by the rite for the earth divinity, the mandala divinities, consecration of the initiation vase, enhancement of the disciples's stream of being, and so forth. As for this last phase (i.e., enhancement of the disciple), this includes the instruction on establishing correct motivation, taking the inner initiation, the disciple's act of making requests and asking to be cared for until enlightenment is attained, establishing the pledges, blessing the three doors (body, speech and mind), tossing the divination stick, drinking of the vase waters, being given the kusha grass and mystical arm-band, giving birth to appreciative joy, and being instructed on how to observe for prophetic dreams.

The disciples make the request for the initiation. They are

then given a blindfold, the deity costumes, and a flower garland. They generate the bodhisattva resolve, take the precepts of the five Tathagata Families, are instructed to generate the all-encompassing yoga mind, and are given the oath of secrecy. This all occurs outside the mandala curtain.

They enter inside the curtain. To establish external merit they circumambulate the mandala, offer prostrations, and are placed in the mystical bond. For inner merit they meditate on receiving a rainfall of wisdom nectars. The master pronounces the words of truth, and the disciples throw the divination flower into the mandala. They are then given the flower garland initiation.

This is the stage of entering the mandala while still blindfolded. Next the disciples are instructed to remove the blindfold. They have now acquired the spiritual maturity necessary in order to be allowed to see the supporting and supported mandalas, and they proceed to receive the four initiations: vase, secret, wisdom and sacred word.

The first of these, the vase initiation, includes the five standard initiations of the five Tathagata Families, and also the exclusive vajra master initiation. They are all called 'vase empowerments' because each stage of the ceremony is concluded with the sprinkling of water from the initiation vase.[1]

Almost all the highest yoga tantra systems contain these six fundamental stages of the vase initiation (i.e., the initiations of the five Tathagatas and of a vajra master). However, some manuals further subdivide these processes, and in these alternative traditions the vase initiation may include as many as nine and even eleven phases.

Through receiving these initiations, the disciples experience purification of all coarse and subtle bodily obscurations, such as grasping at mundane appearances. They are empowered to meditate upon the generation stage yogas and to perform the various mandala activities. The potency for accomplishing the *nirmanakaya* (emanation body) of a buddha is established.

Then follows the secret initiation. Here the disciples rely upon the use of the special secret substance, and experience purification of all coarse and subtle speech obscurations, such as grasping at energy and mantra as being separate. They are authorized to cultivate the illusory body, the conventional reality, and to meditate upon the yogas that accomplish this body, namely, the yogas of isolation of body, speech and mind. The potency for accomplishing the *sambhogakaya* (beatific body) of a buddha is established.

The third of the four highest yoga tantra initiations is called the wisdom initiation. By means of it the mind is purified of all coarse and subtle obscurations, especially the obscuration hindering the perception of all appearance (i.e., all reality) as arising in the sportive play of bliss and emptiness. One is authorized to meditate on the semblant and actual clear light yogas, the highest reality. The potency of the *dharmakaya* (truth body) of a buddha is established.

Fourthly is the sacred word initiation. Here the wisdom of the third initiation is used to point out the nature of the state of great union. All coarse and subtle stains of the body, speech and mind are simultaneously purified. Especially, the instincts of the distortion caused by grasping at duality are removed. One is authorized to meditate upon the completion stage yogas of the inseparable two levels of truth, i.e., the inseparable nature of the illusory body and clear light. The potency is established to actualize the state of perfect enlightenment, and to achieve the *svabhavikakaya*, the quintessence body of a buddha.

These are the four initiations that constitute the body of the empowerment ceremony authorizing practice of an according highest yoga tantra system. All traditions in this tantra class contain these four in one form or another.[2]

As we will see later, the Kalachakra initiation ceremony is more elaborate than that of most highest yoga tantra systems.

The First Panchen Lama refers to the Kalachakra initiations as follows in *An Aspiration to Fulfill the Stages of the Glorious Kalachakra Path:*

Having received the tantric initiations
Of entering like a child, as well as the four worldly
   and four non-worldly initiations
That purify one's continuum of stains
And plant the seeds of the four kayas, may I dwell
Gracefully within the tantric disciplines and trainings.

Thus in the Kalachakra tradition the initiation ceremony consists of three sets. Of these, the first is known as the 'seven initiations of entering like a child,'and incorporates a symbolism considerably different from that used in the mainstream tantras. As for the four initiations in each of the two last sets, these four have the same names as the four presented in the mainstream tantras, although their natures and functions sometimes differ.

The approach that one should take toward the highest yoga tantras, as well as the benefits of doing so, were aptly expressed by the Seventh Dalai Lama:[3]

Draw into the depth of your heart the waters
Of the four tantric enpowerments
That have the potency to purify all faults and stains.
Then under the guidance of a qualified teacher
Enter into a perfect tantric path proved valid
By living oral tradition
And fill the mind with eternal delight.

Inner vision sees the world as mandala,
And the dance of the beautiful consort flows.
The mind settles in meditation focused
Upon youthful awareness of bliss and void,
And the ecstasy that soars freely
In all situations is known.

Having received the initiations, one then proceeds to take up the yogas of the according system.

8   Four Highest Yoga Tantra Systems

It may be useful at this point to take a brief look at each of these four highest yoga tantra systems: first the three mainstream traditions, and then Kalachakra by itself. The Great Thirteenth speaks this way of the three mainstream highest yoga tantra traditions in his *Heart of the Enlightenment Teachings:*[1]

> For those who are not satiated with the Sutrayana trainings there are the four classes of tantras: kriya, charya, yoga and highest yoga tantra.
>
> The quintessence of these four is the highest yoga tantras, or 'great highest tantra division,' through which the full enlightenment of final buddhahood can be achieved in this one short lifetime.
>
> In order to achieve complete buddhahood one requires a path uniting both method (energy) and wisdom (insight) aspects of the path. This produces the state of the great union of evolved body and mind, which is the ultimate attainment. In the highest yoga tantras, 'method' refers to the illusory body yogas and 'wisdom' refers to the clear light yogas.
>
> The highest yoga tantra system that most clearly elu-

cidates the path of the illusory body yogas is that of
Guhyasamaja, 'The Tantra of the Secret Assembly.'
The system most clearly elucidating the clear light
yogas is that of Heruka Chakrasamvara, 'The Tantra
of the Heruka Wheel of Bliss.' The essential points
of both of these systems is skillfully combined in the
Yamantaka tradition, 'The Tantra of the Destroyer of
Death.'

Therefore these three highest yoga tantra systems—
Guhyasamaja, Heruka Chakrasamvara, and Yamantaka
—work very well together as a unified method bringing quick and easy enlightenment.

As we saw earlier, each of these three systems of tantric theory
and practice is constituted of a generation and completion stage
yoga, as is the case with all other highest yoga tantra traditions, including Kalachakra. In all of these systems the generation stage primarily involves the enhancement of the mind
through a radical transformation of the sense of self, and the
cultivation of creative imagination, in which one generates
visualizations of the stages of unfoldment of the mandala.[2]

Here it is said that the two forces one needs to make firm
are inner radiance and divine pride.[3] The former refers to the
ability to dwell within the mandala visualizations with clarity
and a luminous presence of mind; the latter refers to the transference of the ordinary sense of the self, or ego, into self-
identification as the mandala lord. This ego transference, which
produces release from the ordinary sense of the self, together
with all the delusions and limitations thus produced, instantly
places the meditator within the tantric framework.

The first of the highest yoga tantras to surface publicly in
India was that of Guhyasamaja. It is also one of the most extensive of the high tantric systems. In the Tibetan tradition
it is often said that if one understands the generation and completion stage yogas of Guhyasamaja, this comprehension can
be used as an infrastructure for the understanding of all other
tantric systems.

The generation stage yoga is usually defined as follows: A tantric yoga having the effect of preparing (the mind of a meditator) for the completion stage yogas, and that has the characteristic of (incorporating meditation upon) the experiences of death, intermediate state, and rebirth as the paths of the three bodies of a buddha—dharmakaya (truth body), sambhogakaya (beatific body), and nirmanakaya (emanation body). In this context the terms 'the first path,' 'the path of creative imagination,' 'the generation stage,' and 'the path of mental projection' are all synonymous terms and thus refer to this same yogic process.[4]

In the Guhyasamaja tradition, the generation stage yoga begins with the meditation upon the wisdom of the emptiness of the four doors of liberation. This is the time when the universe previously was destroyed and became nothing. Later the universe again began to reform, and the elements once more began to reappear. This process is represented by the arisal of the protection wheel, the *dharmodaya,* the four elemental mandalas, the crossed vajras, the inconceivable mansion, and so forth.

After our universe had once again become developed, the sentient beings began to reappear in it. This was a golden age on earth, and the sentient beings at that time took birth miraculously. To symbolize this, the thirty-two deities of the mandala are visualized as suddenly manifesting simultaneously in a single moment.

Next follows the placement of the tantric divinities at particular sites of the body of oneself as the principal figure in the mandala. One meditates that they become inseparable in nature from the psychophysical aggregates, elements, and so forth. This establishes the basis of the deity visualization.

The world view in the Guhyasamaja traditions is that the sentient beings with the karma to experience birth from a womb on this planet and whose bodies are composed of the six impermanent substances must eventually meet with death. At the time of death they experience the dissolution of the twenty-five coarse substances: the five psychophysical aggregates, such as form and so forth; the five primordial wisdoms, such as the mirror-like wisdom, etc.; the four elements; the six gates of perception; and the five sensory objects. At each phase of this dissolution there is the external sign of the respective sensory power losing its capacity, and also the corresponding element failing in strength. Simultaneously there occur inner signs, such as the mirage-like vision, smoke, fireflies, and the flickering of light like that of a butterlamp. When the elements have thus dissolved there is the threefold phase of absorption of the vital energies, called appearance, increase, and near-attainment. (We will see more on these essential terms later in the Kalachakra translations.) This melts into the experience of the clear light consciousness. A sense of luminosity arises, like the vibrant radiance of a clear dawn.

With this clear light level of consciousness acting as a simultaneously present condition and the flowing energy which is the vehicle of this consciousness acting as the substantial cause, the dying person emerges from the clear light experience and prepares to enter into the *bardo,* or state between death and rebirth.[5]

The three phases (mentioned above) of appearance, increase and near-attainment, as well as the visions of mirage, smoke, and so forth now once again arise. However, this time their order of appearance is reversed. In this way the dying person leaves the clear light and enters into the bardo.

The subsequent Guhyasamaja generation stage meditation involves five phases of unfoldment that represent the five paths as the stages of the life process. These are known as the five clear purifications, or the five enlightenments: suchness, seat, symbol, syllable, and complete deity body.

The meditator contemplates the stages of these five unfoldments and (imagines) arising as a beatific body deity. Then just as the bardo being enters into a womb and eventually takes rebirth, the beatific body deity transforms into the emanation body deity Vajrasattva.

Thus the meditations of the processes of formation, disintegration, birth, death, bardo, and so forth of the world and its inhabitants, and symbolized by the various phases beginning with purification in suchness until the offering of suchness, are known as the perfect accomplishment of one's own purpose. They constitute the meditative absorption known as 'the first application.'

Then to symbolize the physical deeds of the resultant stage of buddhahood, the deities of the space mandala, together with the consorts of their individual families, are summoned to the heart. Clouds of emanations are sent forth and withdrawn in order to purify the world and its inhabitants.

In the subsequent stages of the process, the mental deeds of the resultant stage of buddhahood are symbolized as follows. To arrest mental wandering and torpor one visualizes mystical hand implements, tiny in size, at the tip of the nose. Alternatively, one generates a coarse single-pointed recollection of a drop the size of a mustard seed, within which is envisioned the complete deity mandala. This is performed together with the processes of emanation and absorption, and is known as the yoga of subtle realization supported by meditative tranquility.

Now the buddhahood deeds of speech are symbolized by mental and also verbal mantric recitation.

The Great Thirteenth summarizes the process:

> In brief, from the phase of meditating on the mystical hand implements at the upper door until the phase of establishing the powers, there are forty-nine steps to be cultivated.
>
> There are the three samadhis, such as that called the first application; the four branches, known as propitiation, proximate attainment, attainment and great attainment; four yogas to be cultivated, called yoga, immediate yoga, intense yoga and great yoga; four vajra stages, known as emptiness enlightenment, seed absorption, form completion, and mantric syllable placement; and so forth. These are the processes of the Guhyasamaja generation stage to be cultivated as

a preliminary to entering into the completion stage yogas.

Such is the nature of the Guhyasamaja generation stage yogas, a male tantra specializing in using desire as a path to enlightenment.

As for the generation stage practices of the Yamantaka system, which utilize anger and aggressive forces for enlightenment, one of the better summaries of this system is found in Lama Lobzang Chinpa's *The Two Yogic Stages of the Yamantaka Tantra*, which is a commentary to a small verse work the Second Dalai Lama wrote on Yamantaka practice:

> The two main practices in the Yamantaka generation stage yoga are inner radiance and the cultivation of divine pride. By applying these to the various phases of the generation stage meditation, one becomes familiar with the meditations of taking death as a path of dharmakaya, taking the in-between state as the sambhogakaya, and taking rebirth as the nirmanakaya.
>
> Firstly one accomplishes coarse clear visualization by meditating on the entire mandala. Then one visualizes the mandala in the drop, which is drawn into the lotus of the consort. This is subtle clear visualization.
>
> Meditating upon the mandala in this way strengthens the seeds of the three buddhakayas and thus opens a net of light to dispel darkness from death, the bardo, and the rebirth process.
>
> Through meditating in this way upon the generation stage yogas in four daily sessions—predawn, late morning, afternoon and evening—one quickly lays the foundations upon which the completion stage yogas can be engaged and the state of enlightenment quickly won.

The third of the highest yoga tantra systems studied in the two central Gelukpa tantric monasteries is that of Heruka

Chakrasamvara, which is in the class of female tantras. Lama Tsongkhapa lavishly praised this tradition,

> It is said that the female highest yoga tantras
> Are inconceivably numerous;
> But of all these the central and supreme
> Is that of Heruka Chakrasamvara,
> A tantra like the ornament
> On the very tip of a victory banner.

This is the tradition accepted by Lama Tsongkhapa as the heart of the mainstream female highest yoga tantras.

There were three principal Indian lineages of the Heruka Chakrasamvara tradition, namely, those of the *mahasiddhas* Luipada (Tib., Luipa), Gandhapada (Tib., Tilbupa), and Krishnacharyin (Tib., Nakchopa). Each of these were preserved in separate transmissions. Although the essence of the three is said to be the same, the mandalas of each vary in complexity.

The Second Dalai Lama outlines the Heruka Chakrasamvara generation stage yogas in *The Tantric Yogas of Sister Niguma,*

> Here one should apply oneself to (a mandala practice) such as that of the five-deity Heruka Chakrasamvara cycle, and mentally purify the bases of death, intermediate state, and rebirth, mentally transforming these into the three perfect buddha bodies [dharmakaya, sambhogakaya, and nirmanakaya]. This ripens one's stream of being for the practice of the completion stage methods that accomplish the actual purification and transformation.
>
> In brief, one should accomplish both coarse and subtle aspects of the generation stage yogas for transforming these three states into the three bodies of enlightenment. Moreover, it is said that one should meditate upon as complex a mandala as possible for this purpose. The degree of complexity of the mandala medi-

tated upon in the generation stage yogas affects the degree to which one will purify these three bases [death, intermediate state, and rebirth]; and the more complex the mandala meditated upon the more powerful becomes one's potency of ripening one's continuum through the completion stage yogas.

As we will see in a later chapter, the generation stage yogas of the Kalachakra system are based on the same principles, although they contain a number of unique characteristics.

Once the practitioner has gained stability in these generation stage practices he or she can enter into the completion stage yogas.[6]

9 Completion Stage Yogas in the Mainstream Tantras

The completion stage yogas of each of these four highest yoga tantra systems are somewhat unique. Nonetheless, the Guhyasamaja tradition is taken as the key to the code of the others, with the exception of Kalachakra. The practice in the Gelukpa school[1] is to first look at the completion stage structure of Guhyasamaja as a key to understanding the other two 'mainstream tantras,' and then to use all three of these as a background to approaching the Kalachakra system.

The Guhyasamaja completion stage consists of six yogas. These are known by the names body isolation, speech isolation, mind isolation, illusory body, the clear light, and great union.[2]

Here it is said that the subjects taken as the focal points of practice are the coarse, subtle and extremely subtle levels of the body and mind. By 'coarse body and mind' are meant this ordinary body and the sensory consciousness that it sustains. The subtle body is that constituted of the channels, energies and drops; and the subtle mind includes all conceptual levels of consciousness. Finally, 'extremely subtle body and mind' refers to the fundamental energy that accompanies the extremely subtle mind, the primordial clear light consciousness, from lifetime to lifetime.

These three have to be separated from one another in order for the subtler to be utilized in yogic practice. The completion stage yogas have this as their purpose. As a result of practicing them one gains the ability to enter into meditation uninhibited by the limitations of the coarse levels of body and mind.

The process then is to collect together the most subtle of the physical energies of the body and bring them through the central energy channel to the chakra at the heart. One then applies the specific tantric yogas for 'shaping' them into an illusory body. This illusory body supports a very subtle level of consciousness, which is then directed to meditation on emptiness.[3]

The Seventh Dalai Lama expressed the experience this way in *Songs of Spiritual Change:*

> One bathes consciousness in the innate clear light of
>   mind,
> Shapes subtle energies into the form of a deity,
> And abides unwaveringly in the deep, radiant yoga
> That does not divide meditation from non-meditation.

When first generated, the illusory body is called 'impure.' It is then purified by meditating on emptiness from within the sphere of awareness of the clear light consciousness, until it becomes the 'pure illusory body.' This 'impure' illusory body, created from the most subtle energy, can in turn be used to transform one's ordinary physical body into a 'rainbow body.' Here the gross physical attributes of the body are released, and one's physical base is as though made of rainbow light. (Nonetheless, even this 'rainbow body' is based on subtle material, i.e., subtle light-energy, unlike the utterly immaterial 'empty body' created by the Kalachakra yogas.)

The 'clear light consciousness' referred to in the highest yoga tantras is said to be of two types and also of two levels. The two types of clear light consciousness are called 'mother and child.' The 'mother clear light' refers to the natural clear light level of the mind, the most subtle and primordial aspect of consciousness that we all have. This is the deepest aspect of the subconscious, and thus is not accessible to an untrained person, even though it is the basis of all mental activity. In contrast, the 'child clear light' is the yogic cultivation of a clear light realization; in other words, it is the product of a yogic effort. This 'child clear light' is cultivated through various stages, the two principal being called 'semblant' and 'actual.'

The path of the mainstream tantras thus strives to bring about the perfect union of pure illusory body and actual clear light consciousness, a state called 'Great Union,' synonymous with buddhahood.

The completion stage methods that are used to bring about this rapid enlightenment involve working with what is known as 'the vajra body.' We will see later how this is done in Kalachakra, for the First Dalai Lama describes the meditation in detail in *Notes on the Two Yogic Stages of Glorious Kalachakra*. The process is much the same in Guhyasamaja and the other mainstream tantras, although there are some differences in detail (most of which are listed by the First Dalai Lama).

The topic of the vajra body involves projecting a mentally created image of what is known in Tibetan as *tsa lung tikley,* or 'energy channels, vital energies, and drops.'

In Guhyasamaja the channels are visualized much as described later by the First Dalai Lama in his Kalachakra commentary, although in Guhyasamaja and so forth they do not cross over at the navel. These channels converge at a number of energy centers, or *chakras,* and at each energy center the way in which they converge forms the shape of a lotus flower with petals. In Guhyasamaja and the other mainstream tantras the heart chakra has eight petals, the throat sixteen, the forehead thirty-two, and the navel sixty-four. (Again, Kalachakra exhibits a number of distinctions in this regard.) The Guhyasamaja discussion of the vital energies is also similar to the Kalachakra presentation, with the exception that the former speaks of five vital energies whereas the latter subdivides these into ten.

The subject of *tikley,* or drops, deserves separate mention. In the mainstream tantras these are the male and female forces of the body, the former being symbolized by a droplet of sperm and the latter by a droplet of ovum. These 'drops' are said to strongly influence our emotional and psychological atmosphere. In untrained people these male and female droplets, a word perhaps better translated as 'hormones,' flow through the body at random, driven by the winds of karmic predisposition. The yogi applies the completion stage methods in order to bring these droplets into harmony and to prepare them to serve as a new 'house' for the mind. This physical residence then gives rise to a more subtle and stable level of consciousness, one pervaded by a bliss symbolized by and said to be a hundred times more intense than sexual orgasm. This consciousness pervaded by great bliss is then placed in meditation upon emptiness, inducing a state known in Tibetan as *lhenkyey detong yeshey,* which translates as 'the primordial wisdom of emptiness produced together with bliss,' or perhaps as 'the innate primordial wisdom of bliss and void.'

As we will see later, the Kalachakra system works with four other types of drops not mentioned in the mainstream tantras.

Through working with these channels, centers, drops and energy currents, the meditator progresses along the various levels of the six completion stage yogas.

The completion stage is generally defined as the tantric yoga wherein (the practitioner) trains by means of causing the subtle energies to enter, abide and dissolve within the central channel through meditative application. In this context the terms 'the second path,' 'the path beyond creative imagination,' 'the completion stage,' and 'the path beyond mental projection' are all synonymous terms and refer to the same yogic process. As said earlier, these yogas are sixfold. Each of these in turn has its own definition, but as these are rather technical I will not list them here.

The first of these six is the yoga of body isolation. It is called

by this name because in it all ordinary physical appearances
are dissolved and are made to arise in the forms of mandalas
and deities. Thus in a sense it is a continuation of the generation stage, for the power of visualization is still a primary force
being used. However, because of the intensity of the level of
meditation and also because of the subtle levels of bodily energy
being worked with, it is classified as a completion stage yoga.
The process gives rise to four subtle states of consciousnesses,
known as the 'four empties,' which have the nature of bliss
and are directed to meditation on emptiness.[4] In this context
the four 'empties' are also sometimes called the 'four joys.'

It is said that the objects of the yoga include one's aggregates,
elements, entrances, and sensory objects, each of which is five-
fold, making a total of twenty factors. The five buddha families are then applied to each of these twenty, making a total
of one hundred supreme natures. Here the four elements, together with consciousness, constitute the 'five thatness natures'
to be meditated upon. Body, speech and mind envisioned as
being deities of the three vajras are the three secret natures.
Finally, the practitioner possessing the three doors is envisioned
as being Buddha Vajradhara, which is 'the great secret solitary nature.' All of these factors are 'sealed' with the mark of
bliss and void, and are 'isolated' in the nature of a deity body.
The yogi then meditates on the yoga of the subtle drop at the
tip of the jewel, thus causing the vital energies, followed by
the mind that it supports, to flow into the central channel.
These enter, abide and dissolve at the heart. One achieves absorption in the sphere of bliss and void, and attains the samadhi
of the vajra body isolation in which the hundred natures and
so forth appear as divine forms. This signals the completion
of the yoga of body isolation.

The second yoga is known as 'speech isolation.' Speech here
refers to vital energy, both on the coarse level of the bodily
breathing and the subtle level of the bodily energies. The Thirteenth Dalai Lama speaks of this yoga as follows in *A Guide
to the Buddhist Tantras:*

The basis of the second isolation, or that of speech, involves the root and branch energies in coarse and subtle aspects, and especially the life-sustaining energy at the heart, together with the indestructible drops. This, the basis of all expression, abides as a short syllable *a*, symbol of the ultimate profundity.

The yogi engages the breathing technique known as vajra recitation, while appreciating the inseparability of breath/energy and mantra, thus experiencing yogic isolation in the nature of an illusory body. One moves the indestructible drop to the various places of the body, such as the energy centers at the heart, head, secret place, and so forth. Also, one engages in the vase breathing yoga, taking as objects of concentration the indestructible drop, together with the mantra wheels, the energies in the nature of five radiances, the substances of white and red [i.e., male and female] sexual fluids locked in mystical union and formed into a drop the size of a mustard seed, and so forth.

In this manner all the root energies, with the exception of the all-pervading energy, are brought under control. The yogi then applies the vajra recitation methods and ignites the mystic fire. The vital energies are absorbed into the indestructible drop, and the knots in the channels at the center of the heart are released. This is the process of the yoga of speech isolation, the samadhi of vajra speech.

As we will see later in the First Dalai Lama's *Notes on the Two Yogic Stages of Glorious Kalachakra,* the two yogic techniques of vajra recitation and vase breathing are also very important in the Kalachakra system. As these practices are explained in some detail in that text, there is no need to describe them here.

The third yoga is that of mind isolation. Here it is said that the focuses of the practice are the subtle minds of the three appearances and the eighty conceptual minds. One relies upon the inner condition of vajra recitation and the outer condition of a visualized or actual consort, and 'isolates' into the sphere of semblant clear light focused on emptiness. One then induces the four joys of downward showering and upward rising energies. As an inner condition one focuses the vajra recitation method upon the all-pervading energy. The experience of the body dissolving into clear light at the heart arises, as does the vision of the world and its inhabitants. The dissolution of the eighty natural conceptual minds is experienced: thirty-three in the nature of appearance, forty in the nature of increase, and seven in the nature of near attainment. These eighty natural conceptual minds, that are carried by the coarse and subtle contaminated energies, thus dissolve just as at the moment of death. The wisdoms of the three appearances arise, leading the mind to the experience of the semblant clear light. This is the process of the yoga of mind isolation.

In the Yamantaka tantric tradition 'mind isolation' is referred to as the 'commitment yoga.' Commenting upon it, Lama Lobzang Chinpa writes in *The Two Yogic Stages of the Yamantaka Tantra*,

> Through reliance upon the commitment yoga one brings all energies into the central channel and experiences all the stages of energy absorption, just as at the time of death. This gives rise to the experience of semblant clear light and final mind isolation.

The use of the term 'final mind isolation' is important. This stage is achieved only when the yogi is able to simulate the death process in meditation and enter a state of suspended animation. All the signs of death arise, including that of the clear light of death. The yogi applies the semblant clear light techniques, enters the death state, and shapes the primordial energies into an illusory body.

It is said that final mind isolation, and the creation of the illusory body, can only be achieved in this lifetime through conventional means if one has already achieved it in a previous lifetime; to initially achieve it one has to rely upon a *karmamudra,* or action seal, i.e., a sexual consort, or accomplish the yoga in the bardo. This technique is applied here.

The fourth yoga, that of the illusory body, is described as follows by Lama Lobzang Chinpa in *The Two Yogic Stages of the Yamantaka Tantra:*

> The subtle bodily energies transformed into lights of five colors act as the substantial cause, and the semblant clear light of mind acts as the simultaneously present condition. Then...one transforms one's old aggregates and causes them to emerge as the actual body of the deity embellished with the net of major and minor signs of perfection, like a fish drawn out of the depths of a lake.
>
> This is the impure illusory body of nine stages.... Its nature is described by five images: the body of a dream, a reflection in a mirror, the moon's image in a lake, an illusory person (projected by a magician), and a water bubble.

The basis for producing the illusory body is twofold: the semblant clear light (attained in the previous yoga), which acts as a simultaneously present condition; and the vital energies of five radiances, the vehicle of that clear light, which acts as the substantial cause. It is this that produces the illusory body described by the various similes and having the according qualities. It is this illusory body that substitutes for the merit generated in the exoteric Sutrayana by means of three aeons of practice, and that in the Vajrayana represents the conventional level of truth. It is often said that anyone attaining this level of the illusory body is guaranteed of enlightenment in this very lifetime.

Next is the clear light yoga. Here the Great Thirteenth's *A Guide to the Buddhist Tantras* provides a succinct account of them.

The external time for cultivating the experience of clear light consciousness is dawn, when neither sun nor moon is in the sky and yet darkness has passed. The internal time is the meditative state wherein one experiences subsiding of the three appearances [i.e., appearance, increase and near-attainment], just as at the moment of death. At the conjunction of these two moments, the clear light consciousness is most easily invoked. At a time when these two are possible, the yogi relies upon inner and outer conditions to manifest the clear light, which in the Vajrayana represents the ultimate level of truth and is the remedy that eliminates at once the nine circles of obscurations to knowledge.

The sixth and final completion stage yoga is that of great union. Here one reverses the processes whereby one entered into clear light consciousness, pulling back into the consciousness of near-attainment and so forth. Simultaneously one experiences the path of freedom, the great union of transcendence, which is produced from non-contaminated mind and energy. Arising from that absorption one realizes the inseparable nature of the body and mind. This stage is called the 'great union of a trainee.' One then intensifies the experience by engaging in the three methods known simply as contrived, uncontrived, and utterly uncontrived.

Training in this way one experiences the clear light at the fulfillment of training, thus eliminating all obscurations to omniscience and attaining the 'great union of no-more-training' which is enriched by the seven mystical qualities. This is the stage of complete enlightenment.

Lama Lobzang Chinpa speaks most eloquently of this final yoga in his commentary *The Two Yogic Stages of the Yamantaka Tantra*,

> One arises from this simultaneously born bliss and wisdom. At that time the substantial cause—the subtle energy of the body arising as the five lights, which

is the vehicle of the simultaneously present condition, i.e., the actual clear light of the mind—causes one's aggregates to transform into a fully embellished vajra body. One attains the pure illusory body, which has abandoned all objective obscurations, and one's clear light realization becomes fully manifest.

This pure illusory body then enters into the previous coarse nirmanakaya body, and there arises the union of one taste of the pure illusory body with the pure heart, the wisdom of the actual clear light. This stage is called 'the great union of a trainee.'

When the practitioner on this stage perceives the signs of being ready to approach the stage of 'the great union of a master,' he enters into meditation.... As before, one relies upon the external condition of a karmamudra and the internal condition of meditation upon emptiness, bringing the energies into the central channel and causing them to abide and dissolve. The first instant of clear light mind following this experience destroys the obscurations to omniscience. In the second instant one directly perceives all objects of knowledge, both conventional and ultimate, as directly as a piece of fruit held in the hand.

As we can see above, the Guhyasamaja and Yamantaka completion stage systems speak in much the same language. The only real distinction, as pointed out by the Great Thirteenth's *A Guide to the Buddhist Tantras,* is the manner in which they group the yogas:

As for the completion stage yogas (of the Yamantaka tantra) these are arranged into four categories. Here the yogas of body isolation and speech isolation combine as mantra yoga. Mind isolation becomes commitment yoga. Both impure and pure phases of the illusory body trainings combine as form yoga. Finally, semblant and actual clear light phases become the wisdom yoga.

The Great Thirteenth similarly interprets the Heruka Chakrasamvara completion stage yogas through the key of the Guhyasamaja structure.

> As for the completion stage practices [of Heruka Chakrasamvara], here the yogi fixes the mind at the sound cluster at the navel. The karmic energies are brought into the central energy channel and the four downward showering and upward rising joys are induced. One then relies upon the meditations of the dhyanas of vajra recitation and systematic absorption. In this way, on the emptiness side [i.e., in terms of experience of the ultimate level of reality] one gains an inconceivable experience of semblant and actual clear light; and on the appearance side [i.e., in terms of experience of the conventional level of reality] one achieves the impure and pure stages of the wondrous illusory body. One then manifests the inconceivable state of great union, both that of a trainee and that beyond training.

In addition to the three mainstream highest yoga tantra traditions mentioned above (i.e., Guhyasamaja, Yamantaka and Heruka Chakrasamvara), the buddhist tantric yogis of ancient India also engaged in several other tantric lineages. The two most important of these were Hevajra and Mahamaya. The completion stage practices of these two, combined with those of the three mainstream tantras above, were fused into a single body of practice by the Indian guru Tilopa and transmitted to Tilopa's chief disciple Naropa. Naropa gave the tradition to Marpa the Translator, who propagated it in Tibet as 'the Six Yogas of Naropa.' Naropa also gave a second transmission of these yogas to his principal female disciple, known to the Tibetans as Niguma; this yogini in turn transmitted the lineage to one of her Tibetan disciples, Khyungpo Naljor, who disseminated it widely in the Land of Snows, popularizing it as 'the Six Yogas of Niguma.' These two traditions of completion stage yoga, which were synthesized by Tilopa and transmitted by Naropa and his disciples, eventually spread through all schools of Tibetan buddhism.[5]

As we shall see in the following chapters, Naropa was also a central figure in the transmission of the Kalachakra teachings. Thus his influence on Tibetan buddhism was vast indeed.

Most Tibetan commentaries to the completion stage yogas conclude with a section in which the yogas and the mystical states they induce are compared to the stages and mystical experiences as defined in the Sutrayana.

Both Sutrayana vehicles—the Hinayana and 'Shared' Mahayana—and also the Vajrayana, speak of the path to enlightenment as being comprised of five levels of realization, or stages of spiritual growth. They even use the same names for these five: the paths of accumulation, application, direct vision, integration (or meditation), and no-more-training.

However, because of the varying perspectives, yogic methods and goals of the different vehicles, and also because of their differing usages of key terminology, each of them speaks of these five in a somewhat unique manner.

In the Hinayana, for example, the motivation is personal liberation from cyclic existence and the attainment of nirvana. The principal means used are the three higher trainings of discipline, meditative concentration and the wisdom of emptiness. The focus is the four noble truths and the noble eightfold path. The insight that places one on the first of the five levels of the path, as well as the dynamics that transport one from one level to another, are expressed in according terms.

The Second Dalai Lama discusses one of the most prominent of the early Indian Hinayana schools, the Vaibhashika, in *A Raft to Cross the Ocean of Indian Buddhist Thought*. Here he states,

[For them,] the objects to be understood through the

practice of the path are the four noble truths, together
with their sixteen aspects, such as impermanence and
so forth. By gaining an understanding of these four
truths one travels the five paths leading to liberation:
the accumulation of spiritual energies, application, direct insight, integration, and the path beyond training.

In the Sutrayana branch of the Mahayana, or the exoteric
wing of the Great Vehicle, the basis of practice is the compassionate aspiration to achieve full buddhahood, a state of complete knowledge, love and power, in order to be of maximum
benefit to the world. One seeks to achieve ultimate efficiency
in the task of uplifting the spiritual awareness of sentient beings and thus benefiting them in the highest sense. The path
to this buddhahood is comprised of method conjoined with
wisdom. Here method primarily refers to the cultivation of
the above bodhisattva aspiration, together with the supporting practices of the first five (of the six) perfections: generosity,
discipline, patience, enthusiastic energy and meditative stabilization. The wisdom with which this method must be linked
is primarily that listed as the sixth perfection (i.e., the perfection of wisdom), and its two principal supports are perfections
four and five (i.e., energy and meditative stabilization). Flying the magic bird with the two wings of method and wisdom
operating in balance and harmony (as defined above), the Ma-
hayanist applying the Sutrayana techniques is transported over
the five levels of the path to enlightenment.

The first of the five is achieved when one has cultivated the
bodhisattva spirit to the extent that one cares as much for others
as one does for oneself. This intense love and compassion is
then coupled with various insight techniques, inducing a
glimpse of emptiness in meditation; this glimpse heralds the
second level, that of application. One continues to heighten
both one's bodhisattva aspiration and the experience of emptiness, and eventually in meditation achieves direct perception
of the final nature of all phenomena. This establishes one on
the third level, that of direct vision, and characterizes one as

an arya, or saint. At this point one can directly experience highest reality in one's meditation sessions; but when one leaves meditation and goes about daily life emptiness is no longer directly obvious. This meditational experience of emptiness is cultivated and carried deeper and deeper into all realms of one's being, transporting one across the fourth level, called the path of integration. One ascends the ten stages of an arya bodhisattva, increasingly integrating method (of the bodhi-mind) and wisdom (of emptiness), until the two enter into complete union. This induces the state of buddhahood, the path of no-more-training, last of the five levels.

In the Vajrayana, each of the four tantra classes uses slightly different terminology to describe the process. Here we are interested primarily in the highest yoga tantra class.

As we saw earlier, the three mainstream highest yoga tantras—Guhyasamaja, Yamantaka and Heruka Chakrasamvara—speak in terms of the three isolations (i.e., of body, speech and mind), generating the impure and pure illusory body attainments, and realizing the semblant and ultimate clear light states. In this way the subtle body and mind are separated from the coarse, and then the extremely subtle is separated from the subtle.

The Great Thirteenth's *A Guide to the Buddhist Tantras* outlines how this process is linked to the five levels of the path to enlightenment:

> The 'path of accumulation' is comprised from the period beginning with the time when one acquires the four complete initiations until by the power of meditation one achieves a glimpse of emptiness through dissolving the vital energies into the central channel.
>
> The 'path of application' is experienced from then until the attainment of the impure level of the illusory body yoga that directly perceives emptiness by means of the wisdom of great bliss.
>
> From the first experience of the actual clear light until the attainment of the great union of a trainee is

the 'path of vision,' the first bodhisattva stage.

The 'path of meditation' is comprised of the period beginning with the moment after that until the first moment of the attainment of the stage of the actual clear light of the great union at the end of training.

The yogi then crosses the tenth bodhisattva stage, and in the second moment of that experience achieves complete enlightenment, the 'path of no-more-training.'

Thus in the Vajrayana the first path begins with the receiving of tantric initiation and includes any practices 'shared' with the Sutrayana that are continued after entering the Vajrayana through initiation. It also contains the generation stage yogas of the tantric path, as well as the degree of the completion stage yogas required to induce an initial experience of emptiness by means of bringing the subtle energies into the central channel. The stages of the paths that follow are defined by the ability of the yogi to separate subtle bodily energies and states of consciousness from the coarse, and to abide in meditation within the sphere of the subtle. When one is able to dwell in the most subtle levels, and to bring the pure illusory body thus produced into utter harmony with the actual clear light, the great union of complete enlightenment is attained.

The practices of the completion stage methods have over the centuries inspired numerous Tibetan mystics to break out in song. The Seventh Dalai Lama was one such yogi. In his *Songs of Spiritual Change* he expresses the joy of tantric experience,

> The apparitions of people and things
> Dissolve into light, and the waves
> Of misconception are stilled.
> No longer is the radiance of clear light obscured.
> Even the everyday mind maintains immaculate view.
>
> In the sphere of semblant and innate mahamudra,
> Empty images appear as rainbows.

Flawless method emanates phantom circles,
Erecting the perfect mandala of deities and abodes.

The illusory body merges with clear light
Like clouds dissolving into space.
The fire of innate wisdom arises
And consumes the seed of grasping at a self.

This great union of the glorious vajra body
With the vast clear light of mind
Is called 'the samadhi coursing magnificently,'
A stage not touched by the most profound intellect.

This consciousness, purified of all transient stains,
Gazes clearly and directly at the sphere of truth.
Like a magic gem it manifests the beatific body
Of glorious Heruka for the sake of others
And sends out countless emanations,
Each in accord with the needs of the world.

Thus in this age of short lifespan,
Buddhahood is swiftly and easily attained
By turning lust for sensual objects
Toward the friend who instills great bliss.

10 The Kalachakra Yogas

The Kalachakra tradition emerged publicly in India considerably later than did the various systems of the three lower tantra classes, and also later than the three mainstream tantras. Thus in a sense it has from the time of its appearance presumed knowledge of these, and is a final refinement of them.

As explained earlier, the training in the three lower tantra classes is comprised of the two yogic stages known as the yoga of symbols and the yoga beyond symbols. These work within the context of a coarse level of consciousness, and consequently are not as powerful as the methods of highest yoga tantra; they do not contain methods whereby a practitioner on an initial level can separate the subtle levels of body and mind from the coarse. However, because at the beginning of our training our conscious experience is limited mainly to coarse levels (with exceptions such as at the brief moment of passing into sleep, orgasm, the moment of death, etc.), these simpler tantric systems are considered practical starting points in practice.

In the mainstream highest yoga tantras, the meditator is taught special techniques whereby the subtle body is separated from the coarse. As a consequence, the mind arises solely on subtle levels. These paranormal states of consciousness, aroused through the experience of meditative bliss, are then directed to the observation of emptiness, the final nature of things. The result is near-instant enlightenment.[1]

Kalachakra takes the process a step further, dissolving even the subtle energies and drops, and meditating on the basis of an 'empty body.' It also introduces a number of features and techniques not found in the mainstream highest yoga tantras, as we will see later.

The uniqueness of the Kalachakra doctrines is pointed out by the Great Thirteenth in his *Summary of the Kalachakra Tradition:*

> Another important highest yoga tantra tradition is that of Kalachakra, a system presenting the tantric path in a manner markedly different from the presentation found in other highest yoga systems. This 'clear' tantra is usually taught separately from the other highest yoga paths, for its infrastructure is considerably different from those of the mainstream traditions, such as Guhyasamaja, Yamantaka, and Heruka Chakrasamvara.

Kalachakra is here referred to as a 'clear tantra,' or *selgyu*. This term is set in contrast to 'buried tantra,' or *begyu*. Kalachakra is the former as it speaks in a direct language; the three mainstream tantras are 'buried tantras' because they bury their meaning in a purposely ambiguous language.

A primary characteristic of the Kalachakra doctrine is its presentation of 'three Kalachakras.' His Holiness explains these as follows in *Concerning the Kalachakra Initiation:*

> In the discussion of the Kalachakra generation stage yogas, which ripen and mature the mind for the completion stage, it is traditional to introduce the topic of the three Kalachakras: outer, inner and alternative.
>
> Outer Kalachakra is comprised of the elements of the universe in which we live. Inner Kalachakra consists of the psychophysical aggregates, the sensory and psychic capacities of the living beings, and so forth.

Thirdly, alternative Kalachakra is the path of the generation and completion stage yogas, the yogic methods that have the power to purify the above two Kalachakras.

The Great Thirteenth's *Summary of the Kalachakra Tradition* adds,

Alternative Kalachakra is the actual practice of the yogas of the Kalachakra system whereby the world and its beings are purified. The basis of the purification is the person possessing the six elements with the karma to be born from a human womb here in this world.

Also, the First Dalai Lama writes in *Notes on the Two Yogic Stages of Glorious Kalachakra,*

Of the three Kalachakras mentioned above, outer and inner Kalachakras are the bases to be purified, whereas alternative Kalachakra refers to the yogic practices that effect this purification and produce the three purified results.

Thus of the three Kalachakras—outer, inner and alternative—it is the last that refers to the actual yogic path of the Kalachakra tradition. Because this yoga purifies the world and its inhabitants, all three can be subsumed under the classification of 'alternative Kalachakra.'

The uniqueness of the Kalachakra system becomes evident from the very beginning of the path, which is demarcated by receiving the initiations.

Quoting the Indian mahasiddha Gandhapada (Tib., Tilbupa), the First Dalai Lama describes the mandalas[2] that can be utilized as the basis of the initiation ceremony in the mainstream highest yoga tantras:

There are three types of mandalas that can be used as the basis of the initiation (in the mainstream tantras): those made from colored particles, those painted on cloth, and those visualized in the body.

The First Dalai Lama then points out that Guhyasamaja and some other systems also allow a fourth type of mandala, that of dhyana, or stabilized meditation.

However, the Kalachakra differs from these traditions in that it only allows initiation on the basis of a mandala made from colored powders; in other words, a sand painting. This is confirmed by Naropa in his commentary to the only section of the *Kalachakra Root Tantra* to have survived, the chapter entitled "The Treatise on the Initiations."

Secondly, the actual initiation process itself is considerably different in Kalachakra. As we saw in an earlier chapter, the mainstream tantric initiations are comprised of four individual empowerments, known as vase, secret, wisdom, and sacred word, each of which is given only once during the ceremony.

In Kalachakra, however, the initiation process is in three separate sets: 'entering like a child,' which is comprised of seven phases; the four higher initiations; and the four higher-than-higher initiations. The four phases of each of the last two sets have the same names as the four initiations of the mainstream tantras, and the meditations pursued during them are similar to those in the mainstream tantras. Nonetheless, their nature and function differ somewhat, as we will see in the commentaries of the First and Thirteenth Dalai Lamas.

The seven initiations of 'entering like a child' essentially take us back to the time of our birth and start us on the path of life anew. Thus they are symbolized by the seven experiences that a child undergoes in being introduced into this world: being washed; having the hair cut; having the ears pierced; learning to laugh and speak; learning to use sensory objects; being given a name; and learning to read, write and so forth. The seven are called water, headdress, silk ribbon, vajra and bell, activity, name, and permission initiations. To receive them the disciple comes before each of the four faces of Kalachakra—white, red, black and yellow in color. These initiations introduce one to the experience of purification of the five aggregates, ten energies, right and left energy channels, ten sensory powers and their objects, the activities of the five bodily functions, the three doors, and the element of primordial wisdom.

The second set of initiations is known as the four conventional higher initiations, and also the four worldly initiations. These establish the disciple on the path of the four joys, using as their means the vase waters, tasting the secret substances, experiencing melting of the mystic drops and the resultant bliss, and being introduced to the innate bliss and void.

The third set are known as the four higher-than-higher initiations, and also as the four beyond-worldly initiations. These introduce the disciples to the consciousness which directly perceives emptiness while abiding in supreme unchanging bliss, a consciousness characterized by transcendent ecstasy abiding in full awareness of highest reality, which is of one taste with the empty body arising in the form of Kalachakra and Consort in sexual union.

The First Dalai Lama outlines the nature and functions of these three sets of initiations:

> The main purpose of the seven initiations is to transform the spiritual aspirant into a vessel suitable for practice of the generation stage yogas and to provide a path for the cultivation of dhyana. However, the initiations of the silk headdress and of the vajra and bell also have the function of transforming the disciple into a vessel capable of successfully practicing the completion stage yogas, which gain control over the energies flowing through the secondary channels of the body and redirect them into the *dhuti*, the central channel.
>
> The next set of initiations, known as the four higher initiations, have both generation and completion stage associations. . . .

The first three of the higher-than-higher initiations that follow are as in the previous set, with the exception that on each occasion the visualized sexual union is performed with nine consorts rather than only one. The manner of inducing (the bliss that confers) the initiations is much the same. However, here the fourth initiation, which reveals the full meaning of what is to be accomplished and what transcended, possesses the full characteristics of a fourth initiation and thus is called 'the non-worldly fourth initiation.'

Having gained these eleven initiations (or fifteen, depending on how one counts them), one is empowered to enter into the generation and completion stage yogas.

The next distinct feature of the Kalachakra system is its treatment of the list of *samaya*, or tantric commitments, that are adopted at the time of initiation. In the mainstream tantras this involves the pledge of the bodhisattva resolve, the nineteen commitments of the five Tathagata Families,[3] and the set of fourteen root and eight secondary general commitments. The female tantras, including Heruka Chakrasamvara, add to this a number of extras, such as beginning activities with the left part of the body (i.e., taking things in the left hand rather than in the right, and so forth), as well as the commitment to perform a tantric feast (involving the consumption of meat and alcohol) at least once a month.

As the Thirteenth Dalai Lama points out, the Kalachakra system includes these general tantric disciplines, although its version of the fourteen root samaya differs, with seven being the same as in the mainstream traditions and seven being uniquely interpreted.[4] In addition, the Kalachakra system contains an extra set of twenty-five special samaya, which are in five groups of five.

These add up to a considerable number of precepts; more, perhaps, than most people can even remember. The Tibetan tradition is not to worry about them too much at initial levels of training, and to gradually grow into them as one's training matures. The custom is to begin by adopting just one or two of the fundamental guidelines, and at that the ones most comfortable with one's present lifestyle. One then slowly expands from that basic starting point.

In general, precepts are divided into three types in accordance with the three vehicles: Hinayana, Mahayana and Vajrayana.

The discipline in the first of these is known as 'the resolve of individual liberation.' It involves the eight types of 'ordinations,' such as lay practitioner, monk or nun, and so forth. Its essential purpose is to create an environment of simplicity and moderation for the practitioner to achieve individual spiritual growth. Each of the various levels of ordination has its own number of precepts, but the central maxim underlying all of them is the commitment to non-violence and the concomitant resolve to follow the path that avoids harming others.

The discipline of the second of the three vehicles—the Mahayana—is known as 'the resolve of the bodhisattva.' This is of two types: 'aspirational,' which is the resolve to hold as a priority the aspiration to achieve highest enlightenment as a means of benefiting the world; and 'practice,' which is the resolve to live by the bodhisattva code of the six perfections. Some Tibetan scriptures speak of sixty-four bodhisattva precepts; the essence of all of these is the maxim to always try to be solely of benefit to others.

Again, the precepts of the third vehicle—the Vajrayana— are similarly numerous. All of these, however, condense into two essential maxims. These are given by His Holiness the Dalai Lama in *Cultivating a Daily Meditation:*

> The main precepts [in tantric practice] are [twofold:]
> to restrain from ordinary appearances, and to restrain
> from grasping at ordinariness.

The actual practice of the Kalachakra path begins with the generation stage yogas. These exhibit a number of differences from the approach and terminology of the mainstream tantras, as revealed by comparing what the First and Thirteenth Dalai Lamas say of these yogas with what was said earlier about the similar stages in the other three major traditions.[5]

The principal distinction, however, is that all three mainstream tantras place great emphasis on the process known as 'taking the three occasions as the path of the three kayas,' i.e., the meditations on transforming the experiences of death, the intermediate state and rebirth into the paths of dharmakaya, sambhogakaya and nirmanakaya, the three 'bodies' of a buddha. The Kalachakra system replaces this threefold approach with a division of the generation stage into four phases. These are known as the supremely victorious mandala, the supreme activity practice, the yoga of the mystic drop, and the subtle yoga.[6]

Although the first two of these are common (at least in name) to other highest yoga tantra systems, the latter are unique to Kalachakra, due to this tradition's theory of 'the four drops of the four occasions.' As the First Dalai Lama points out in *Notes on the Two Yogic Stages*, in Kalachakra these drops (called the drops of the waking state, dream state, deep sleep, and sexual ecstasy) act as the basis of all our experience.

The theory in Kalachakra is that by purifying these four drops we purify the entire spectrum of our perceptual process, transforming consciousness at the focal points of its arisal. This process is not matured and taken to finality until we engage in the completion stage yogas; but the seeds are planted by the generation stage practices. The topic of these four drops becomes more pronounced in the completion stage applications.

As with the other highest yoga tantras, in applying the Kalachakra generation stage yogas there are a variety of mandala forms that one can choose from as the foundation of the practice. We find a list of the major forms in the Great Thirteenth's *Summary of the Kalachakra Tradition*,

As for the various mandalas that can be used as the

basis of the generation stage yogas, *The Kalachakra Root Tantra* speaks of the mandala of glorious moving stars containing 1,620 mandala deities. *The Abbreviated Kalachakra Tantra* speaks of 722 divinities in the mandalas of body, speech and mind. Other optional traditions are the mind mandala of thirty-six divinities and the mind mandala of thirty-two divinities. Then there are the smaller mandalas of twenty-five, twenty-three, nineteen, thirteen and nine divinities. There is also a mandala with only Kalachakra and Consort, and a mandala of Solitary Kalachakra alone.

Commenting on the same point the eighteenth-century Kalachakra yogi of Amdo, the illustrious Longdol Lama, an important disciple of the Seventh Dalai Lama's pupil the Third Panchen Lama, writes in his *Lexicon of Kalachakra Terms according to the Views of Lama Tsongkhapa,*

There are eleven principal mandala forms on which the *sadhana* [of the Kalachakra generation stage training] can be accomplished: the mandala of 1,620 deities of glorious heavenly bodies as described in *The Kalachakra Root Tantra*; the mandala of body, speech and mind together, as described in *The Abbreviated Kalachakra Tantra*, which contains 722 deities; a mind mandala of either thirty-six or thirty-two deities; then the mandalas of twenty-five close deities and twenty-three close deities; the mandalas of nineteen, thirteen, and nine deities; and also the mandalas of five blissful deities; of male and consort alone together; and of Solitary Kalachakra, without a consort.

These are the different mandala forms that can be adopted as the basis of the practice of the generation stage. Traditionally the choice would be made in consultation with one's meditation teacher. Most trainees would begin with one of the simpler mandalas, such as that of Kalachakra and Consort, or even the mandala of Solitary Kalachakra, developing familiarity with the Kalachakra generation stage environment before going on to any of the more complex mandala forms.

The structure of the generation and completion stages in Kalachakra is somewhat different from that of the mainstream traditions. Therefore the definitions of these two yogic stages differ somewhat.

The Buriati lama Kalzang Tenzin provides the following definition of the Kalachakra generation stage application in *A Message from Lama Norzang,* a work on the Kalachakra yogas in accordance with the tradition of the Second Dalai Lama's guru Khedrup Norzang Gyatso:

> [The Kalachakra generation stage yoga is defined as] the yogic application of the first tantric stage, taken up by one whose mindstream has been ripened by receiving the (Kalachakra) initiations; this path is characterized by (the practice of) alternative Kalachakra as the essence of all three Kalachakras [outer, inner, and alternative], within the context of a mentally projected meditation on how the various stages of unfoldment of the enlightenment experience are symbolized by the processes of arisal and dissolution of the ordinary world we experience, with the effect of establishing identification with a unique form body of enlightenment.
>
> Here four synonymous terms are used: the first tantric stage, the yoga of fabrication, the generation stage, and the yoga of mental projection.
>
> When we subdivide the generation stage meditations they are said to be twofold. Firstly there is the process of meditation on how at the time of death the bodily elements withdraw and the clear light of death arises; to symbolize this, one intensifies one's accumulation of meritorious energy and contemplates the four doors of liberation. Secondly, to symbolize the process of crossing through the intermediate state and entering

into a womb of rebirth there is the yoga of meditating upon the four branches of approach and accomplishment.

This second phase involves four (visualized) processes, known as the supremely victorious mandala, the victorious activities, the yoga of the drop, and the subtle yoga.

As we can see by comparing this definition and breakdown to those of the generation stage yogas of the mainstream tantras given earlier in Chapter Eight, the Kalachakra emphasis is quite unique.

Chapters Eighteen and Nineteen of the present work contain two meditational texts that belong to the generation stage level of Kalachakra training. The first of these is a short six-session guruyoga liturgy, meant to be recited and contemplated three times each day and three times each night by a Kalachakra initiate, in order to fulfill the nineteen pledges of the five Tathagata Families as taken at the time of initiation. It was written by Kyabjey Khangsar Dorjey Chang, an important Gelukpa saint born in 1888 who passed away in the middle of this century. This lama taught the Kalachakra doctrines to both tutors of the present Dalai Lama, and is thus His Holiness' 'spiritual grandfather.' The Tibetan text used for translation here was adapted for the Dalai Lama's 1976 Kalachakra initiation in Ladakh, where a generous patron sponsored the printing and distribution of ten thousand copies to the crowd. Consequently the Dalai Lama's name mantra has been incorporated into our source text.

The second and considerably longer meditational text, given here as Chapter Nineteen, is a sadhana, or method of accomplishment, of the type used in the actual generation stage yogas. It describes the four stages of the mandala process that a practitioner should contemplate once, twice or four times a day, together with the mantra recitations. The author, Buton Rinchen Druppa (1290-1364), a Sakya monk of Zhalu Monastery, was perhaps the greatest Tibetan master of his generation. His collected works contain five volumes of writings on Kalachakra, and include titles covering all major aspects of the tradition. It was from Buton's disciple Chokyipel that Lama Tsongkhapa received the transmission.

Dedicated trainees of highest yoga tantra are generally advised to cultivate a practice routine incorporating the daily recitation of both a six-session guruyoga and a sadhana, such as those given here.

There are in Tibetan thousands of texts in the categories of six-session guruyoga and sadhana manuals. Over the centuries Tibetan lamas have continued to write works in this genre. Some of these are hundreds of pages in length; others are but a few lines or paragraphs. The examples printed here are quite brief.

It is interesting to note that although the tradition today is to recite this type of text, it is possible that such was not always the case. One of my principal lama teachers, the Ven. Doboom Tulku, once commented to me that he felt these types of meditation manuals were not actually chanted in the olden days, such as in the time of Lama Tsongkhapa. It was Ven. Doboom's opinion that instead the Indians and early Tibetans would memorize the essential structure of the process; then during actual practice they would silently generate the phases of visualization and contemplation, and quietly recite the mantras.

As in the other highest yoga tantras, once the practitioner has gained proficiency in the Kalachakra generation stage methods, he or she should take up the yogas of the completion stage. There are six of these: individual withdrawal, dhyana, energy concentration, retention, subsequent mindfulness, and samadhi. Although the names used as labels of these six completion stage yogas can also be found in the Guhyasamaja literature, their application in the Kalachakra tradition is quite different.

Because of the unique nature of the Kalachakra path, the completion stage yoga is given a somewhat different definition than was seen earlier in the mainstream systems. In *A*

Message from Lama Norzang the Buriati lama Kalzang Tenzin provides the following definition:

> [The Kalachakra completion stage yoga is defined as] the yogic application of the second tantric stage, taken up by one whose mindstream has been ripened by receiving the [Kalachakra] initiations; this path is characterized by (the practice of) alternative Kalachakra as the essence of all three Kalachakras [outer, inner, and alternative], within the context of meditations that focus upon the unfabricated vajra body.
>
> Here four synonymous terms are used: the second tantric stage, the yoga beyond fabrication, the completion stage, and the yoga beyond mental projection.
>
> When we subdivide the completion stage yoga, it is said to be sixfold: the yogas of individual withdrawal, dhyana, energy control, retention, subsequent mindfulness, and samadhi.

The opening section of the First Dalai Lama's *Notes on the Two Yogic Stages of Glorious Kalachakra* reveals several of the unique features of the Kalachakra system. For example, the manner in which the energy channels of the vajra body are envisioned demonstrates a number of distinctions from the manner in which they are imagined in Guhyasamaja and the other mainstream tantras. There are slight differences in the precise placement of some of the chakras, and in the number of 'petals' formed by the converging channels at the energy centers. A quick comparison of texts from the two systems—such as the First Dalai Lama's *Notes on the Two Yogic Stages* and, say, the portrait of the mainstream tantras as drawn by the Second Dalai Lama in *The Tantric Yogas of Sister Niguma*—reveals a number of innovations in the Kalachakra presentation.

The next major topic introduced by the First Dalai Lama in his discussion of the completion stage yogas is that of the four drops. Here he points out,

The site of the drop of the waking state occasion, the body, and form is at the forehead. The site of the drop of the dream state, speech, and sound is at the throat. The site of the drop of deep sleep, mind, and thought is at the heart. Finally, the site of the drop of sexual ecstasy, wisdom, and primordial awareness is at the navel. . . .

For ordinary beings the drops of the four occasions —waking, dream, deep sleep and sexual ecstasy—carry the potencies that induce perception of the impure objects of the world, the potencies that generate confused appearances and sound to arise, the potencies giving rise to obscurity of mind and ignorance, and the potencies arousing dissipating ecstasy.

These potencies are purified by the Kalachakra yogas. To be specific, they are transformed into the empty body, unconfused sound, non-conceptual wisdom and unchanging bliss. These are cultivated to perfection, giving rise to the vajra body, speech, and mind of a buddha, and to fully manifest gnosis.

Thus the Kalachakra takes as its central approach to the path the purification of the four drops. To effect this it applies the technology of the Kalachakra 'empty body' doctrine, together with the force of 'unchanging great bliss.' The structure of the application is that of the six yogas.

There is also a tradition of speaking of the four drops as eight, by placing four in the upper region of the vajra body and four in the lower. The First Dalai Lama does not mention this separately in his *Notes,* although his treatment of how the drops move in the body and the effects this has on consciousness indicates that he was well aware of the discussion. The Amdo master Longdol Lama writes in *A Guide to the Structure of the Kalachakra Generation and Completion Stage Yogas,*

In the upper region of the vajra body, the drop of the waking state is at the forehead, the drop of dreams at the throat, the drop of deep sleep at the heart, and the drop of sexual ecstasy at the navel. These four are dominated by the life-sustaining energy.

As for where these four drops are located in the lower region of the vajra body, the drop of the waking state is at the navel, the drop of dreams at the secret place, the drop of deep sleep at center of (base of) the jewel, and the drop of sexual ecstasy at the tip of the jewel.

It is extremely important to understand how these eight drops operate and the effects that they have on consciousness. Everything that is to be transcended is supported by them: both the obscurations to omniscience and the obscurations to liberation.

The six yogas that are utilized are applied sequentially rather than simultaneously. Each has its specific objective to accomplish, and when this is realized one enters into the succeeding yoga. This is strongly stated by the First Dalai Lama in *Notes:*

The six yogas are practiced in the order listed above. That is, one gains proficiency in the first before proceeding to the second, and so forth. To practice the later yogas before accomplishing the earlier ones will not produce the desired results. It is the impact of each one that carries the yogi successively across the stages of the path, and that prepares one for the next yoga to be approached. It is important to understand how this process works, and to engage in practice accordingly.

As in the mainstream tantras, the Kalachakra completion stage yogas are based on meditations that work with the vajra body of energy channels, subtle energies, chakras and drops. However, this 'vajra body' exhibits a number of differences from that utilized in the mainstream systems. The First Dalai Lama describes the unique nature of the Kalachakra vajra body in his *Notes.* With this as the fulcrum the yogi engages in the completion stage yogas.

The first of the six yogas is called 'individual withdrawal.' It has this name because its function is to cut off the flow of vital energies in each of the six sensory organs and six spheres of sensory perception.[7] The meditator concentrates on 'the drop of the waking state,' which is at the forehead, and brings the bodily energies into a state of increased stillness. This gives rise to the ten signs indicating progress, such as smoke and so forth. These appear as inner visions, and are similar to the images seen at the time of death. After their successive arisal there appears an eleventh sign: a small black outline, the size of a hair, that radiates within the drop. This signifies the attainment of a coarse sambhogakaya, or beatific body, possessed of the five characteristics. These five are that its timing occurs after the ten inner signs have been experienced; its place is inside the central channel; its nature is that it is not based on physical matter; its form is that of a Diamond Being; and its aspect is the bliss arising from the union of the inner male and female forces. This is the 'substitute' empty body.

As the First Dalai Lama points out, the yoga of individual withdrawal is to be practiced in darkness. In Tibet it was the tradition to engage in this yoga in solitary retreat, in an area near one's teacher. The retreat would be made inside a hut especially designed to keep out all light, and would continue for some months and perhaps even years, until the signs of accomplishment appeared.

The second yoga is called *dhyana*, meaning the stabilizing of the mind.[8] This is because its purpose is to stabilize the accomplishment produced by the first yoga. In other words, it serves to integrate and intensify the experience of the inner signs as well as the yogic states that they signify. Again the meditator concentrates upon the drop in the crown chakra, dissolves the entire world into mandala deities and into the coarse beatific body previously generated, projecting divine tantric pride until it effortlessly arises. The yoga is applied in five branches, the first two having the nature of insight meditation (vipashyana) and the last three having the nature of meditative tranquility (shamatha). The focus includes the coarse body, the joy that arises in the mind, the bliss that arises in the subtle levels of the empty body, and the interrelated nature of form and consciousness. The fulfillment of the five induces the absorption which is the inseparable union of insight and meditative tranquility.

When the six yogas are divided into three branches, these two are said to be the branch accomplishing form. This is because the first yoga produces a special physical base for meditation, and the second reinforces this accomplishment. The 'special body' being discussed here is called a 'coarse sambhogakaya.' The term 'sambhogakaya' is shared with the Sutrayana, where it refers to a special level of emanation of an enlightened being, a level that can only be perceived by beings on high spiritual stages.

Another name for the 'body' created through these yogic methods is the 'substitute empty body.' It is generated inside the drop at the center of the crown chakra.

The third Kalachakra yoga is called energy control.[9] The previous two yogas calmed the energies moving in the sensory organs and spheres; the third will cause the subtle energies to enter the central channel. The two principal yogic techniques here are the vajra recitation and vase breathing, which are applied in order to bring the life-sustaining and downward-moving energies into union at the navel chakra. The mystic heat at the navel is ignited, causing the drop at the forehead chakra to melt and descend through the central channel, giving rise to bliss as it passes through the chakras. This bliss fulfills the yoga of energy concentration.

Thus in this third yoga we see the term 'mystic heat' used for the first time. This differs from the placement of the technique in the mainstream highest yoga tantras, where it is incorporated in the first of the Guhyasamaja six yogas.

The two breathing techniques used in this yoga have similar applications in the mainstream tantras, although in Kalachakra the focus is the production of a particular type of higher energy aimed to facilitate the creation of an actual 'empty body.' The word 'energy' here also corresponds to breath, and as the meditation progresses the yogi is able to hold the breath for increasing periods of duration. Eventually the breath can be held for days, or even weeks, without any damage to the meditator.

The fourth Kalachakra yoga is called 'retention.'[10] Here the meditator retains the energies inside the central channel. The elements are first dissolved one by one, bringing the subtle energies back up through the chakras. They are retained at each chakra for a period of time, giving rise to the four joys. One creates an inseparable union of the two principal energies, one's mind, and the empty body; this is then retained at each of the six chakras. The mystical experiences thus induced transport one through the stages of this yoga.

This and the previous yoga combine as the branch that accomplishes higher energy. They are also known as the 'vajra speech yogas.'

Next is the yoga of subsequent mindfulness,[11] a method whereby the special Kalachakra bliss is induced. It is called 'subsequent mindfulness' as it is accomplished by recollecting the subtle form previously accomplished and applying a mindfulness technique to this image.

The yogi engages in either actual, visualized or subliminal sexual union in order to generate the unchanging bliss. Here it is said that practitioners are of three types: sharp, medium and dull. The first meditates in sexual union with a subliminal knowledge woman, and the second visualizes entering into sexual union in order to induce the requisite experiences. As for the third type of practitioner, the dullard, it is said that he or she has to meditate while in sexual union with an actual consort. But no matter at which level one begins, eventually all three practitioners are led to mahamudra, the great seal.

The white drop at the crown melts and descends to the tip of the sexual organ, and the red drop at the navel rises to the crown, giving rise to the supremely great unchanging bliss. This brings one to the threshold of the sixth Kalachakra yoga, called the 'yoga of samadhi.'

In this sixth and final Kalachakra yoga[12] the meditator amasses the drops in the central channel, inducing flashes of bliss. Each moment of this bliss is said to dissolve one of the 21,600 components of the physical body, and to carry the meditator to higher and higher states of transcendental ecstasy. Eventually the entire physical base, together with all elements and objects connected with it, are freed from obscuration, and the obstructions to knowledge are eliminated, transporting one to the buddhahood state symbolized by Kalachakra and Consort.

Thus the ordinary physical body is evaporated and replaced with an 'empty body' embellished with the marks and signs of perfection. The mind is filled with great bliss and transformed into the innate unchanging wisdom.

The First Dalai Lama puts it this way in *Notes on the Two Yogic Stages:*

> The meaning...is that the Kalachakra yogi accomplishes enlightenment in one lifetime in such a way that his or her body attains the characteristics of the form of Kalachakra and Consort; a vast empty body adorned with all the marks and signs of enlightenment, a body similar to space itself. It is 'clear and lucent' because it is intangible and immaterial, being empty of a mundane atomic structure.
>
> This is the bodily attainment. As for the mental attainment, its essential nature is compassion arising as the supreme, unchanging bliss locked in eternal union with the one taste of wisdom perceiving the emptiness of non-inherent existence, which is beyond characteristics.
>
> When in this way the body and mind are experienced as an inseparable entity based on the supporting empty body and the supported wisdom of unchanging bliss, this is what is meant by 'Primordial Kalachakra.'

Elsewhere in the same text the First Dalai Lama explains

how the six Kalachakra yogas combine to form a complete path
to enlightenment:

> The six yogas can also be otherwise arranged into three
> branches, wherein the yogas of individual withdrawal
> and dhyana combine as the branch that accomplishes
> form; the yogas of energy control and retention com-
> bine as the branch that accomplishes higher energy;
> and the yogas of subsequent mindfulness and samadhi
> combine as the branch that accomplishes bliss....
>
> As we can see from the above description, by ac-
> complishing the first four yogas one engages the fifth
> (the yoga of subsequent mindfulness) and gains the
> ability to arise in the qualified empty body. The
> strength of that attainment in turn provides the basis
> for success in the sixth and final yoga, that of samadhi.
>
> Thus (the six yogas by themselves have the power
> to generate the attainment of full enlightenment, and
> so) there is no need to supplement them with various
> assortments of other practices, nor to practice anything
> on top of them. On the other hand, to omit any of
> them will impair the system's potency (to produce en-
> lightenment).

As was said earlier, the Kalachakra system omits many of
the key terms found in the mainstream highest yoga tantras—
such as the three isolations (of body, speech and mind), the
impure and pure illusory bodies, the rainbow body,[13] the semblant and actual clear lights, and the yoga of great union—
and instead uses terms like the substitute and actual empty
bodies, purification of the four drops, generating the unchanging bliss, and so forth.

A principal distinction of the Kalachakra completion stage
yogas is the doctrine of the 'empty body,' in contrast to the
mainstream highest yoga tantra doctrine of an 'illusory body.'
It is difficult to say what terms like this really mean, because
of the self-secret nature of mystical experience and the limita-

tions of the means by which it can be verbally conveyed. The statement usually made in the Tibetan writings in this regard is that the illusory body (and its product, the rainbow body) is composed of matter—the most subtle form of energy; whereas the 'empty body' achieved by a yogi of the Kalachakra system is immaterial and insubstantial, a mere projected image.

The First Dalai Lama compares the illusory body doctrine of the mainstream tantras with the empty body technology of the Kalachakra tradition:

> The Kalachakra doctrine of the extraordinary empty body is somewhat similar to the illusory body doctrine of the mainstream yoga tantra systems, although the basis of this accomplishment must be affected by means of the first of the six yogas, that of individual withdrawal. The second yoga, that of dhyana, then makes this attainment firm. The empty body that has thus been produced by these two yogas, which are categorized as the branch accomplishing form, becomes one's extraordinary body (used as the basis supporting the mind in meditation). The third and fourth yogas—those of energy control and retention—are then applied in order to gain control over the subtle energies. Next, in reliance upon the external condition of a mudra one applies subsequent mindfulness to one's own attainment, and arises in the empty body form of Kalachakra and Consort. This gives rise to the bliss that is the yoga of samadhi abiding in union.
>
> Here the empty body produced by the yoga of subsequent mindfulness is similar to the third stage illusory body attainment of the completion stage yogas of mainstream tantric paths such as Guhyasamaja....
>
> According to the illusory body doctrine in systems like Guhyasamaja, the basis of the accomplishment is established by the very first yoga, i.e., that of body isolation. This is then gradually intensified by means of the yoga of speech isolation, until eventually one

comes to the third stage and arises within an illusory body.

If we compare this to the process of the empty body discussed in the Kalachakra tradition, here a stabilized similitude of this special body is established in the second yoga, that of dhyana. From that point until the yoga of retention (i.e., the fourth yoga) this accomplishment is gradually intensified, but the empty body itself is not actually produced until the fifth yoga is applied, that of subsequent mindfulness. The empty body produced here has no equivalent on the stage of the yoga of individual withdrawal (for this one is utterly non-material). Having applied the yoga of subsequent mindfulness, in the occasions that follow one relinquishes all physical attributes and arises solely on the basis of the Kalachakra empty body.

He then looks into the Kalachakra teachings for an equivalent of the clear light theory discussed in the mainstream tantras.

In the Kalachakra literature one sees a lot of discussion focused on the topics of 'emptiness with characteristics,' and 'true emptiness without characteristics.'

In the first of these, the mind directly perceiving the empty body arises within a subtle light of dual appearance. It is nonetheless called 'emptiness' because in it the object of negation, the coarse and subtle atomic structure of the body, has been eliminated, and is altogether empty of physical matter.

In the second case [i.e., emptiness without characteristics], this refers to the mind directly perceiving the emptiness of its object of negation, i.e., the emptiness of inherent existence. Because that mind has reversed all dual appearance, it is called 'without characteristics.'

Thus (in the Kalachakra tradition) the discussion

of the empty body as explained above, wherein the wisdom of emptiness is brought into one taste with supreme, unchanging great bliss, is a substitute for the clear light and illusory body doctrines found in the other highest yoga tantra systems [that is, the empty body substitutes for the illusory body doctrine, and the one taste of unchanging bliss and wisdom substitutes for the clear light doctrine]. The assembling of these two [i.e., the empty body and the unchanging bliss absorbed in the wisdom of emptiness] within the stream of one's body and mind substitutes for the Great Union [of the clear light and illusory body] spoken of in the other highest yoga tantras.

Earlier we saw how the yogas of the mainstream tantras propel the yogi over the five paths leading to enlightenment. Because in the Kalachakra tradition the emphasis is on creating an 'empty body' and then meditating on emptiness with the blissful consciousness that arises, the process is described in considerably different terms.

The Second Dalai Lama's guru Khedrup Norzang Gyatso explains that, as in Guhyasamaja, one enters the path of accumulation through receiving the initiations. After that, however, all similarities with Guhyasamaja end.[14]

The First Dalai Lama explains how the experience of the Kalachakra yogas transports one over the final stages of the five levels of the path:

When one thus simultaneously brings the white and red substances to the tip of the jewel and to the chakra of the crown protrusion [i.e., one brings the white drop down to the tip of the sexual organ and the red drop up to the crown], and retains them there with stability, this gives rise to a momentary flash of stabilized bliss. Of the 21,600 factors of which our coarse form is composed, one is dissolved. Simultaneously, of the 21,600 karmic energies coursing through the nostrils, one part of (the twelve sets of) 1,800 are halted.

When (in the first set) 1,800 experiences of bliss have been fulfilled and 1,799 of the vital drops piled up, one attains to the 'great supreme dharma' stage of the path of application [i.e., the fourth and final stage of the second level of the path to enlightenment]. A further one part of 1,800 such moments places one on the stage of an arya, the path of direct vision [third level of the path to enlightenment].

If in this way one can draw 21,600 (white) male drops, the supports of bliss, to the tip of the jewel, and stack them in a stable column that extends up to the crown chakra, and also bring 21,600 red drops up and form them into a red column beginning at the crown (chakra) and extending down to the tip of the jewel, on the basis of each of the (21,600 sets of red and white drops) one experiences a moment of stabilized bliss. In this way 21,600 moments of 'supported' unchanging bliss arise. Each of these cuts off one part of the 21,600 karmic winds, and this in turn causes the utter dissolution of one of the 21,600 factors of the physical body.

One's form aggregate, together with the elements and objects connected with it, becomes freed from obscuration. One transcends all obscurations to knowledge, and simultaneously in this very lifetime attains the state of enlightenment in the aspect of the Primordial Buddha Kalachakra.

Sometimes in Kalachakra literature we see the state of enlightenment referred to as 'the twelfth stage,' or as 'the Kalachakra twelfth stage.' The word used for this in Tibetan is *sa*, a translation of the Sanskrit *bhumi*, meaning earth, ground, stage, or level. The same term is applied in the Sutrayana, or general teachings of the Buddha, where we see it in reference to the ten levels of an arya bodhisattva. These are the stages in a high bodhisattva's experience, beginning with the moment he or she first achieves direct meditational perception of emptiness and thus becomes established on the path of direct vision, up until (but not including) the first moment of full enlightenment.

Thus the ten constitute the third and fourth of the five paths to enlightenment (the fifth being enlightenment itself). Most Sutrayana schools accept the first bodhisattva level to be equivalent to the path of direct vision, and the other nine to belong to the path of integration (or meditation), fourth of the five paths.

The Mongolian lama Lobzang Tayang, commenting on the way in which the Kalachakra enlightenment experience relates to the bodhisattva levels, states in his *Legacy of the Sun-like Masters,*

> Another way to speak of the yoga of samadhi is as consisting of the twelve levels. The first of these is still on (the non-arya) stage of aspiring activity. The next ten are the ten levels of an arya in training, from (the first, which is called) 'The Joyous,' until (the tenth, called) 'Dharma Cloud.' The twelfth level, which is also known as the Extraordinary Path, refers to the Path Beyond Obstacles [i.e., full enlightenment].

The same text then concludes with a review of how the stacking of the white and red drops in columns up and down the body carries the practitioner across the paths and stages, using the same number combinations as does the First Dalai Lama in *Notes:*

> Thus in reliance upon arising at the core of the navel chakra inside the central channel as an actual 'empty body' of male and female forces in sexual union, and by arousing the mystic heat located at the navel area of this ordinary body produced by the forces of karma, a red drop is brought up the central channel from below and is retained at the crown.

Simultaneously a white drop is brought down the central channel to the tip of the jewel. These drops are held here and not allowed to transfer to other sites. They are made to abide, and are firmly retained. Based on this, one achieves an initial experience of a single moment of supreme unchanging bliss, inspiring a moment of primordial wisdom of bliss and emptiness that releases one part of its own sphere of obscurations to be abandoned. At the same time one part of the 1,800 karmic winds (in this 'set' of 1,800) is stilled, and one of the 21,600 factors of the physical body [i.e., one part of twelve times 1,800] is consumed.

In this way one builds a string of 21,600 white and red drops (in reversed columns) inside the central channel and generates 21,600 experiences of supreme unchanging bliss. This in turn arouses 21,600 experiences of the primordial wisdom of bliss and emptiness, which causes transcendence of the 21,600 obscurations to be abandoned, and the stilling of 21,600 karmic energies. The 21,600 assembled drops consume all 21,600 factors of which the bodily atoms are composed, causing the body to totally dematerialize. In this way (in twelve sets of 1,800 drops, moments of bliss, experiences of the wisdom of bliss and emptiness, stilling of karmic energies, and dissolutions of bodily factors) one ascends the twelve Kalachakra stages.

Referring to the writings of Lama Tsongkhapa, Lobzang Tayang summarizes the Kalachakra enlightenment process as follows in *Legacy of the Sun-like Masters:*

In brief, of the first set of 1,800 experiences of unchanging bliss, 1,799 arise on the path of application [i.e., second of the five paths to enlightenment]. The 1,800th moment of this bliss marks the beginning of the path of direct vision [third of the five paths], and the first arya level, that called 'The Joyous.' Another

1,800 moments of bliss arise, the last of which marks the beginning of the path of integration (the fourth path), and the second arya level, called 'The Stainless.'

In this way one ascends each of the twelve Kalachakra levels, each of which is comprised of 1,800 factors, and eventually arrives at the twelfth level, the Path Beyond Obstruction.

There is also a tradition of linking the process of 'stacking' the columns of drops inside the central channel and the experiences thus induced, to the opening of each of the six chakras. Again, Lobzang Tayang comments upon this:

Thus the process of building up columns of drops begins at the tip of the jewel. As the column moves from the jewel chakra to the secret place, the meditator experiences the first two Kalachakra grounds: the (non-arya) stage of aspiring activity, and the (arya) stage known as the 'Joyous.' The column is then increased from the secret place to the navel, and the next two Kalachakra stages are experienced: the 'Stainless' and the 'Radiant.' The column extends from the navel to the heart: one experiences the two stages known as the 'Luminous' and the 'Pure.' It builds from the heart to the throat: one experiences the stages of the 'Manifest' and the 'Durable.' It builds from the throat to the forehead; one experiences the 'Unmoving' and 'Sublime Wisdom.' It builds from the forehead to the crown; one experiences the stages of 'Dharma Cloud' and the 'Path Beyond Hindrance'. . . .

In this way one builds the column of drops from the jewel to the crown and retains them without letting them dissipate, taking to fulfillment the experience of great unchanging bliss. Then just as when one applies a magic elixir to coarse metal the iron entirely disappears and in its place appears pure gold, through the fulfillment of the Kalachakra yogas one's previous physical aggregates completely fade away, and in their place the empty body of Kalachakra and Consort manifests like a rainbow in the sky.

Lobzang Tayang provides a similarly succinct description of the enlightenment state characteristic of the twelfth stage of Kalachakra:

All the qualities of buddhahood are explained as being subsumed within the four kayas, or bodies of a buddha.

The first of these is the innately produced body. This is the experience of the drop of the fourth occasion [i.e., sexual ecstasy] free from all distortion. It provides instant enlightenment, and is the primordial vajra wisdom. Purified by emptiness, it is the attainment of omniscient knowledge and omniscient vision.

The second is the truth body of primordial wisdom. This is the drop of sleep purified of all distortion. It provides the aspect of enlightenment that is characterized by the five aspects, and is the vajra mind. Purified by abiding in a state of signlessness, it brings knowledge of the enlightenment path, and dwells within the supreme, unchanging great bliss.

The third is the beatific body. It is the drop of the dream state, purified of all distortion. It provides the fulfillment of the twenty stages of unfoldment of enlightenment, and is vajra speech. Purified by wishlessness, it is imbued with the power to teach the Dharma to the sentient beings in accordance with their own means of communication.

The fourth is the emanation body. This is the drop of the waking state, purified of all distortion. It provides the enlightenment powers able to emanate magically throughout the world, and is the vajra body. Purified in the unconditioned, it brings knowledge of all things, and the ability to emanate forth in various forms at will....

Each of these four 'bodies' can also be said to be comprised of body, speech, mind, and great bliss, and thus becomes fourfold.... In this way the Kalachakra doctrine speaks of sixteen kayas.

11   The Lineage of Transmission

Who were the early teachers of the Kalachakra tradition?

His Holiness the present Dalai Lama throws light on the subject in *Concerning the Kalachakra Initiation:*[1]

> From the point of view of the personage at whose request the Kalachakra Tantra was taught, unlike any other tantra it was transmitted as a result of a request from Suchandra, spiritual chieftain of the legendary land of Shambala.
>
> It is said that in order to benefit the subjects of the ninety-six principalities of his country Suchandra traveled to India and requested just such a teaching from the Buddha. Kalachakra therefore has a special relationship with Shambala.
>
> From Suchandra the lineage was passed down (in Shambala) through a line of seven great masters, beginning with Suchandra, and then twenty-one *kalkin* masters, beginning with Manju Yashas. (We are presently in the era of the twenty-first kalkin). In future, during the era of the twenty-fifth kalkin, the special connection that the people of this earth share with Kalachakra will manifest strongly in world events.

Thus the initial Kalachakra exponent in our world era is said to be the Buddha himself. The place of the teaching was Dhanyakataka Stupa, South India, and the recipients are said to have been accomplished yogins, not mere ordinary people. They, as Buddha, traveled to Dhanyakataka Stupa by means of yogic powers. The principal recipient was Suchandra, the illustrious Dharmaraja, or 'spiritual chieftain' of Shambala, a kingdom to the northwest of India. In addition, representatives of six other kingdoms are also said to have been present.

As His Holiness mentions in the Foreword to this book, the tradition of the Second Dalai Lama's guru Khedrup Norzang Gyatso establishes the time of the teaching as the full moon day of the fourth month, in the year of Buddha's passing. The First Dalai Lama's guru Bodong Chokley Namgyal held the same view. A second (and perhaps more widespread) tradition is that Buddha gave the teaching on the full moon of the third month in the year following his attainment of enlightenment.

Even though the Buddha taught the Kalachakra tradition in India, it is not possible to say just when the system began to surface publicly in that country. It is known, however, that the lineage of transmission that came to Tibet did not have a long Indian history, having been carried out of India to Shambala when Suchandra returned to his homeland almost immediately after receiving the transmission from the Buddha, and not being returned until only sixty years before capturing the attention of the Tibetan spiritual community. As for the lineages of the six other countries represented at the original teaching, nothing seems to be known (or at least said) about what became of them.

The Great Thirteenth's *Summary of the Kalachakra Tradition* describes the Kalachakra lineage and early literature this way:

> Buddha Shakyamuni originally taught this tradition
> at the Dhanyakataka Stupa in South India. The teach-
> ing had been requested by King Suchandra of Sham-

bala, who was an actual emanation of the bodhisattva Vajrapani. Emissaries from six different kingdoms were also present. On that occasion Buddha transmitted *The Kalachakra Root Tantra* in twelve thousand lines, and shortly thereafter Suchandra composed his extensive commentary in sixty thousand lines.

However, the only section of *The Kalachakra Root Tantra* to come down to us is the chapter known as *The Treatise on the Initiations.* Later, Manju Yashas, who was the first of the twenty-five kalkin masters of Shambala, wrote a summary of *The Kalachakra Root Tantra* that came to be known by the title *The Abbreviated Kalachakra Tantra,* which is in five chapters. . . . Another important text is *The Great Commentary: A Stainless Light,* which elucidates *The Abbreviated Kalachakra Tantra . . .* by another of Shambala's kalkin masters, Pundarika. . . . In addition, Kalachakrapada's extensive and abbreviated commentaries to the Kalachakra generation stage yogas are fundamental reading, as are the writings of the Dro masters.

The Great Thirteenth here has provided us with a list of many of the important tantric masters and texts, most of them Indian, others from Shambala and then Tibet, associated with the early Kalachakra transmission. His *Summary* also lists numerous other people and scriptures, but I have not quoted these here. Those quoted will suffice to give us a sketch of the early tradition.

After receiving the Kalachakra teaching from the Buddha it is said that Suchandra transcribed it into a text known as *The Kalachakra Root Tantra: The Primordial Buddha,*[2] consisting of twelve thousand verses. Shortly thereafter he composed an extensive commentary to this, in sixty thousand lines.

Neither of these, however, was ever widely known in India in its original form. Only *The Treatise on the Initiations,* a quintessential section of *The Kalachakra Root Tantra,* seems to have been carried to Central India from Shambala, along with a number of important treatises written by later Shambala masters. These, together with the oral tradition, were deemed all that was necessary for the enlightenment of human beings in this degenerate age; more would have been superfluous.

Nonetheless, the essence of both *The Kalachakra Root Tantra* and Suchandra's commentary to it were carried to India, and thereafter in translation to Tibet, in the form of *The Abbreviated Kalachakra Tantra*, and the elucidation to it, *The Great Commentary: A Stainless Light*, two texts that were composed (in the Sanskrit language) in Shambala.

The former of these two texts, *The Abbreviated Kalachakra Tantra*, was composed by Kalkin Yashas (often erroneously identified as Manjushrikirti[3] in Western literature), the eighth lineage master (in the line transmitted) from Suchandra. Arranged into five chapters—entitled "World," "Entity," "The Initiations," "The Application" and "Primordial Wisdom"—the work was conceived as a condensation of all the essential teachings contained in Buddha's original Kalachakra discourse and Suchandra's commentary to it. Thus his text today stands as the most complete guide to *The Kalachakra Root Tantra*. The First Dalai Lama repeatedly quotes from it, generally identifying the source solely by the chapter title.[4]

The latter text, *The Great Commentary: A Stainless Light*, was written as a clarification of *The Abbreviated Kalachakra Tantra*. Its author, Kalkin Pundarika, was the principal disciple and spiritual heir of Kalkin Yashas. He is also believed to have been the latter's blood son. Pundarika's work still serves today as the principal key to *The Abbreviated Kalachakra Tantra*.[5]

A Stainless Light, together with two other texts mentioned elsewhere by the Great Thirteenth, constitute the trilogy known in Tibetan as *Sems 'grel skor gsum*, or *Trilogy of the Bodhisattvas*. The other two are *The Vajrapani Commentary*, and *The Vajragarbha Commentary*, both of which the First Dalai Lama quotes several times in his *Notes on the Two Yogic Stages of Glorious Kalachakra*.

These three, together with *The Treatise on the Initiations* (from

The Kalachakra Root Tantra taught by Buddha) and Manju Yashas' *The Abbreviated Kalachakra Tantra*, are considered by the Tibetans as being the most fundamental Kalachakra literature. Hopefully over the next few decades these five fundamental works will receive the attention from Western scholars that their antiquity merits. It is auspicious that the original Sanskrit of several of them still exists. The Tibetan and Mongolian translations are also available, of course, to people who can read those languages.

The master Manju Yashas propagated the Kalachakra widely in Shambala. To him and all succeeding Shambala lineage holders is prefixed the title *kalkin*,[6] meaning 'lineage master,' and also 'master of the clans.' As he was the first to bear this epithet, he is known as the First Kalkin. Pundarika, who composed *The Great Commentary: A Stainless Light*, is known as the Second Kalkin.

In summary, the principal early Kalachakra teachers referred to by the Great Thirteenth in the passage quoted above are the Buddha, who was from India, and the three most important early lineage holders—Suchandra, Manju Yashas, and Pundarika—all of whom were from Shambala.

The Great Thirteenth does, however, make two other references, these being to Kalachakrapada and the Dro family. The former name is linked to the story of how the Kalachakra tradition was retrieved from Shambala and brought back to India, the land of its origin; mention of the Dro masters invokes the story of how knowledge of the Kalachakra tradition was carried to Tibet.

Only sixty years transpired between the time the Kalachakra tradition was carried back to India from Shambala (most Western scholars fix this at 966/7 A.D) and the time that it was first carried to Tibet (1026/7 A.D.). In that brief period, two Kalachakrapadas appeared. The first is known as the Elder, the second as the Younger. Most prayers to the masters of the lineage of transmission usually put one name between these two, that of Pindo Acharya.

The first of the two Kalachakrapadas was better known in

India as Chilupa, the mahasiddha of Orissa who journeyed to Shambala and retrieved the Kalachakra tantric tradition. The second Kalachakrapada most probably can be identified as Naropada, known to Tibetans as Naropa, who in the early eleventh century served as abbot of Nalanda Monastery.

Traditional Tibetan histories comment that the Kalachakra doctrine must have also existed in India before Chilupa retrieved it from Shambala, for it is said that Chilupa purposely set out for Shambala after having seen a text of the Kalachakra system. Be this as it may, the lineage that came to Tibet, as well as the lineage widely propagated throughout India from the late tenth or early eleventh century onward, was exclusively inspired by the transmission from Shambala. Nothing further seems to be said in any of the Kalachakra historical literature about the text that had originally so inspired Chilupa; from the time of his return to India he seems to have propagated solely the Shambala teachings.

Kalachakrapada the Elder (that is, Chilupa) taught the Kalachakra doctrines to numerous disciples. Foremost amongst them was Pindo Acharya.[7] He in turn had numerous accomplished disciples, the most important being Kalachakrapada the Younger, otherwise known as Naropa. It is possible that Naropa also met Kalachakrapada the Elder and received the Kalachakra transmission directly from him.

As mentioned earlier, even though Chilupa and Pindo Acharya had numerous disciples, it was the lineages of their disciple Naropa that were to be transmitted to and consequently preserved in Tibet and Central Asia. Thus the lineage of Naropa is probably the only Kalachakra tradition that has come down to us today in an unbroken transmission.

The Tibetan *Tengyur* contains almost a dozen works by Naropa on various aspects of the subject of Kalachakra. One of the most important of these is his *Commentary to the Treatise on the Initiations,* which the First Dalai Lama quotes several times in his *Notes on the Two Yogic Stages of Glorious Kalachakra.*

Naropa in turn transmitted his lineages to numerous Indian

disciples, several of whom would be particularly important in the development of Kalachakra in Tibet.

The first of these was Shribhadra, who from 1026/7 worked with the Tibetan translator Jyojo Dawai Ozer. This lineage did not become important in a direct spiritual sense, but it did draw the attention of the Tibetan tantric intelligentsia to the existence and nature of the Kalachakra materials.

The second of Naropa's disciples in the Kalachakra teaching was the master Somanatha, who traveled to Tibet in 1064 and worked with Dro Lotsawa to translate much of the basic Kalachakra material into Tibetan, including Pundarika's extensive commentary. This is the Dro referred to above by the Thirteenth Dalai Lama. The transmission coming down from this meeting is known as the Dro Tradition.

Another of Naropa's disciples, Manjukirti, produced a disciple by the name of Samanta Shribhadra. This second master later transmitted the Kalachakra doctrines to Rva Chorab, a disciple of Rva Dorjey Drak.[8] Samanta Shribhadra and Rva Chorab also translated numerous important Kalachakra scriptures.

The above two traditions, the Dro and the Rva, are said to be the most important lineages of transmission in the early spread of the Kalachakra in Tibet. Eventually they were fused into one by Buton Rinchen Druppa, an important fourteenth-century master (and, incidentally, the author of the sadhana translated in Chapter Nineteen of this volume). It is the two-fold lineage from Buton that eventually came down to Lama Tsongkhapa, and that therefore constitutes the tradition preserved in the Gelukpa school today.

Another important Indian teacher to study Kalachakra under Naropa was Atisha, who came to Tibet in 1042 and whose doctrines almost four centuries later became fundamental to the tenets of the newly established Gelukpa school. Atisha did not write on the subject, but he is said to have taught it widely.

In addition to studying Kalachakra with Naropa, Atisha also studied it with a master called Pindo while in Indonesia. In the autocommentary to *A Lamp for the Path to Enlightenment*

Atisha states that his mention of "the great *Adibuddha Tan-tra*" (i.e., *The Kalachakra Root Tantra*) refers to the oral trans-mission of this text as received from his guru Acharya Pindo of Java. Could this master be identical with the Bengali-born Pindo Acharya who transmitted the lineage to Naropa? Even though Naropa was Atisha's guru there was not a great differ-ence in their age. To further complicate the issue, one of Atisha's six principal Indian disciples was named Pindo. Also, one wonders if "Pindo of Java" could point to a link with Borobudur, the enormous Buddhist stupa in central Java said to be modelled on the original Dhanyakataka Stupa of South India, where Buddha gave the first Kalachakra teaching.[9]

As stated earlier, in Tibet the Kalachakra tradition was propagated in two lines, known as the Dro and Rva, that were fused in the late thirteenth century by Buton Rinchen Druppa. Buton wrote prolifically on the subject,[10] and from him it spread throughout all schools of Tibetan buddhism to some extent, but achieved its greatest popularity in the Gelukpa. Lama Tsongkhapa and most of his immediate disciples studied, prac-ticed, taught and wrote extensively on Kalachakra.[11]

It is often pointed out that even though Lama Tsongkhapa and his two principal disciples Khedrupjey and Gyaltsepjey were heavily involved in the Kalachakra tradition, Kalachakra was not fully incorporated into the principal study programs of either Gyumey or Gyuto, the Lower and Upper Tantric Col-leges.[12] The two tantric colleges instead specialized in the other three of the four highest yoga tantra systems, namely, Gu-hyasamaja, Heruka Chakrasamvara, and Yamantaka. The study of Kalachakra was included only as a reference point. As a result, those in the tantric colleges who wished to learn the Kalachakra system had (and have) to do so privately. Kalachakra was preserved not in any of the large central monasteries, but by private lineage holders (such as Kyabjey Ling Rinpochey, the late Senior Tutor to H.H. the Dalai Lama), and in numerous other Gelukpa communities across Central Asia.

It is possible that the Kalachakra doctrine was kept outside

of the curriculum of the central Gelukpa monasteries for political reasons. Oral tradition has it that after Tsongkhapa passed
away his followers broke into two factions. The elderly Gyaltsepjey, who succeeded to Tsongkhapa's throne at Ganden Monastery, was not involved in the controversy; this distinction fell
to another of Tsongkhapa's chief disciples, Khedrupjey, who
later succeeded Gyaltsepjey to the Ganden Throne.

It is said that many Gelukpa monks resented Khedrupjey's
aristocratic background and the glamorous style that seemed
to characterize his activities. Many of them also questioned
the importance that he placed on the Kalachakra doctrines,
charging that it was at the expense of study of the mainstream
tantras.

One of the most outspoken of Khedrupjey's critics was the
monk Gungru Gyaltsen Zangpo. After Khedrupjey composed
his extensive commentary to Pundarika's *The Great Commentary: A Stainless Light,* Lama Gungru is recorded to have
laughed at the attention the text received, and to have ex-
claimed, "As for this so-called 'Glorious Kalachakra Tantra,'
the root scriptures do not even begin and end with the syllables *e-vam,* the seal marking every other highest yoga tantra.
The explanatory scriptures are full of contradictions. And as
for its source, this is as unclear as the paternal lineage of a
child born to a prostitute."

Surprisingly, the Kalachakra tradition nonetheless remained
strong in the Gelukpa school, more so than in any other sect
of Tibetan buddhism. Certainly its popularity increased and
decreased with the generations, probably because of the
charisma and energy of the Kalachakra lineage teachers of a
given era; but it not only survived, it often flourished with
a popular intensity outshining that of the three 'establishment'
highest yoga tantras.

Frequently overlooked by Tibet enthusiasts as well as by
academics is the variety of spiritual and intellectual life that
existed in the thousands of Gelukpa monasteries found
throughout Central Asia before the days of the Communist
destructions. Many of these had unique study programs focus-

ing on specific topics quite other than those of the half dozen specially accredited monasteries of Lhasa and its environs.

An example is Amchok Tsennyi Gonpa, located in Amdo, Eastern Tibet. This is the hereditary monastery of Ven. Amchok Tulku, with whom I translated a number of the works included in Part Two, and whose story I mentioned in the Preface. This institution was in fact a community of five independent monasteries, each of approximately five hundred to a thousand monks. Four of these five sub-monasteries each specialized in one of the four tantric systems listed above: Guhyasamaja, Heruka Chakrasamvara, Yamantaka, and Kalachakra. The fifth specialized in astrology and medicine.

Kumbum, another large and important monastery in Amdo Province, had a similarly varied study program within its different departments, with Kalachakra again playing a significant role. Tashi Lhunpo in Shigatsey, southwest Tibet, also maintained an important Kalachakra lineage, as did Namgyal Dratsang, the Dalai Lama's private monastery in Lhasa. A lineage was also maintained in one of the *khamtsens* (departments) of Ganden Shartsey, the monastery founded by Lama Tsongkhapa himself near Lhasa.

Most of the Dalai Lama and Panchen Lama incarnations, Tibet's two highest ranking spiritual leaders, were strongly involved in the Kalachakra teaching. For example, the passion exhibited by the First Dalai Lama in his *Notes on the Two Yogic Stages of Glorious Kalachakra* speaks for his sentiment in this regard.

The Second Dalai Lama was as expressive in his praise of the Kalachakra yogas. His enthusiasm is reflected in a poem he wrote one day when thoughts of his principal tantric teacher, the controversial yogi Khedrup Norzang Gyatso (mentioned by His Holiness in the Foreword), overwhelmed him during a meditation session:[13]

Here I sit in Rinchen Gang, in a hermitage
Where meditation spontaneously achieves results,

A Dharma site at the foot of Ode Gungyal,
A magnificent mountain rivaling Mount Kailash itself.

Thoughts of my guru Khedrup Norzang Gyatso arise
And I recollect his immeasurable kindness.
A flood of emotion surges up from within me
And every hair on my body trembles with joy.

I call out to him with a plaintive voice:
Pray, come forth from the sphere of the unmanifest.
Emanate the radiant countenance of your holy body;
With speech, release a great rainfall of the Dharma;
And lead sentient beings to the state of enlightenment
That is inseparable from your peerless mind.

O most holy root guru, under your kind guidance
I mastered the yogas of the two tantric stages
Of glorious Kalachakra, king of the tantras,
And also the branches of Kalachakra,
Such as astronomical knowledge of the heavens,
That facilitate higher spiritual knowledge.

Without relying on words alone you led me
To a naked understanding of the profound teachings
Of Arya Nagarjuna, Aryadeva and Lama Tsongkhapa
Concerning the ultimate mode of Being:
That all things abide in the nature of emptiness;
That nothing exists in its own right;
That things are mere mental projections
Imputed on their bases of imputation.

You helped me to see the great inner enemy,
The I-grasping habit that sees things as real,
And to see its limitlessly harmful effects.
You also showed me how to destroy it;

So now everything that occurs in the sphere of
  perception
Effortlessly arises within the path of the void.

Yet you did not let me fall into nihilism,
But pointed out to me the relevance of how
All the things that appear, though mere names,
Nonetheless continue to function conventionally
According to the laws of relativity and causation.
Thus you freed me from the terrible cliffs
Of grasping at the extremes of "is" and "is not."
O most kind root guru, it was you who taught me
How to extract the quintessential meanings
Of all the profound sutras and tantras
And helped me to find the inner strength
Of a mind well trained in the wisdom tradition.

The Third Dalai Lama also received and taught the
Kalachakra lineage. In 1578 this incarnation traveled to Mongolia, where he converted the Mongols to buddhism. He spent
the remainder of his life traveling and teaching throughout
Mongolia and Eastern Tibet, building the foundations of buddhism and the enlightenment tradition. These areas still remain
firmly dedicated to the study and practice of the Kalachakra
doctrines, and some of the best Kalachakra literature of Central Asia has been produced by lamas of the Amdo-Mongolia
borderlands.

The Seventh Dalai Lama's contribution to the Kalachakra
legacy is said to be particularly significant. This was Gyalwa
Kalzang Gyatso, who was born in 1708 in Litang in Kham,
East Tibet.[14] He studied with numerous gurus, including the
Second Panchen Lama. One of his most intimate spiritual
preceptors was the Gelukpa Throne Holder Trichen Ngawang
Chokden, and it was from this lama that he first received
detailed teachings on the Kalachakra six yogas.

Later in his life he realized that the Kalachakra teachings
had become dangerously fragmented. He requested his elderly

guru to collect together all the fragments before anything was lost, and then to transmit the complete tradition to him, to ensure its preservation.

The biography of the Seventh Dalai Lama found in Tsechokling's *Lives of the Lam Rim Teachers,* speaks thus of his contribution: [15]

His Holiness (the Seventh Dalai Lama) at this time repeatedly requested his guru Trichen Ngawang Chokden to collect together the complete Kalachakra lineage, that had been painstakingly gathered by Lama Tsongkhapa and his disciples several centuries earlier, but that now was in danger of becoming fragmented and lost.

Although very old, out of respect for His Holiness and his spiritual vision, and in order to try and help preserve the full legacy of Lama Tsongkhapa, the aged Throne Holder traced down and collected the various fragmented traditions with great effort. He then internalized the meanings of all the teachings received by performing the according meditational retreats. Later he passed the complete package of lineages to His Holiness Gyalwa Kalzang Gyatso. His Holiness himself then made retreat and accomplished the trainings, thus becoming fearless in giving initiations into and teachings upon Kalachakra.

The closeness of the Seventh Dalai Lama with his Kalachakra teacher Trichen Ngawang Chokden remained firm until the latter's death. Tsechokling poignantly recalls this event:

When Ngawang Chokden was in his seventy-fifth year his body became very heavy to him and he even had trouble in rising from his seat unassisted. His Holiness went to the lama's residence. . .and requested him to use his powers to extend his lifespan.

His old guru replied, "From childhood I have lived

as a buddhist monk. . . . I have had the good fortune to study, contemplate and meditate in accordance with the teachings to my utter satisfaction, and to have served as a tutor to Your Holiness, the protector of the Tibetan people. It has been a great joy to me to be able to transmit to you many sutra and tantra branches of the buddhist path. . . . But now my mind is ready to meet with death. This haggard body is worn out. All this old man wants is to be in solitude in Redeng Monastery when the time of death descends.''

On the morning of the departure His Holiness went to the great guru and spoke with him at length of spiritual matters. As his teacher was about to leave, His Holiness placed the crown of his head against the old man's chest for several moments and then, shedding tears, offered prayers for their continued spiritual bond. His Holiness immediately requested ceremonies to be performed in the three great Lhasa monasteries, in order to effect his teacher's safe arrival at his hermitage. Tsechokling's account continues,

> Trichen Ngawang Chokden reached Redeng Monastery, and not long thereafter passed away. . . . His Holiness retreated into an upper chamber of the Potala and entered into intensive prayer and meditation. . . . From this time onward each year he performed an extensive Kalachakra practice in honor of his deceased guru.

From the Seventh Dalai Lama's time until today the Kalachakra doctrine has remained a priority with the Dalai Lama office.

The Seventh Dalai Lama had offered Redeng Monastery to Trichen Ngawang Chokden, and thus this tutor is now better known to history as the First Redeng Rinpochey. Toward the end of the last century, when relations between Lhasa and Shigatsey became strained because of the latter's innocent yet illicit dealings with the British Raj (and in particular with the spy Sarat Chandra Das),[16] the traditional spiritual father-son relationship that had existed between the Dalai and Panchen Lamas, with the elder serving as guru to the younger in any given generation, was largely transferred to the Redeng Rinpochey. After the death of the previous Dalai Lama the incumbent Redeng Rinpochey was appointed regent, and ultimately became the person in charge of overseeing the search for the new incarnation. He seems to have done a very good job indeed. It is unfortunate that his tragic death lead to a rewriting in Tibet of his role in this respect, and generally to a campaign of character assassination perpetrated by the very Lhasa aristocrats responsible for his most cruel murder. It is also unfortunate that most Western scholars have been so misled as to the character and contribution of this wonderful man, whose only real faults were his good-naturedness and his love of beauty.

The Panchen Lama incarnations, who rank second only to the Dalai Lamas in the Tibetan spiritual hierarchy, were also very much involved in the Kalachakra transmission. The First Panchen Lama, who was the guru of the Fifth Dalai Lama, and whose *An Aspiration to Fulfill the Stages of the Glorious Kalachakra Path* constitutes Chapter Twenty of this volume, dedicated tremendous energy to teaching Kalachakra, as did his successor the Second Panchen Lama. The Third incarnation achieved even greater popularity for his Kalachakra writings, his *Guide to Shambala*[17] becoming an instant success throughout Central Asia. Subsequent incarnations continued the legacy. The Sixth, whose verse work on Kalachakra is included in Chapter Thirteen, was also an active teacher of the Kalachakra doctrines.

In Tibet the Kalachakra tradition was also taught outside the Gelukpa school, although not with the same enthusiasm. The Kargyu school, for example, holds a unique Kalachakra transmission coming from the Jonangpa school. The Jonangpa lamas, whose most famous exponent is Taranatha, wrote widely on the Kalachakra tradition, and many of their works can still be found in Tibetan libraries around the world. Also, the Sakya school has maintained a Kalachakra tradition from the earliest days of that order's existence.

One terrible aspect of the destruction of the great monastic libraries of Central Asia by the Communists over the last few decades is that many of the texts destroyed were single copies of hand-traced manuscripts, of which no second copy existed anywhere in the world. Many of the large monasteries of Kham and Amdo that specialized in the Kalachakra transmission must have produced extensive literature of this nature. Some of this was saved, of course, and more will continue to emerge from time to time. But unfortunately this is merely a fraction of what existed only half a century ago.

The writings of Bodong Chokley Namgyal, an important Jonangpa guru of the First Dalai Lama, come to mind. Although Bodong was quite famous as a philosopher and teacher during his lifetime, in fact he was so prolific a writer that nobody could afford to publish him. A single handwritten copy of his collected works (in a hundred and thirty-seven volumes) managed to escape the Chinese destruction in Tibet. The collection contains half a dozen thick volumes of texts associated with Kalachakra. The entire corpus of his writings, with hundreds of titles covering every important topic in the Buddhist world, was eventually published in India by Tibet House, New Delhi, in association with the U.S. Library of Congress.

Tibet undoubtedly had thousands of literary collections of this nature, mostly kept as single copies in the home monastery of the original author. Anyone wanting a copy would traditionally have to contact the monastery and hire a scribe to prepare a hand reproduction, or visit the monastery and personally trace the original. Consequently much of this wondrous produce of a most unique human endeavor has now been lost to posterity.

The Chinese invasion of Tibet and the scattering of the Tibetans across the world is certainly a tremendous tragedy from the viewpoint of the suffering inflicted upon the Tibetan people and the genocidal assault upon their culture. It has, however, had the positive side-effect of throwing the lamas and their Tibetan buddhist culture onto center stage of the international arena, at a time in world history when mankind is more in need of spiritual inspiration and guidance than ever before.

This very hopeful note was expressed by the late Prof. A. L. Basham, probably the greatest indologist of the twentieth century, in the foreword to *The Tantric Yogas of Sister Niguma:*

> One of the unexpected results of the Chinese occupation of Tibet was the emigration of thousands of Tibetan lamas, who joined His Holiness the Dalai Lama in voluntary exile. Bringing with them copies of their scriptures and the rich traditions of their own brand of buddhism, they quickly adapted themselves to new environments and found many students in both America and Europe. The spread of the knowledge of Tibetan religion in the West within a few decades is in some ways comparable to the spread of knowledge of Greek and classical culture in Europe after the capture of Constantinople by the Turks and the diaspora of Byzantine scholars. It is as though a new dimension has been added to the stock of world civilization.

Certainly the impact of the lamas on world culture has been extremely positive, as symbolized by His Holiness the Dalai Lama receiving the Nobel Peace Prize in 1989. Possibly it will even eventually translate into some of the lineages of transmission being passed into Western hands, as Western maturity in tantric theory and practice grows from mere emotional and/or intellectual curiosity to actual inner realization.

A lama friend of mine in England, the Ven. Chimey Rinpochey, once commented to me, "We Tibetans regard this introduction of tantric buddhism into the West as something of an experiment. We're still waiting for the first Westerner to achieve enlightenment through these methods, and prove the experiment successful."

That was twelve years ago. Perhaps by now the patience of Rinpochey and the other Tibetan lamas who have given time and energy to the training of Western students has begun to bear the desired fruit within the mindstreams of one or two practitioners somewhere on the face of this planet.

The Buddha is said to have prophesied that "Two thousand and five hundred years after my passing the Dharma will spread to the land of the red-faced people."[18] Most Tibetans today take this to refer to North America, home of the American natives.

In 1956 India hosted the celebration of the 2,500th anniversary of Buddha's passing. Amongst the chief guests of honor was His Holiness the Dalai Lama, who was on his first trip abroad (excluding his forced trip to Peking a few years earlier). This was his first real contact with the international buddhist community, and it set the stage for the mass Tibetan exodus to India that would follow the Chinese crackdown three years later. It also could be interpreted as an omen of the spiritual contribution that His Holiness and the other Tibetan spiritual leaders have made to the international community since that time.

12   The Shambala Connection

The tantric scriptures speak of a number of places of power located on this planet, magical places where the auric energies of different dimensions cross through one another's fields, and diverse realities overlap. These are mystical sites, and the experience of those who visit them varies according to the level of spiritual and karmic maturity of the pilgrim. The tantric tradition of Heruka Chakrasamvara, for example, identifies twenty-four such locations in India.

Two places of power receive extraordinary attention in the classical buddhist tantric literature of both India and Tibet.

The first of these is Oddiyana,[1] usually identified with modern-day Swat, Pakistan, where many of the mainstream tantras were stored and preserved from the time of Buddha until the world was ready for their wider dissemination. Many tantric traditions are still said to exist in Oddiyana, secretly safeguarded in the hands of tantric families who pass them from generation to generation; and there they will stay, until their need manifests in the world. Only then will their keepers reveal them.

The second is the mystical land of Shambala, located to the north of the Sita River[2] somewhere in what is now the central section of the southern Soviet Union. It is from here that

Suchandra traveled in order to receive the Kalachakra transmission; to here he returned and propagated the teaching; here where the lineage was transmitted for some twelve centuries before being returned to India by the mahasiddha Kalachakrapada the Elder, or Chilupa; here where the eighth lineage holder and first kalkin, Manju Yashas, wrote *The Abbreviated Kalachakra Tantra*, and the second kalkin, Pundarika, composed *The Great Commentary: A Stainless Light*; here where the tradition is still maintained in its purity on another dimension, with the twenty-first Kalkin Master presiding as chieftain of the mystical clans; and here where Kalachakra practitioners who do not achieve enlightenment in this lifetime can take rebirth to continue their yogic path.

It is also from here, sometime in the not too distant future, when the world is in danger of being taken over by hordes of violent barbarians, that the great warrior Raudra Chakri, Bearer of the Wheel, the twenty-fifth kalkin, will ride forth with his heroic followers and save the day for the forces of light.

Thus on one level Shambala is (or was) an ordinary country populated by humans; but on another it is a pure land, occupying the same space as the worldly Shambala but existing entirely on a different etheric frequency. Those on the extraordinary dimension can be contacted by devotees of pure karma from this world, and when conditions are ripe the mystical heros of Shambala can emanate forth and help subdue the forces of evil.

Addressing this aspect of the Kalachakra mythology the Ven. Garjey Khamtrul Tulku commented,[3]

> As for. . . Shambala, its appearance varies according to one's karma. For example, one and the same river will be seen by the devas as nectar, by man as water, by hungry ghosts as pus and blood, and by some animals as a place to live in. . . .
>
> Three hundred and fifty years after the earth horse year of the present sixteenth cycle, the twenty-fifth royal Holder of the Castes, Dr'ag-po Khor-lo-chan

(i.e., Raudra Chakri, Holder of the Wheel), will ascend
the golden throne of Shambala.... Then...there will
be a great war with the *la-los*.... In this way they (the
barbarians) will be defeated. The human lifespan will
gradually increase...and the perfect age will dawn
anew, better than anything that happened before.

The presence of prophecies such as this in the Kalachakra
literature is no doubt one of the reasons for the tradition's
tremendous popularity with the Central Asian masses. It is
an aspect of Kalachakra that has also attracted considerable
attention from Western scholars. In addition, much of the recent dialogue between the Tibetan lamas and the Native North
American spiritual leaders, especially the Hopi and the Iro-
quois, has focused on these prophecies and how they compare
to those handed down in the North American native traditions.

As for the question of just who the *la-los* or 'barbarians'
are, there is little doubt that the Indian and Tibetan masters
of the past took the term to refer to a fundamentalist Muslim
group from the West Asia area.[4] The Kalachakra tradition
prophesies that Islam will endure on the earth for eighteen
hundred years from the time of its inception, and in the end
will destroy itself through its own aggression and fundamen-
talism. Raudra Chakri, Bearer of the Wrathful Wheel, will play
an important role at that time. There is also a Central Asian
tradition that claims Raudra Chakri will in fact be none other
than the reincarnation of the First Panchen Lama, Lobzang
Chokyi Gyaltsen, guru of the Fifth Dalai Lama.[5] Should this
be the case, no doubt we are all in good hands.

As the Third Panchen Lama suggests in his *Guide to Shambala*, the legendary country of Shambala is really three different things: a yogic symbol of the state of Kalachakra attainment, a pure land, and an actual physical place.

It is, however, its role as a pure land that has most captured
the hearts of Central Asians. In the minds of high yogis and
simple nomads alike, Shambala stands resplendent as a place
where those of a clear heart and positive karma can take re-

birth in an environment of happiness and enlightenment.

As a consequence, numerous 'Shambala prayers' emerged in Tibet, often uniting in their symbolism the yogic concepts of the Kalachakra tradition, the mythology of Shambala, and the prophecies related to the heroic work of the twenty-fifth kalkin, Raudra Chakri.

The Sixth Panchen Lama, for example, wrote half a dozen short verse works of this nature. These are all in the form of guruyoga liturgies intended for daily recitation and meditation. Each begins with the visualization of Raudra Chakri, the twenty-fifth lineage master of Shambala. He is sitting in the central courtyard of the palace of Malaya, capital of Shambala, and has the look of a powerful hero. One offers auspicious thoughts, and makes the request to be cared for by the enlightened forces of the Wrathful Holder of the Wheel,[6]

Homage to the kind spiritual master
Inseparably one with glorious Kalachakra,
Who has attained to the state of the empty body, with
The great unchanging bliss possessing all excellences
In constant embrace with the beautiful dharmadhatu
    lover.

To the north of India lies the fabulous land of
    Shambala,
With the city of Kalapa a jewel at its heart.
There at its center, seated on a throne studded in gems,
As though riding a magical flying horse
Is Raudra Chakri, Wrathful Holder of the Wheel...

I call to him, an embodiment of the Three Jewels:
Come forth with your weapon of inconceivable
    wisdom;
Slay from within me my every delusion
And my habit of grasping at a truly existent self.

Bless me that I may behold you in Shambala,
Wisely guiding your throngs of devotees.
And when the time comes to tame the barbarians,
May you keep me in your inner circle.

Should I die before achieving enlightenment
May I be reborn in Shambala, in the city of Kalapa,
And have the good fortune to drink the honey
Of the sublime teachings of the kalkin masters.

May I take to completion the profound non-dual
    message
Of the two yogic stages of tantric practice as taught in
Guhyasamaja, Yamantaka, Heruka Chakrasamvara and
    Kalachakra;
Thus in this very lifetime may I achieve realization of
The clear light and illusory body in perfect union,
Or the empty body conjoined with the unchanging
    bliss.

Thus the Sixth Panchen's prayer makes references to all three
aspects of Shambala: as a symbol of the Kalachakra yogic system, as a pure land, and as representative of the Kalachakra
prophecies.

The Shambala myth has been known to the West for some
time now, although until a century ago only to an elite group.
However, Madame Blavatsky, the Russian mystic who founded
the Theosophical Society, widely popularized the legend
throughout Europe and North America during the end of the
last and the first half of this century. It was probably from
a Theosophical influence that James Hilton learned of it and
subsequently embodied it as Shangrila in his highly successful novel *Lost Horizons*. Thus by the time Western academics
finally came around to seriously looking at it, the mystical legend of Shambala had already become something of a household concept.

Myths and symbols, of course, change with time and usage, and also change with the evolving experiences of those who use them as vehicles of understanding. Should the Kalachakra tradition ever take root in the West, no doubt we will develop our own understanding of it, as well as our own vision of the essential sense of the Kalachakra doctrine.

Until then, we have the wonderfully inspired Kalachakra literature of India, Shambala, Tibet, and the Mongol regions to fire our imaginations, and to provide us with grist for the spiritual mill.

Earlier in the analysis of fundamental Kalachakra literature it was said that the original *Kalachakra Root Tantra*, otherwise known as the *Paramadibuddha*, or *The Primordial Buddha*, no longer exists; that it was never carried from Shambala back to India, and consequently was never translated into Tibetan. Only that section known as *The Treatise on the Initiations* was returned to India, and therefore Manju Yashas' *The Kalachakra Abbreviated Tantra* has come to serve as a 'proxy' root tantra.

Nonetheless *The Kalachakra Root Tantra* does still exist in Shambala, on a dimension perceivable only by the pure. There it is held in secret, perhaps to be revealed in a future age if conditions should become ripe.

It is possible that it may also emerge from elsewhere in the world. For example, Atisha mentions having seen it in Java, when he visited in the early eleventh century, before coming to Tibet.

In fact, the Kalachakra doctrine may have spread in the Golden Islands (i.e., Indonesia) even before it became widely known in India. Certainly it would seem that in the eleventh century buddhism in Indonesia was more vibrant and energetic than it was in India at the time. When Atisha saw the text, it had been known in India for less than half a century.

Another source of our knowledge of *The Kalachakra Root Tantra* may come from the many passages in which it is quoted. For example, Dvakpo Gomchen Ngawang Drakpa's *A Commentary to the Kalachakra Generation Stage Yogas* opens by quoting a series of verses, said to be from the root tantra, that tell the story of how Suchandra received the Kalachakra teaching from the Buddha:

> Then from the famed land of Shambala there came
> A man said to be an incarnation of Vajrapani.
> Using his yogic powers he traveled
> To the Dhanyakataka Stupa of South India.
> He circumambulated Buddha three times to the right,
> Took a seat at the master's lotus feet,
> Offered precious jewels and flowers,
> And made prostrations repeatedly.
> Placing his hands together in supplication,
> Suchandra then requested this sublime transmission.

Also, Buton Rinchen Druppa's text on the Kalachakra method of conducting death and cremation rites, which includes enshrining the ashes in a special Kalachakra stupa, opens with a quote that Buton ascribes to *The Kalachakra Root Tantra,*

> Construct a mandala of colored powders,
> Summon the deceased's consciousness to it,
> And perform the empowerment ceremony.
> Even if the deceased has already taken rebirth
> In any of the three realms of misery,
> Have no doubt that he or she will be liberated.
>
> Take an image of the deceased,
> Or a piece of paper inscribed with the deceased's
>   name;
> Consecrate this according to the tradition,
> And place it inside of a stupa.
> The beneficial effects are inconceivable.

Another oft-quoted passage used to support the Kalachakra theory of the world as a macrocosm of the human mind is said to come from the first chapter of *The Kalachakra Root Tantra,*

> As it is with the outer world,
> Just so it is with the inner world of man.

It is possible that as a coordinated effort is made to check the Kalachakra materials found in the various repositories around the world we may one day be able to recreate a more complete picture of the contents of Buddha's original Kalachakra discourse.

PART TWO:
SELECTED TIBETAN READINGS

13 Prayer of the Kalachakra Path

by Lobzang Tubten Chokyi Nyima,
the Sixth Panchen Lama (1883-1937)

O great treasuries bestowing all realizations,
Supreme gurus embodying all objects of refuge,
Masters of knowledge, beings greater than the gods,
I direct my spiritual aspirations to you.
Grant me your gracious guidance, blessings and care.

A flash of lightning cuts through the night,
Eliminating the darkness for but a moment.
This human incarnation too endures for but an instant;
It is rarely found and is easily lost.[1]
Accomplished gurus, may I be inspired by this insight
And turn my mind always to the enlightenment path.

Like a stream flowing over a cliff and
Like the clouds of autumn, our time steadily passes
And there is nothing we can do to stop it.
May I be inspired to generate within my mindstream
Awareness of this impermanent nature of things,
The transient quality of life in samsara.

At the time of death one cannot look for help
To friends, relatives, wealth or possessions.
The only companions able then to follow
Are the karmic seeds of the black and white actions
Accumulated during one's lifetime;
And these are like a shadow trailing the body.
May I be inspired to give rise within myself
To certain knowledge of the workings of karmic law.

To a mind bereft of wisdom this world of samsara
Offers little but suffering interspersed with short
    refrains.
Sea monsters of pain ravage body and mind
As one's boat tosses in the waves of karma and
    delusion.
May I therefore be inspired to lose interest
In the vain fancies of ephemeral pursuits
And aspire instead to spiritual freedom.

In my countless lifetimes since beginningless time
Each living being has often been a mother to me,
Caring for me then with great kindness;
And now they are afflicted by great suffering.
Unable to endure the thought of their torment,
May I be inspired to experience the sublimely
    meaningful,
The aspiration to achieve highest enlightenment
As a means of becoming most useful in this world.

Vast indeed are the bodhisattva practices,
Such as the six perfections and four ways of
    benefiting trainees,
That mature the mindstreams of both oneself and others.
May I be inspired to step forth with undaunted daring
Into this Great Way leading to enlightenment,
And apply myself single-pointedly to the bodhisattva
    path.

Having thus trained the mind in the methods
Shared by both the sutra and tantra vehicles,
One becomes a suitable vessel for tantric practice
And enters through the door of the Vajrayana
By receiving the according initiations.
Having done this may I be inspired to guard
The disciplines and trainings of the tradition,
And to achieve proficiency in the yogas
Of both the generation and completion stages.

Especially, may I be inspired to accomplish the
  meditations
Of the supreme yogas of the profound tantric path
Of Kalachakra, the king of tantric traditions,
And thus purify and dissolve all physical materiality,
Giving rise to the dance of the empty body
In union with the great unchanging bliss
That in turn induces highest enlightenment,
The state of the primordial Buddha Kalachakra.[2]

I send this prayer to the sublime gurus,
Embodiments of the Three Jewels of Refuge,
Regents of Buddha Vajradhara:
Whatever comes to me in this life—
Joy or hardship, things good or things bad—
I look only to you for my strength and inspiration.
Feverently I focus my attention upon you;
Prove your compassion to me.

The colophon: Composed by the Buddhist Monk Lobzang
Tubten Chokyi Nyima Gelek Namgyal Palzangpo while residing on the Five Mountain Peaks,[3] a holy place blessed by the
bodhisattva Manjushri, embodiment of the wisdom of all the
buddhas.

14 Concerning the Kalachakra Initiation
by the Buddhist Monk Tenzin Gyatso,
the Fourteenth Dalai Lama (born 1935)

THE SEARCH FOR INNER HAPPINESS

The notion and sense of 'I' is a mere projection on the four or five psychophysical aggregates which make up the person. Yet this sense of I, which is possessed by us all, even the smallest insect, innately seeks to find satisfaction and to avoid misery.

In order to establish desirable states of happiness and to eliminate undesirable states of frustration and sorrow, the various kinds of living beings apply themselves, according to their individual capacities, to the activities that will achieve these goals.

The happiness which is to be produced and the sorrows to be eliminated are of many types. For example, people gain a type of happiness from food, shelter and social success, and they experience much suffering when these are taken from them.

However, were one to ask whether the limits of joy and sorrow end here, the answer is to the negative. No matter how much food, shelter and social success one has, these external conditions alone will not produce a lasting happiness if the mind is disturbed by spiritual unease.

This indicates that in addition to concerning ourselves with physical and environmental well-being, we must try to create an inner basis of peace and spiritual balance.

Which happiness is stronger, that arising from external conditions or that arising from inner spiritual harmony?

When one has the latter, then suffering does not arise in the mind even when the external conditions of happiness fail to converge. Alternatively, when one is bereft of inner peace the most pleasant external situation is unable to bring happiness to the mind.

THE SPIRITUAL SOLUTION

In this sense, the inner state of the mind is much more important than external conditions.

Therefore it is essential that we ourselves know the means by which a state of inner peace is created and cultivated. Not only would this benefit us individually in a very immediate, practical and down-to-earth sense; but also in this era when there is so much social tension on the earth, when the nations of the world are themselves so intensely concerned with competition and with efforts to overpower one another—even at the threat of nuclear devastation—it is most urgent for us to try to develop spiritual wisdom.

At present the world is not lacking in technological or industrial development. What are we lacking? A basis for inner harmony and joy.

Were we to cultivate the gentle pleasures of a loving and compassionate mind inspired by wisdom, the result would be that we would continually experience peace and happiness, even when confronted by external hardships, and we would have a pacifying effect on our chaotic environment rather than merely being caught up in and perpetrating it.

On the other hand, when our mind is bereft of spiritual qualities and instead we are controlled by inner forces such as greed, jealousy, aggression, pride and so forth, then even the most positive external conditions will fail to bring any significant comfort to the mind.

Hence this inner peace and joy not only benefits the individual who develops it; it also benefits the entire human community, and by extension this entire world in which we live.

THE FOUR NOBLE TRUTHS

What does buddhism have to contribute to the human quest for spiritual knowledge?

The root of the buddhadharma is the teaching of the four noble truths discerned by the Enlightened Beings. These four are: the nature of suffering, its causes, liberation from or the cessation of suffering, and the path to such liberation.

The truth of suffering invokes the topic of the various levels of hardship, frustration and pain that we living beings experience and that we must learn to recognize. Usually we mistake suffering, especially in its subtle forms, and mis-identify it as pleasure or entertainment. When the nature of suffering has been understood, the mind takes on a quality of indifference toward it.

Therefore after speaking of suffering the Buddha taught its source, its cause.

First of all we must investigate the question of whether the undesirable states of suffering that we experience arise from causes, or if they arise without causes. Secondly, if they have causes and these can be identified, can they also be eliminated? These are important questions.

When one perceives that in fact there are various ways to eliminate all inner causes of misery, one gains a certain conviction in one's own spiritual potential. From this is born a mind that will work for liberation.

Therefore, the Buddha taught the third truth of cessation, or the liberation from suffering.

By understanding that a state of inner illumination totally

beyond suffering can be generated, one appreciates the fact that liberation is something to be achieved within the mind itself, and not through any other object. Once the stains and aberrations of one's own mind have been purified in the mind's own final nature, liberation is achieved.

This being so, we should cultivate the liberating techniques within our own mindstream and eradicate all distorting factors and obscurations, such as attachment and the other delusions, that so strongly influence our present mode of existence. We must reverse deluded habits of thought born from misunderstanding reality, and actualize the pristinely clear level of mind.

Here 'pristinely clear mind' refers to the consciousness that has totally eradicated the mental habits of incorrectly apprehending objects of knowledge.

To accomplish this, one must generate an awareness of emptiness, the way things actually exist. When this awareness arises, the mind that mistakenly apprehends its objects can be put to rest.

We should use our ability to destroy from within ourselves the confused habits of thought of wrongly perceiving things—of seeing them other than the way they exist—by generating this awareness of the ultimate mode of existence of reality.

The Buddha taught that by generating this awareness of the ultimate mode, and then meditating on it single-pointedly, all forms of mental distortion are destroyed.

APPROACHES TO TRUTH

This ultimate mode of things has been explained by various means in order to suit the individual capacities and needs of the various kinds of disciples.

The Buddha's words suggest themes for four different trends in philosophical thought. In India these developed into four major schools. In this way the Buddha provided a diverse range of paths to spiritual growth and enlightenment. Trainees should begin their spiritual careers by first gaining proficiency in the simpler methods, before going on to the higher.

In Tibet we regarded these four schools as offering, from the lower to the higher schools, a diversity of philosophical and spiritual attitudes that the trainee can work with in a disciplined sequence, beginning with the lower and going on to the higher.

When put to the test of reason, it soon becomes obvious that several important doctrines accepted by the lower schools fail to withstand the rational scrutiny of an intensive investigation. A number of crucial faults become evident.

We should always carry reason and investigation as our tools. Critically examine all teachings that you hear. You must discern which of them are intended to be taken directly, and which are lower doctrines given by the Buddha in accordance with a specific time and need, and therefore are in need of interpretation.

Any teachings which, when tested, reveal logical flaws must be approached with the attitude that they require a non-literal interpretation.

Of the four schools of Indian buddhist thought, the most direct description of the ultimate nature of being is found in the Madhyamaka, or Middle View School. This ultimate nature is a phenomenon they call emptiness.

We should therefore try to understand this school's teachings on the ultimate nature of being by carefully studying and meditating on its authoritative traditions.

METHODS OF APPLICATION

In order to be able to generate inner spiritual forces which are strong enough to destroy the various mental distortions, one must engage a powerful method. The more powerful the method, the stronger becomes one's application to the view of emptiness. When one's method is strong, one's meditations on emptiness become very powerful and one's ability to destroy mental and spiritual distortion is intensified.

On the basis of the vastness of the methods used, the

Buddha's teachings are divided into two main vehicles: the *Bodhisattvayana* and the *Shravakayana,* generally known as the Mahayana and Hinayana, respectively.

In the Bodhisattvayana method one meditates that everything one does is for the benefit of living beings. Once it has been understood that all living beings, just like oneself, want happiness and dislike suffering, the attitude which assumes responsibility for their well-being arises. This attitude is an amazing, wonderful and most courageous force, more precious than anything else in existence.

When one uses it as a basis for one's meditation upon the ultimate mode of things, the forces that destroy delusion and distortion are easily cultivated.

What are the methods of meditating on this altruistic and compassionate aspiration to highest enlightenment in conjunction with meditation on emptiness as explained in the great Madhyamika works?

These are classified in accordance with the coarseness or subtlety of the level of consciousness performing the meditation. Factors such as the subtlety, the force and nature of one's mind, and so forth, strongly influence one's experience of the view of emptiness.

How so? The coarse levels of consciousness will not produce an experience of emptiness as quickly as will the subtle; and whether the coarse or subtle mind engaged in meditation is doing so on the basis of a union of method and wisdom also affects the impact of the practice. A meditation in which method and wisdom are not held in union will not produce tremendous results. When the mind is absorbed in method and wisdom conjoined, meditation on emptiness is most effective.

According to the schools of buddhist thought that accept six spheres of consciousness (the five sensory consciousnesses together with purely mental consciousness), there is both a coarse or ordinary level of consciousness that can perform meditation on emptiness on the basis of method and wisdom combined, and a subtle level of consciousness able to perform this meditation. Once one has cultivated a subtle level of consciousness propelled by the vast aspiration to highest enlightenment and applies it to realization of emptiness, the meditation becomes extremely powerful and is able to instantly destroy the host of destructive mental traits.

THE TANTRIC PATH

Where can be found the practices of the coarse and subtle levels of consciousness that counteract delusion by means of undivided method and wisdom? This leads to the subject of the buddhist tantras.

According to the *Tantra of the Two Forms* (of the Hevajra cycle), there are four classes of tantra: kriya, charya, yoga, and anuttarayoga. Kalachakra belongs to the last of these four.

In the three lower tantra classes one generates a coarse consciousness combining method and wisdom, and then meditates on emptiness.

The yogic techniques for engaging the powerful, subtle levels of consciousness focused in meditation born from the inseparability of method and wisdom are found only in the texts of highest yoga tantra.

To generate this subtle level of consciousness one must first eliminate the agitation of the coarse level of conceptual thought. Many methods for effecting this end have been taught.

One such method found in the highest yoga tantras involves arresting the deceptive projections of conceptual thought by means of channeling the vital energies of the nervous system. In a second method one cuts off the movements of conceptual thought and engages in totally non-conceptual meditation in order to eliminate the elements that distort the mind.

THE KALACHAKRA TRADITION

A number of different approaches to this yogic path have been expounded. Here I will speak briefly about the meditative techniques found in the Kalachakra system, which belongs to the highest yoga tantra class. It is a tantric system with several unique characteristics.

Generally, highest yoga tantra systems are of two types: 'buried tantras' such as Guhyasamaja, and 'clear tantras' such as Kalachakra.[1] The difference between these two styles appears in the fourth initiation. In the buried tantras the fourth initiation is revealed in a very concealed or hidden manner, whereas in the clear tantras it is presented openly.

Although basically all the individual systems found in the highest yoga tantras are equally profound, they each have their own approach which renders them more effective as a practice in accordance with the specific nature of the individual practitioners, their karmic tendencies and so forth. If one practices the highest yoga tantra system most appropriate to one's personal situation, the effect will be far more powerful than meditating on any other system of the same tantra class.

It is important that the practitioner engages in the system most suited to him or her. To demonstrate this metaphorically, a sick person takes a medicine appropriate to the specific illness and to the general condition of his or her being. In the same way, all systems in the highest yoga tantras are equally powerful, but a difference between them appears in their application to the physical, psychic and karmic situation of the individual practitioner.[2]

This is obvious from the different ways in which people experience the manifestations of the subtle consciousness and energies, such as in the visions of smoke and so forth at the time of death.

The yogic path of Kalachakra provides a very special method for those who have the correct body, mind and karmic predispositions. These special qualities become apparent after one has completed the imagined generation stage yogas and engages in the unfeigned completion stage practices. Here again the Kalachakra system reveals a unique presentation of the six yogas that constitute the completion stage.

In the discussion of the Kalachakra generation stage yogas, which ripen and mature the mind for the completion stage, it is traditional to introduce the topic of the three Kalachakras: outer, inner and alternative.

Outer Kalachakra is comprised of the elements of the universe in which we live. Inner Kalachakra is the psychophysical aggregates, the sensory and psychic capacities of the living being, and so forth. Thirdly, alternative Kalachakra is the path of the generation and completion stage yogas, the yogic methods that have the power to purify the above two Kalachakras.

Outer Kalachakra is generally explained in the context of this universe. Then when one meditates on the mandala, inner Kalachakra is seen as the body, faces, hands, feet, and so forth (of Kalachakra and Consort), as well as all the surrounding deities of the mandala, conceived as symbols of the stars, planets, constellations and so forth. From this we can know that Kalachakra has a special connection with all the living beings of this world system.

THE KALACHAKRA LINEAGE

From the point of view of the personage at whose request the Kalachakra doctrine was expounded, unlike any other tantra, Kalachakra was taught at the request of Suchandra, spiritual chieftain of the fabulous land of Shambala.

It is said that in order to benefit the subjects of the ninety-six regions of his country Suchandra traveled to India and requested just such a teaching from the Buddha. Kalachakra therefore has a special relationship with Shambala.

From Suchandra the lineage has been passed down through a line of seven spiritual leaders, beginning with Suchandra himself, and twenty-one kalkin masters, beginning with Manjushri Yashas. (We are presently in the era of the twenty-first kalkin.) In the coming of the twenty-fifth kalkin, the special connection that the people of this earth share with Kalachakra will manifest strongly in world events.

In general the Kalachakra system, like any highest yoga tantra, is meant for practitioners of the highest faculty. Nonetheless, because of the above considerations it was the tradition in Tibet to give the initiation openly to very large gatherings.

Although Shambala is a place located somewhere on this planet, it is a place that can be seen only by those whose minds and karmic propensities are pure. This is how it remains hidden from the everyday world.

The Buddha taught in accordance with the predispositions of mental focus and the qualities existing within the practitioners. It is said that for general trainees he taught the paths of the *Shravakayana* and *Pratyekabuddhayana,* that is, the ways of the Hearers and the Solitary Sages; and for the practitioners of a more vast karmic predisposition he taught the Bodhisattvayana, or the general Mahayana. Finally, for the few of highest potential and faculty he taught the Tantrayana, which is also known as the Vajrayana. Here he manifested in various forms, sometimes as a monk and sometimes as a tantric deity, to teach the three lower of the four classes of tantras. Then in the forms of various mandala deities embodying the inseparable union of method and wisdom he taught the highest yoga tantras.

Because these teachings were given in mystical manifestations of the Buddha to those in transcendental states of purified karma and perception, it does not matter much whether or not any specific tantra was expounded during the lifetime of the historical Buddha himself.

However, in fact *The Kalachakra Root Tantra* was set forth by Buddha Shakyamuni himself during his very lifetime.

The principal recipient of Buddha's original Kalachakra discourse, Suchandra of Shambala, transcribed the teaching (into *The Kalachakra Root Tantra*) and also composed a clarification of it, entitled *A Commentary to the Root Tantra.* Later Manju Yashas, the first kalkin master, composed an abridgement entitled *The Abbreviated Kalachakra Tantra.* Manjushri Yashas' son and spiritual successor, Kalkin Pundarika, then composed an extensive elucidation of (*The Abbreviated Kalachakra Tantra),* entitled *The Great Commentary: A Stainless Light.*

Consequently knowledge of the yogic and philosophical systems of the Kalachakra tradition became widespread throughout Shambala.

Eventually Chilupa, a master from eastern India, traveled to Shambala in search of the Kalachakra tantric doctrines. On the way he met an incarnation of the Bodhisattva Manjushri, and received from him the initiation, scriptures, commentaries and oral transmissions of the Kalachakra system.

Chilupa eventually passed the lineage to the Bengali-born master famed as Pindo Acharya. In this way in India it was propagated by such illustrious masters as Kalachakrapada the Elder; Kalachakrapada the Younger; the Nalanda sage Manjukirti; the Tibetan monk Sangyey Yeshey, who had come from Kham Province of Tibet, worked his way up the hierarchy of Bodh Gaya Monastery,[3] and became its abbot; and the Nepali pandit Samanta Shribhadra.

In this way the lineage gradually spread throughout India and Nepal.

The Kalachakra tradition came to Tibet in a number of lines of transmission. One of the most important of these was that of the Tibetan yogi Rva Chorab, who traveled to Nepal to study the Kalachakra doctrines under Samanta Shribhadra. He later invited this teacher to Tibet, where they translated many of the major scriptures related to Kalachakra. Rva Chorab passed the lineage to his principal disciple, Rva Yeshey Sangyey, and eventually it came to Buton Rinchen Druppa. Another important lineage is that of Dro Lotsawa, that also came to Buton. Buton united and transmitted these two lines of transmission, as well as systemizing and elucidating the tradition as a whole.

Thus the lineage has been passed from generation to generation until the present day.

ATTENDING A KALACHAKRA INITIATION

The higher meditations of the Kalachakra tradition can be practiced only by a select few. But because of past and future events, and in order to establish a strong karmic relationship with Kalachakra on the minds of the people, there is now a tradition of giving the initiation to large public gatherings.

The following are qualifications of someone who wishes to receive the Kalachakra transmission for actual practice.

The first qualification is that of the bodhichitta, the altruistic aspiration to highest enlightenment, which cherishes others more than oneself. Here it is said that the best disciple dwells in an unfeigned experience of this sublime mind; the medium disciple has had a small glimpse of it in his or her meditations; the lowest should have at least an appreciation for and interest in developing it.

The second qualification is given in terms of the special insight training, i.e., one's experience of emptiness. Here it is said that the best disciple has an undistorted experience of the nature of ultimate reality as explained in the Madhyamaka or Yogachara schools of Mahayana thought; the medium disciple has a correct understanding based on study and reason in general; and the lowest disciple should at least have a strong appreciation for and interest in learning the philosophical views of either of the two above-mentioned schools.

In addition, a disciple seeking the Kalachakra initiation should have a feeling for and interest in this particular tantric tradition. The purpose of initiation is to plant special karmic seeds in the mind of the recipient; but if he or she does not possess the openness born from a basic degree of spiritual interest, it will be very difficult for the seeds to have any impact.

Should anyone wish to attend an initiation ceremony merely as a blessing, that is to say, in order to establish a karmic relationship with the Kalachakra lineage, initiation can be given on this basis to those who can appreciate and respect the opportunity. People attending solely within that perspective should not imagine taking on the commitments or disciplines of the system, such as the bodhisattva or tantric precepts. Rather, they should feel that they are present solely for purposes of enjoying the spiritual inspiration that the event provides.

Even if one has more faith than knowledge, and does not comprehend the principles of the path combining method and wisdom as explained above, the seeds of initiation can still be firmly planted on the mindstream of a trainee if he or she has even a small basis of spiritual conviction.

Therefore this is the minimum qualification required to attend the Kalachakra initiation. One should have at least a small particle of spiritual interest, even if one is not a formal practitioner.

CULTIVATING A DAILY PRACTICE

For those who attend the initiation and wish to cultivate a daily training, it is common to begin by performing a six session guruyoga method. A number of texts of this nature exist. This type of practice presents a concise review of the important points in the generation stage yogas of the Kalachakra path, within the context of a guruyoga prayer and meditation. Practices of this nature are called 'six-session yogas' because they are meant to be recited and contemplated three times during the day and three times at night. If this is not possible then one should try to read and meditate on the guruyoga text at least once each day, blending the meaning of the words with one's mindstream.

This is how we should begin our training. However, we should not limit our practice to this level of endeavor alone. To best fulfill the purpose of the initiation, we should take a six-session guruyoga method as the basis of our daily meditation and then month by month, year by year, we should try to constantly expand our minds in knowledge of the practice.

At the beginning we should study in depth the nature of the Kalachakra path, its generation and completion stage yogas, paying special attention to those aspects that we find most difficult to understand. Then, having heard and reflected upon the instructions, we should try to generate realization of them within our own stream of being.

As explained above, at the moment our minds are bound by habitual modes of perception, modes that are distorting and impure. We must dissolve these impure patterns of thought and this false posturing into the dharmadhatu reality, the nature of emptiness.

Should we accomplish that task then we automatically fulfill the purposes of Buddhadharma, of the Mahayana, of the Vajrayana, of highest yoga tantra, and of having received the Kalachakra initiation.

Although the path to enlightenment is a somewhat rigorous undertaking, it is well worthwhile. The wise, therefore, energetically apply themselves to it.

15 The Prerequisites of Receiving Tantric Initiation

by Gyalwa Kalzang Gyatso,
the Seventh Dalai Lama (1708-1757)

The highest of all Buddhist paths is that of the esoteric Vaj-rayana, the path of secret mantras taught by Buddha Shakya-muni in a mystical form as the mighty Buddha Vajradhara.

Yet one cannot enter into the practice of this vehicle with-out first acquiring the empowerments that ripen one's body, speech and mind for tantric training as well as the initiations and blessings that give birth to various abilities, such as the ability to generate qualities as of yet undeveloped, the ability to increase whatever qualities one may have, and so forth.

Teachers who wish to lead fortunate trainees through the meditations and scriptural transmissions of this secret path should be qualified by an understanding and depth of experience that accords with the views of the great tantric treatises.

One's ornament should be the jewel of having received the appropriate lineage transmissions in accordance with clear ex-planations from qualified masters and yogis. One should not lead disciples in accordance with personal fancy, but should guide them through all phases of empowerment and tantric meditation precisely as outlined in the traditional scriptures.

Without distractions or mental wanderings, at the time of the actual empowerment ceremony one should thoroughly perform the generation of the vision of oneself as the deity of the mandala, and also the generation of the external mandala.

The disciples may then wash, enter the mandala, and offer the flower. Visualizing the guru as being inseparably one in nature and appearance with the deity of the mandala, they should make an imaginary offering of all valuable things in this world, such as one's own and other's bodies, possessions and so forth, as well as all goodness of the past, present and future.

The most important precept for the guru is found in the words of the incomparable Lama Atisha,[1]

> When giving spiritual advice to others,
> Have the altruistic mind of compassion.

That is to say, the teachers' preliminary in preparing to elucidate the spiritual path is to transcend all superficial thoughts, such as desiring personal gain or fame, and instead to dwell within the sublime thought of benefiting others.

The disciple's basis is given in a sutra:[2]

> Listening correctly brings knowledge of all truth;
> Listening correctly leads away from negativity;
> Listening correctly brings freedom from misery;
> Listening correctly results in nirvana.

Another sutra adds,

> O child of noble family, if one listens well, wisdom will arise. If one has wisdom, mental distortion will subside. When one has no mental distortion, Mara the Evil One is unable to gain victory.

As this passage suggests, if one dedicates energy to listening to the spiritual teachings one will gain an understanding of the inner qualities to be cultivated and the negative to be overcome. Once this basic knowledge is generated one can begin to work on engendering spiritual qualities such as generosity, ethical discipline, and wisdom.

In this context the master Vira wrote,[3]

> The highest spiritual aspirant
> Constantly listens to a few teachings.
> By continually collecting the few,
> Before long much is acquired.

> What happens to a vessel
> Placed outside in a rain
> Of tiny droplets of water
> Falling in an unbroken stream?

> From this clear illustration
> We can, O King, clearly see
> That one should constantly delight
> In listening to spiritual instructions.

We should listen most enthusiastically to every line of teachings that we have the opportunity to hear, so that before long we can go to the other side of listening and of knowledge.

The value of striving to hear the holy Dharma was stated by the great Lama Tsongkhapa,

> When listening to the sacred teachings
> Consider yourself most fortunate.
> Show a face radiant with joy
> And a smile exuding delight;
> Listen with a mind free of the three pot-like faults.

Whenever we attend a Buddhist discourse or empowerment ceremony, we should first generate a joyous mind by contemplating the beneficial effects of hearing the Dharma. The external sign of this contemplation is a face radiant with joy, a smile exuding delight, and a manner of reverence.

This is the basis for listening with a mind free of the three faults, which are likened to three pots—an overturned pot, a pot contaminated with poison, and a pot with a hole in its base.

Letting the mind wander to external objects in a deluded manner while attending a Dharma event is like pouring water into an overturned pot. Listening to Dharma while holding impure thoughts, such as imagining faults in the teacher, becoming haughty with pride, entertaining thoughts of gaining transient happiness or worldly occult power through misuse of the teachings, and so forth, is like pouring water into a poisoned pot. Finally, if the student has an attentive mind and a creative motivation but does not attempt to retain what he or she has learned, giving him or her the teaching is like pouring water into a pot with a hole in its base.

Guard yourself against these three faulty attitudes if you would gain maximum benefit from your involvement with the holy Dharma.

One should listen to Dharma teachings in order to be able to gain a state of realization that would contribute to freeing living beings from the ocean of misery. The motivation should be to gain the wisdom of a buddha, a fully enlightened being, not to gain wealth or prestige; to triumph over the enemy which is one's own delusion, not to be able to learn as a means of becoming more successful in debate and argumentation; to respectfully master the essence of Dharma, not to steal an occult trick from the spiritual friend.

This is how the sutras instruct us to listen.

If we were to abbreviate from the sutras and tantras all the essential advice on how to listen to Dharma, the most crucial precept would be to maintain the thought, "By all means possible I must strive to achieve the precious stage of perfect buddhahood, the peerless awakening, the highest spiritual attainment, in order to benefit the limitless sentient being who are as vast in number as the extent of space. Solely to actualize this goal am I engaging in this wondrous Dharma activity."

In the case of a tantric empowerment or initiation one replaces the last line with, "Solely to actualize this goal am I attending this event of the Vajrayana Dharma, the Secret Path."

This thought establishes the perfect motivation, first of the four perfect conditions for tantric practice.

Secondly we must create the perfect environment. Visualize that the place of the tantric event is the inconceivable celestial mansion produced from the spontaneously appearing primordial wisdom of the meditational deity. At the center of this fantastic palace, seated upon a throne upheld by eight fearless lions, is one's tantric master. He is inseparably one in nature and appearance with the meditational deity.

The third perfect condition is perfect company. Visualize that you and all others present are the five meditational buddhas, the various bodhisattvas and so forth.

Lastly we should try to experience perfect activity. Visualize that the master's voice resounds like the melodious song of Brahma, sending out clouds of teachings to the various disciples in accordance with their individual spiritual needs.

The general attitude toward the subject one is listening to, the holy Dharma, is described in *Selected Sayings of the Buddha,*

> The wise people of this world
> Make firm their conviction and wisdom,
> For these are supreme jewels
> Outshining all others.

The two greatest jewels in this world are unshakeable purpose of direction and penetrating vision. These excel even wishfulfilling gems, for they eradicate all the sufferings of samsara and the lower realms of existence, and bring quick attainment of high spiritual status and final realization.

Of these two qualities (namely, conviction and wisdom), it is very useful to begin by cultivating the former, for conviction makes one into a vessel suitable for receiving Dharma.

To be more specific, one should cultivate the three types of conviction: stabilizing conviction, that comprehends the significance of the unfailing laws of cause and effect, and recognizes that positive and negative actions of body, speech and mind produce happiness and misery respectively; clear conviction, that arises by perceiving the excellent qualities of the spiritual masters, the Triple Gem, etc., and brings clarity to the mind; and wishful conviction, that attempts to strive at progressing along the stages of the path to spiritual liberation.

These are the three general types of conviction to be cultivated.

The special conviction of the tantric path is given in a passage from *The Tantra of Susiddhi,*

> One should see one's tantric master
> As being in fact a perfect buddha.
> Disciples with such wise respect
> Hold attainment in their very hands.

All the sutras and tantras proclaim that cultivating a spiritual direction is the root of all religious experience. Therefore generate clear conviction toward your teacher and meditational deity, and make firm the stabilized conviction in the Dharma of the Secret Path.

This type of spiritual confidence is to be maintained during all Dharma events, and also throughout all daily activities. Otherwise one will not have the ability to clear away the mud of the mind, and consequently will gain no grip on the basis of the path. Strive therefore at the methods that imbue conviction for the Dharma.

What are these methods?

The principal one is mentioned in the chapter on conviction in the text *Selected Sayings of the Buddha.*

> Do not rely upon those of no conviction,
> Who are like dry wells.

By digging in a dry well
We extract only a foul stench.

The wise rely upon those with spiritual conviction,
Who are like vast lakes
Of waters clear, cool
And free of all mud.

Beginners should try to associate mostly with creative people in possession of both conviction for and mindfulness of the Dharma. They should repeatedly listen to Mahayana teachers expounding the holy Dharma, and should contemplate the meanings of what they have heard until they arrive at a definite understanding.

The scripture *Advice Given by Vajrapani to the Mahasiddha Karmavajra* states,

O Karmavajra, to think that one has experienced a vision of one's meditational deity and generated a sublime experience when one has not even developed an effective working relationship with a qualified spiritual teacher is to deceive oneself. To think one has renounced worldly indulgence when one has no conviction in meditation upon impermanence and death is to deceive oneself.

Similarly, it is mere self-deception to think one does not create negative karma even though one has no real conviction in the karmic laws of cause and effect; to think that one's back is turned to samsaric addictions although one has not meditated thoroughly upon the faults of samsaric indulgence; to think that one has generated love, compassion and the bodhimind when one does not have an atom of concern for others; and to think that one understands emptiness when one has not seen the untrue nature of conventional things.

O Karmavajra, if you have interest in the supreme Dharma, approach it with conviction.

What are the causes engendering conviction? It is aroused when one visualizes one's spiritual teacher as being a second Buddha. It is aroused when one associates with spiritual people. It is aroused when one contemplates impermanence and death. It is aroused when one looks at the shortcomings of samsara.

And if on the basis of these understandings we see the guru as a boat by which we can free ourselves from samsara and subsequently we attempt to practice as instructed and not to degenerate our spiritual relationship with the teacher, great benefits will accrue.

Especially, at the time of receiving tantric empowerments or initiations we should not see the guru and meditational deity as being superior or inferior to one another. Approach the various phases of initiation, such as requesting the empowerment three times and so forth, with a visualization of the two as being of one inseparable nature.

It is very important to appreciate these fundamental causes of a spiritually meaningful life. In this context the incomparable master Atisha wrote:

This incarnation with the freedoms and endowments
So difficult to find has been gained.
To achieve it again will be difficult.
Therefore use it to practice the Dharma
And thus make your life meaningful.

Buddha has come, a spiritual community is flourishing;
You have won a rare human incarnation,
And have met with the difficult-to-meet teacher.
Do not make it all for nothing.

That is to say, we have achieved a precious human incarnation having the freedoms and endowments necessary for Dharma practice, a form difficult to win and, once won, most

meaningful. We have also met with the precious sutra and tantra doctrines of Buddha and with the spiritual friends and
teachers who are able to explain these to us. Now that we have
the opportunity to listen to Dharma, to contemplate its meaning
and to meditate upon it, we should strive to take its essence.

Were life such that we could be assured of continually regaining a human form after death, perhaps there would be no need
to make a great effort in practice now. We could work to attain liberation and the path to omniscience in a future life.

But in actual fact the possibilities of regaining a human body
in future lives indeed are slender if we do not make use of
the life we presently have.

Now that we have met with the Dharma we should try to
generate the light of wisdom able to cultivate goodness and
to eradicate negativity from within ourselves.

As for the practice of Dharma, remember the words of the
great and omniscient (First) Panchen Lama,

> When we point a searching finger
> Down our throats to analyze
> The nature of our previous ways,
> We see a fox wearing a lion's skin:
> We feign Dharma but don't really practice it.

When the mind is lost and overpowered by delusion, how
can spiritual thoughts arise? Let alone a positive thought, even
a neutral thought is rare. Rather, the body, speech and mind
flow on in an unbroken stream of darkness and negativity.

With motivation controlled by forceful delusion, even our
attempts to practice Dharma usually end up in collecting nothing but negative karma with the spiritual teachers.

Negativity is like a huge river cascading downhill, but goodness like struggling to pull water uphill: one pulls and pulls
but progress is small and intermittent. Even when we strive
intensely with strong conviction it requires much effort to pass
beyond lower cyclic patterns.

The master Nagarjuna said,

From negative activity comes suffering
And all lower cyclic realms.
From creative activity comes self-improvement
And happiness in all future lives.

In other words, when the karmic cause is negative, the karmic fruit is lower rebirth and misery; and when the karmic cause is creative, the karmic fruit is higher rebirth and happiness. This law is unfailing.

Perhaps you will think that rebirth in the lower realms is not so bad because, after that life-form has ended, you will again die and will then once more take a high rebirth.

Remember the words of (Shantideva in) *A Guide to the Bodhisattva Ways:*

If one continues in negativity,
A human rebirth will not be gained.
If a human rebirth is not found,
Negativity rather than goodness ensues.

If we do not now generate creativity
While we have the power to do so, then
When later we are obscured by the misery
That pervades the lower realms,
What will we be able to do?

If now I create no goodness
But only collect more negativity,
Then for a hundred million aeons
I will not hear even the sounds of happiness.

Those reborn in the lower realms do not have the wisdom able to understand what to cultivate and what to avoid. Much negative karma is then collected, and it becomes very difficult for merely the thought of goodness to arise. Consequently, even when one's lifespan in a lower realm is over one just takes another lower rebirth and becomes lost for aeons in a vicious circle. How will the cause of high rebirth then be cultivated?

Rather than let yourself go from light to endless circles of darkness, use this human life to go from light to greater light, from happiness to a more profound happiness.

You may think, "Fine, I will strive to accomplish the eternally beneficial; but later. First I should set straight the concerns of this life."

Remember the chapter on impermanence in *Selected Sayings of the Buddha:*

> I did that, I am doing this,
> And then will do that:
> Thus people lay their plans.
> But death strikes suddenly
> With sickness and old age.

We can draw up a plan to fill the next hundred years, yet there is no certainty that any of it will be accomplished. However, this body degenerates and comes closer to death every year, every month, every day, every moment. Its lustre is fading, the powers of its senses are waning, and the mind is losing its vitality.

These are but a stream of the sufferings of the ageing process. And in the end we can expect only death.

We are like a person living in a jungle inhabited by lions, tigers, poisonous snakes and other such terrible, ferocious animals that are unable to live in harmony with one another and love to take life.

When one finds oneself in such a place, where death can strike at any moment, it is not wise to sit complacently.

Externally, all the various human and non-human harmful forces sit watching us, waiting for the fruit of our negative karma to ripen so that they can create interferences to our body, life, possessions, happiness and so forth. Internally, the four elements of the body—earth, air, fire and water—and the essential triad—wind, bile and phlegm—by nature hold the constant possibility of disease, and like wild animals of the jungle are continually fighting with one another for supremacy. When one gains power over the others, the suffering of disease and perhaps even death falls upon us.

You may think, "But my body and mind are healthy at the present moment"; yet this also is not a valid reason for complacence. As the omniscient Great Fifth (Dalai Lama) put it,

Black hair turns white as snow,
A white face turns black as night,
A body grown straight bends like a bow,
And sensual objects give no pleasure.
This is the pressure of old age.

Neither loved ones nor professional aids can help;
The things of the past also are lost, and
Friends and relatives just await their inheritance.
This is the messenger bearing
An invitation from the Lord of Death.

Investigate the present condition of your body. The fact that it has never in the past ceased growing and evolving is an omen that it is held in the clutch of the agents who lead us to the other shore, the land of the Lord of Death.

Especially in this degenerate age when the human lifespan is so short it is rare to meet a person more than fifty or sixty years of age: and even were we to live this long ourselves, when we deduct the time spent in childhood, old age, sickness, sleep and so forth, not much is left for Dharma practice. Perhaps the equivalent of a year or two is given to serious practice. And most of one's life already has been spent on the meaningless. To quote *A Letter to King Kanika,*

The Lord of Death comes suddenly
To those who lack awareness.
Do not wait for tomorrow;
Practice the holy Dharma now.

Saying "I will do this tomorrow"
Is not the way of a wise person.
Have no doubt that death is sudden,
And that you will be reduced to nothing.

There is no certainty that the unpredictable hand of the merciless Lord of Death will not fall on us this year, this month, this day or even this very hour. The sun that will rise tomorrow morning may find our body in a charnel ground or on the funeral pyre surrounded by friends and relatives performing our death rites. Who can know this will not happen to him?

The great Lama Tsongkhapa said,

What living being can say
He will not be swallowed by the demon of death?
When this is my sure fate,
O mind, how can you sit complacent?

Leave aside essenceless works
That anyway at death must be abandoned
No matter how much energy one gives to them.
Think instead of how to progress
Along the path of enlightment.

With this thought make firm
Spiritual qualities like humility,
Mindfulness, alertness and mental clarity,
And tame the difficult-to-tame mind.
Then at death the mind will abide in joy.

Whether one is a monk scholar who has mastered the five categories of knowledge, a mahasiddha who has occult powers, a king who rules with total control over many people, a warrior with strength and skill in fighting, or a farmer who lives his life under the weight of household commitments, in the end one will not escape death.

From the very moment of birth all people enter into the path leading to death, regardless of whether they are high, medium or low.

Nor is there any certainty when that death will come to us. Therefore to become distracted in worldly work is like a criminal condemned to death tomorrow wasting time today on works which benefit this life alone. How tragic!

What benefits and what harms both this and future lives? As the chapter on karma in *Selected Sayings of the Buddha* advises,

> If you fear misery
> And do not enjoy pain,
> Then create no negative karma
> Openly or in secret.

And also,

> Negativity is not like milk,
> That can suddenly change in nature.
> It is like hot coals covered in ashes that
> Burn the immature, who have long forgotten them.

> Negative karma is not like a weapon,
> That perhaps may not harm its bearer.
> It is a force carried into the future,
> That sooner or later strikes its carrier.

A very intense negative karma produces the fruit of suffering within this very lifespan. But even karma that does not ripen in this life will not lose its potency in a hundred countless aeons. The time shall come when it will manifest and bring suffering down upon its carrier.

Alternately, positive karma immediately brings a degree of creative energy and happiness to the mind, and in the future produces a rebirth conducive to further Dharma practice.

Ask yourself, "What positive karma have I generated? What negative karma have I generated? What am I doing now, and what do I plan to do in the future?''

The doors through which we collect both black and white karma are the body, speech and mind. Yet whether an action of body and speech is positive or negative depends solely upon the state of the mind.

This was pointed out by the great master Aryadeva in *Removing the Veils of the Mind:*

> Placing two boots on the head of Buddha
> Out of a positive motivation
> And taking them off again:
> Both lead to rebirth as a king.
> Therefore an action is meritorious or evil
> Solely in dependence upon the state of the mind.

This refers to the famous story of a man who, on seeing water dripping onto the head of a Buddha image, placed boots on its head to protect it. A second man who saw this thought it improper because boots are unclean, and so removed them. It is said that both men produced an equal amount of positive karma, and both were reborn as great beings.

Thus it is most important to be clear on the nature of our motivation in all our activities.

The significance of establishing the basis of a positive attitude in all activities is stressed by the great spiritual master Geshey Potowa:

> All teachings by Buddha and the buddhist masters
> Are said to be methods for improving the mind.
> When the mind is unchanged, practices of body and
>   speech
> Do not cause freedom, though one perseveres a
>   hundred aeons.
> All practice of study, reflection and meditation
> Are but tools to transform the mind.

In brief, all teachings of the three vehicles elucidated by Buddha, which includes all the doctrines of the Hinayana and Mahayana sutras and the four classes of tantras, are in reality only methods and techniques for training the mind. Hence we should use them solely for that purpose.

Our every Dharmic activity—be it study, reflection, meditation or merely reading a scripture—should be used as a method for taming our mind. Then Dharma in theory and the reality of the practitioner's way of life will never contradict one another. This is extremely important.

If we take this pragmatic approach ourselves then whatever we study is useful, every teaching is relevant, and we can see how every line of scripture is of immediate and far-reaching benefit to sentient beings.

Yet of all the high, medium and low teachings given by Buddha in accordance with the capacities, attitudes and karmic inclinations of the diversity of living beings, most expedient is said to be entering the Mahayana teaching from the very beginning.

The nature of the Mahayana is described by the great Indian master Shaddhakaravarma:

> The Bodhisattvayana has two paths: the Paramitayana, or the causal Transcendent Wisdom Vehicle; and the Guhyamantrayana, the resultant Vehicle of Secret Mantras.

That is to say, the Mahayana is comprised of two distinct vehicles: the Paramitayana, or vehicle (which provides meditation) on the causes (of enlightenment), also the Vehicle of Signs; and the Guhyamantrayana, or Vajrayana, the vehicle (which provides meditations) on the results (of enlightenment).

Yet practice of solely the former of these produces enlightenment only after three countless aeons of difficult practices. In short, it is a long and arduous journey.

But if in our practice we couple the Vajrayana with the Paramitayana then after a short comfortable practice we can go to the end of cultivating goodness and overcoming negativity, and can quickly and easily gain the state of all-pervading Vajradhara within one lifetime.

Vajrayana is a very quick path; but in order to embark upon it we must first train our mindstream through the disciplines of the common path, the Paramitayana, until a degree of stability has been gained. Only then should we enter into the path of secret mantras.

As *The Root Tantra of Glorious Chakrasamvara* states,

> When the practices of the sutras (are strong), the horizon of the secret yogas is (in sight).

Also *The Vajra Song* states,

> The kriya tantras are for simpler practitioners.
> Above this are the charya tantras;
> Then is the supreme yoga tantra for supreme beings;
> And above this is the anuttara tantra.

The master who gives a tantric empowerment or initiation should explain to the disciple the exact nature and classification of the tantric system which is being introduced. He or she should also explain the distinguishing characteristics of the numerous lineages of transmission extant, and should relate a brief history of the lineage. It is also useful to elucidate the benefits and purpose of the transmission ceremony, the nature of the mandala being introduced, the function of the empowering Vajra Master, the characteristics required of the disciples receiving the empowerment, and the stages of the procedure to be followed. These procedures can be understood either from the general tantric treatises or specific lineage manuals.

If the master does not have time for such elaborate preparations then he can reduce the above to a concise explanation of the specific qualities of the meditational deity in question.

One of the most important preliminary steps in the empowerment and initiation ceremonies is the taking of the bodhimind pledge, the vow to make one's aspiration to enlightenment a priority. This is such an important point because the practice of any Vajrayana system is a Mahayana method only when the practitioner applying himself to it does so on the basis of the bodhimind.

This was clearly pointed out by the great Lama Tsongkhapa:

> When practice of spiritual discipline
> Is not coupled with the bodhimind,
> It does not produce the bliss of buddhahood.
> The wise therefore cultivate the supreme bodhimind.

And also:

> It is not enough to have a Mahayana teaching. The practitioner must have the Mahayana perspective. Furthermore, the quality that gives one this is nothing other than the bodhimind: if one has the bodhimind one is a Mahayanist; if one doesn't have it one is not on the Great Way. Therefore dedicate yourself to cultivating the bodhimind.

As said here, if we have the bodhimind we are Mahayanists and all our practices become Mahayana.

On the other hand, to use a so-called Mahayana method without having the basis of the bodhimind is of little value. Even if our renunciation is so great that we see samsaric indulgence as a terrible pit of fire, or we have meditated for a hundred aeons upon the ultimate nature of being, the view vast as the sky, or have applied ourselves diligently to the profound tantric systems by means of receiving empowerments, attending discourses and engaging in the powerful tantric yogas, our consciousness does not touch the Mahayana path when it is devoid of the bodhimind.

As is said in *The Gandhavyuha Sutra,*

O son of noble family, the bodhimind is the very essence of the teachings of the Buddha.

If we wish to have a flower or fruit, we have to plant the corresponding seed. One cannot plant an apple seed and expect to get a marigold. The bodhimind is the seed giving birth to all Mahayana paths; it creates, maintains and fulfills the qualities of a buddha.

The beneficial effects of the bodhimind are described in many sutras, tantras and shastras. The great bodhisattva Shantideva gives an elequent account of them:[4]

It is a supreme elixir
To destroy the Lord of Death,
An inexhaustible treasure to remove
The poverty of living beings.

It is a supremely powerful medicine
To pacify the diseases of beings,
A tree giving shade to pilgrims
Long wandering on the roads of life.

It is a ladder leading out
Of terrible states of suffering,
A moon shining in the mind
To disperse the pain of delusion.

It is a great sun to clear away
The ignorance clouding the minds of beings,
And the essence of butter produced
By churning the milk of Dharma.

When the disciples do not have this inner spiritual basis, then let alone giving them a tantric empowerment or initiation, they should not even be permitted to see a mandala or mudra. As is said in *The Tantra of the Vajrapani Empowerment*,

O Manjushri, if any disciples have meditated upon and attained a measure of the bodhimind, they are bodhisattvas who stand in the gateway of the Vajrayana because of their bodhisattva ways. They should be given the empowerment of great wisdom and introduced into the mandala. But disciples without the qualification of the bodhimind should not be permitted to see the mandala. They should not even be shown mudra or secret mantra.

Therefore prior to receiving a tantric empowerment or initiation one should generate a pure motivation based on the bodhimind.

This does not mean merely reciting certain verses, for how can words substitute for a state of mind? It means actually generating the bodhimind step by step, like a carpenter builds a house.

What exactly is the bodhimind? This is elucidated by the Venerable Maitreya:

The bodhimind is the wish for perfect enlightenment
In order to accomplish the welfare of the world.

The thought aspiring to attain the state of perfect Buddhahood in order best to be able to benefit all other sentient beings is the phenomenon called the bodhimind.

In order to develop this state of consciousness one must cultivate two qualities: the thought concerned with sentient beings, and the thought concerned with enlightenment. As for the first of these, *A Letter to a Disciple* states,

Animals eat plentiful grass when hungry
And drink cherished water when thirsty;
Why say they do it to benefit others?
But there are supreme beings concerned
Solely with the benefit of the world.

Like the sun they illuminate the entire earth,
Like the earth itself they support
The weight of all living beings.
These great beings, free from personal interests,
Strive to give the taste of happiness to others.

A horse's motivation is always simple: it seeks grass with which to chase away hunger, and water with which to chase away thirst. In brief, it thinks only of its own needs. This is a quality common to most creatures.

But the quality of a supreme being's mind is that it has turned its back on self-interests and thinks only of ways to benefit others.

Thus it is like a sun untiringly illuminating the lives of sentient beings dwelling on the four continents, and like the great earth which carries the weight of all that lives upon its surface. The bodhisattvas who possess it no longer have any liking for self-centered works. They concern themselves solely with methods to produce benefits and happiness for the limitless sentient beings.

Why should we develop an altruistic attitude towards others? Because in all samsara there is not a single living being who does not want happiness and does not want to avoid even the smallest suffering. However, delusions and mental distortion have overpowered us and we are helplessly propelled into destroying our own happiness and well-being.

Each of us is our own worst enemy. Forced by our own ignorance, attachment and aversion, we collect a constant stream of negative karma. Our every action of body, speech and mind seems to produce only further causes for rebirth in the lower realms of existence.

As a result, there are many living beings who have taken rebirth in hell, where the great suffering of heat, cold and violent torture are experienced; pain one moment of which exceeds the total suffering of all humanity.

Others have become tormented ghosts who, although they search for a hundred years, rarely find even a dry gob of spit to eat or drink. Their sufferings of hunger, thirst, cold, heat and so forth are unimaginable.

Still others have taken birth as animals and suffer terribly because of stupidity, domestication and so forth. Unable to generate spiritual trainings, they have little chance of working for enlightenment.

Even those sentient beings who have been reborn in the so-called higher realms must endure tremendous suffering.

For example, in the human realm there is the suffering of not getting what one wants, of having to nervously guard the things one has collected, of meeting with unpleasant people or circumstances, of being parted from loved ones, and so forth.

The supreme (Indian) sage Vasubandhu wrote,

> All the sufferings of the lower realms
> Manifest in the life of humans.
> We have the hell of intense pain,
> The tormented ghost quality of destitution,
> And the animal sufferings of being controlled
> By others of superior strength and cunning.
> These sufferings flow constant as a river.
>
> Some humans are physically poor,
> Others, though rich, are poor in contentment.
> These intense sufferings of destitution
> Attack and kill rich and poor alike.

The mental and physical sufferings of man are his hell experiences, and his poverty and destitution are his experiences as a tormented ghost. The person who is used by others of superior strength or intelligence, who is too poor to secure his food or shelter, or who although wealthy knows no contentment or satisfaction with his material state, or who fights with or is killed by other men, knows the nature of an animal's suffering.

Concerning the power and glory of rebirth as a deva, or celestial spirit, Vasubandhu also wrote,

When delusion is present,
Negative karma continues to arise
And in the end comes a fall.
Are these heedless ones not objects of pity?
The patient chronically ill
Knows not his own condition.

The person who is overpowered by attachment, anger, pride, jealousy, or the like has been struck down by the worst of enemies. Based on his loss he collects a steady stream of negative karma. Then at the end of his life he falls into the lower realms like an arrow plunging down to earth. This is the nature of the death of a celestial spirit of the sensuous realm.

Even during their lifetime the devas experience much misery. They have the physical suffering of continually warring with the antigods, the various mental frustrations inherent in celestial life, the sorrow of witnessing their vitality wane, and so forth.

The devas in the lower of the sensuous realms also suffer terribly. As well as the miseries described above, they know anguish in their old age because of the signs of death that appear to them. They understand that soon they must leave their celestial palace, friends, lovers, and state of constant pleasure, and must descend once again into the lower realms of existence, where suffering completely embraces life.

The true nature of life in the heavens above the sensuous realms is described by the great master Vira:

Everything in these three realms
Burns in the flames of impermanence;
A fire blazing in a forest
Consumes flowers as well as trees.

The gods on the peak of samsara,
Whose minds are constantly distorted,
Become captured by the noose of death
Like an elephant tied by a chain.

Brahma, lord of the Brahma Heaven,
Who dwells in the bliss of meditation,
Becomes struck by impermanence
And falls like a river over a cliff.

A thousand gods and
A hundred universal emperors
Meet with the time of death
Like open butterlamps in a windstorm.

Even should one be reborn in the formless realms above the peak of existence, when the time of death falls one is led away like an elephant with a chain around its neck. The great god Brahma himself, who experiences only the bliss of meditative absorption, evolves toward death from the very moment of his birth, like a river flowing to the ocean.

They all die, leaving nothing and taking nothing with them. Like a butterlamp in the face of a savage wind, the life of even a universal emperor is suddenly extinguished. When the time comes, his lustre bears the signs of death. Therefore the exalted Nagarjuna wrote,

After happiness comes misery,
After misery comes happiness.
This world of living beings constantly rotates
Between these two poles.

No matter what pleasure one gains in samsara, one day it will end and pain will take its place. This is the nature of the world. *The Elimination of Suffering* says,

In this life we suckle
Upon our mother's breast,
But in another we drink her blood
And eat flesh from her back.

Thus turning on the wheel of becoming,
We forget a hundred people
Who once did serve us well,
Who are the same hundred people
Whom we ourselves did once serve.

As the wheel of karma carries us through life upon life, a woman whose breast we once sucked becomes an animal that we eat, and a servant becomes a lord with great power over us.

Even in this life our relationships with people change drastically. A little flattery turns an enemy into a friend; and a few heavy words make a friend into an enemy.

Relationships with friends and relatives are at best unstable. The great master Chandragomin wrote:

In the beginning, samsaric indulgence
And sweet poison are the same:
Both give pleasure when consumed.

In the end, samsaric indulgence
And sweet poison are the same:
Both produce unbearable suffering.

Both samsaric indulgence and poison
Represent the darkness of confusion,
And the effects of both are equally difficult
To counteract and turn away.

If we analyze the nature of both
Poison and samsaric indulgence,
Both are poisonous and both are terrible.
Poison poisons us in this lifetime;
Indulgence poisons us in another.

All living beings naturally utilize sensual objects, such as form phenomena and so forth, in the quest to maintain happiness. Yet when we mix craving and clinging in with this natural process the result is like mixing poison into food. The food will still taste good, but rather than sustaining life it will lead to death.

Samsaric indulgence based on clinging harms us in this life. It deadens and binds us, destroys our social relationships and creates hindrances to our own success and happiness. It gives birth to endless chains of anger towards those who threaten us, worry that our standard of life will degenerate, endless hopes to improve our material standing, and so forth. Finally the mind is left with no space in which to know peace and clarity.

The process is difficult to reverse. The more one indulges in samsaric addictions the greater becomes one's attachment to them, and the process eventually becomes so strong that it blinds the wisdom-eye knowing what to engage in and what to avoid.

This in turn results in the accumulation of all the various negative karmas, which produce a hundred rebirths in places of misery in future lives. Thus, like ingesting poison, indulgence is a cause of great suffering.

Furthermore, sensual gratification is something that can only last for a limited time. It depends upon outer circumstances, and these are constantly in flux.

When this is not fully understood, the craving for indulgence sets in and we become lost in the fantasy of eating sweet poison for its good taste. What could be more deserving of our compassion! *Expressing the Experience of Seven Youthful Maidens* states,

> There is not a single pleasure
> We have not experienced in previous lives
> As gods of the higher realms,
> But still we wander meaninglessly.

There is not one amongst us who can say that he or she has never before taken rebirth as a human or as a god of the sensuous, form and formless realms.

Yet although we have been everything a hundred times we

still have not found satisfaction. It is as though we have become immune to being benefited. How sad to permit ourselves to continue to wander fruitlessly in circles!

No matter what life-form we take, if it is born from the causes of karma and delusion then we will have to undergo the physical sufferings of birth, sickness, fighting with enemies, obstacles and so forth, as well as the mental sufferings of frustration and confusion.

Thus it is said that our worst enemy is the collection of our own contaminated aggregates. The great Acharya Aryadeva wrote,

> The body which gives us pleasure
> Is also a vessel for suffering.
> Indulging one's body and indulging an enemy
> Are two equal actions.

Also the mighty Bodhisattva Shantideva said,

> The one cause increasing all that harms me,
> The enemy who has harmed me for long,
> Resides constantly within my heart.
> How then can I be complacent in this world?

> If the guardians of the prisons of hell
> And all the evil forces that harm me
> Exist within the net of my own mind,
> How can I ever be content?

No matter how terrible an external enemy may be, his ability to affect us ends with this life. But the enemy known as Delusion has flowed within our minds in an unbroken stream since beginningless time, and will continue to do so until we eliminate it.

An external enemy can only harm us in certain times and situations. But the enemy Delusion creates all the infinite sufferings found within the three realms. Thus its strength is incomparable.

The external enemy will not find an opportunity to harm us if we move to another country. But the enemy Delusion resides within our very heart, so moving out of its reach for even a moment is difficult.

Through making friendly advances we can turn an enemy into a friend; but the more kindness we show to our delusions, the more they harm us.

They are like merciless assassins always watching us from their own distance, waiting vigilantly for an opportunity to strike.

When this is our constant situation, how can we sit complacently? As *The Tantra Requested by Subahu* states,

> Swept along by the forces of karma and delusion,
> They are powerless, helpless, and insecure.
> Aimlessly they drift from life to life
> In accordance with the forces of karmic instinct.

Although the self does not substantially exist and therefore does not have any truly existent power over us, nonetheless we are overpowered by delusion and grasp at a self. This has dominated our stream of thought since beginningless time, leading us from life to life. Helplessly we have wandered throughout samsara, being born alone, dying alone and experiencing suffering alone.

No one else can take our fate for us. No one can really protect us. Whether we stay or move is determined not by the strength of our determination, but by our karma and delusion. *The Four Hundred Verses* states,

> Impermanence harms everything,
> And they harmed by it know no joy.
> Therefore it is said that everything
> Impermanent is by nature suffering.

All realms and life-forms of samsara, evolving from moment

to moment, are impermanent. Whatever is impermanent has the fault of continual disintegration. Anything having a fault has the potentiality to agitate an imperfect mind. Mental agitation is by nature frustration and suffering.

Thus all the infinite sentient beings of the three realms are by nature enmeshed in frustation. Yet each of them has been a mother to me in countless previous lives, carrying me in her womb and caring for me more than for even herself.

At that time she protected me from all harmful elements and did all she could to help me. In many previous lives every sentient being as my mother has sacrificed limbs of her body and even her very life for me.

But now our memories of these lives are clouded by the impact of death, transmigration and rebirth.

How should I relate to all these sentient beings, my all-kind mothers? *The Aspirational Prayer in Seventy Stanzas:*

> When I see pleasure delighting others
> May I generate higher joy that shares in their delight,
> And remain meditating on joyfulness
> As if my only beloved child were happy.
>
> May I transcend anger and attachment,
> The causes of harming or favoring others;
> And may I care for all living beings of the three worlds,
> Like tending to the needs of my own child.

We should rejoice in the good fortune of the sentient beings who previously gained a pleasurable position or experience, even if it is something that one could have had for oneself. Look toward others who succeed with the glad love of a mother for her only child. Wish solely for the happiness of others.

To regard some beings with attachment and others with aversion is ignoble. We should instead wish that the aspirations and needs of them all be fulfilled, and should exert ourself in the methods that eliminate their sufferings and improve their happiness.

A Guide to the Bodhisattva Ways gives the following advice,

> Whenever your eyes see a sentient being,
> Look upon him with integrity and love.
> Think, "In dependence upon living beings
> I can attain perfect buddhahood."

All good things that exist, from the ephemeral pleasures of this life to the ecstasy of perfect buddhahood, arise purely in dependence upon the kindness of other sentient beings.

Regard everyone you meet as a friend and relative. See all beings through eyes of joy, and take every initiative in the quest to bring happiness to them.

Yet although the happiness and welfare of sentient beings are to be fulfilled, a person himself bound in the chains of worldly existence can forget about being able to do anything substantial to help others.

The Bodhisattva Tokmey Zangpo wrote,[5]

> What worldly god has power to protect us
> When he himself is shackled
> In the prison of cyclic existence?

The most powerful worldly god, being limited by the fetters of cyclic existence, has no ability to fully benefit other sentient beings. Nor do Shravaka Arhants or Pratyekabuddhas, who are free from all chains.

Who has this capacity? The answer is given in a verse by Arya Nagarjuna.

> Homage to the omniscient ones, the buddhas,
> Who are always friends to living beings,
> Who are free from all faults
> And are adorned with every perfection.

If one could attain the state of perfect buddhahood that is free from all faults, that sees directly all aspects of the qualities to be cultivated and faults overcome in the quest for enlightenment, and that is physically adorned with the marks and signs of perfection, the mere perception of which is beneficial, then one would be beyond the distinction of feeling attraction or aversion toward the infinite sentient beings. One would regard all beings with an equal compassion, and would have the ability to really benefit them. Think, "I should make every effort to attain this all-beneficial state."

In brief, the motivation should be, "For the ultimate benefit of the sentient beings, who are as infinite as the sky is vast, I must attain the state of a peerless, perfect, pure buddha." This is the aspirational aspect of the bodhimind.

In particular, at the time of receiving an empowerment or initiation, one should generate this aspiration by means of the appropriate liturgy.

It is important in the initiation ceremony to maintain a pure vision unstained by attraction to ordinary appearances. The house of the empowerment should not be seen as it ordinarily appears, but as the inconceivable celestial mansion embodying the meditational deity's wisdom.

The master should be seen as having the actual form of the deity. The ritual cakes arranged on the altar should be envisioned as being the mandala deities themselves.

Then imagine inviting the entire lineage of present and past gurus, the meditational deities, buddhas, bodhisattvas, dakas, dakinis, hosts of dharma protectors and all objects of refuge into the sky above. Generate firm conviction in the unfailing power of the objects of refuge, and take refuge in them.

Next contemplate the negative effects of the previous unskillful karma you have collected in this and previous lives, until you feel regret as intensely as though you had eaten poison. Resolve never again to engage in negativity even at the cost of your life. On the basis of this determined mind acknowledge all shortcomings and failures in the presence of the visualized assembly.

Then meditate with delight on rejoicing in the goodness of yourself and others, until you feel as ecstatic as a beggar who has found a huge treasure.

With these as preliminaries you then give rise to the thought, "For the sake of the sentient beings infinite in number as the measure of the sky, I must try by every means possible to attain the precious state of complete, perfect, peerless buddhahood."

This is the contemplation to be pursued while reciting the verses of bodhimind in the preliminary processes of every tantric ceremony.

As for the actual empowerment itself, because its basis is the transformation of the disciple into a meditational deity, a buddha, he or she should perform the appropriate visualizations throughout the rite precisely as described in the tantric treatises of the transmission being given.

Obscure points of the rite should be made clear (by the master) by drawing from tantric supplementary literature free from the faults of excess, omission and erroneous information.

The ceremony should follow the traditional stages of taking the tantric pledges and commitments of the system being imparted, offering the thanksgiving mandala, making aspirational prayers, and adorning the conclusion with verses of auspiciousness.

When the empowering master is a highly realized tantric adept, the usual procedures need not be followed. It is quite permissible for such a teacher to conduct the ceremony as deemed most appropriate to the minds of the disciples and the nature of the time.

Thus I conclude this brief elucidation of the fundamental spiritual qualities that must be cultivated as a preliminary to receiving the tantric initiations, which ripen and prepare the body, speech and mind of disciples and open the gateway to the powerful Vajrayana.

This text can be used as a manual to be read to disciples as a preliminary to an empowerment or initiation ceremony.[6] Should it seem too lengthy for certain occasions it can be abbreviated by deleting the various quotations and just reading the actual body of the work, interspersing bits of commentary as is deemed appropriate to the understanding of the particular disciples.

When the seeds of detachment and the bodhimind
Are firmly planted in the soil of eager disciples,
They should moisten their minds with the nectars of
    wisdom
By entering into the esoteric Vajrayana,
And grow the tree of the three enlightenment kayas.

May the pure waters of spiritual knowledge
In its three aspects of the three paths
Flow forth from the mouths of qualified teachers,
And reveal to the living beings of this world
The path that brings transcendence of all imperfection.

May this world become filled with practitioners
Accomplished in study, contemplation and meditation
Of the supreme tantric teachings given by the Buddha;
And may the flame of spiritual knowledge and
    endeavor
Blaze forth with an unextinguishable strength.[7]

16 Summary of the Kalachakra Tradition

by the Thirteenth Dalai Lama,
Gyalwa Lobzang Tubten Gyatso (1876-1933)

One very important highest yoga tantra tradition is that of Kalachakra, a system presenting the tantric path in a manner markedly different from the presentation found in other highest yoga systems.

This was expressed in verse by the incomparable Lama Tsongkhapa,[1]

> Another important highest yoga tantra system,
> And one with a unique manner of presenting the path
> Is that of Kalachakra, 'the Wheel of Time,'
> Which is based upon *The Abbreviated Kalachakra*
>   *Tantra*
> Together with *The Great Commentary: A Stainless Light.*

This 'clear' tantra is usually taught separately from the other highest yoga paths, for its infrastructure is considerably different from those of the mainstream traditions, such as Guhyasamaja, Yamantaka, and Heruka Chakrasamvara.

Kalachakra, or 'the Wheel of Time,' is spoken of in three aspects: outer, inner and alternative.

Outer Kalachakra is comprised of the six elements of earth, water, fire, air, space and wisdom; the world of Mt. Meru, the four continents, the eight sub-continents, and so forth, together with everything above, below and in all the directions; and also all objects of smell, sight, taste, touch, sound and dharma.

Under the topic of inner Kalachakra are included the three realms of living beings, the sixteen worlds, the ten planets, the twenty-eight principal heavenly bodies, the five places of rebirth, the six types of living beings, the time cycles of years, months and days, the six energy centers of the body, the ten vital energies, the eight drops that carry the instincts of the two obscurations, and so forth.

In other words, (in these two categories) are included all the living beings, and also the external world as understood in an astrological context.

Alternative Kalachakra is the actual practice of the yogas of the Kalachakra system whereby the world and its beings are purified.

The actual basis of the purification is the person possessing the six elements with the karma to be born from a human womb here in this world.

The process begins by taking initiation into a mandala made from colored powders. This initiation commences with the nine preliminary steps of invoking the earth spirits, consecrating the vase, the conch of great victory, the action lines, vajra, bell, enhancing the disciple, establishing the seat, and the analysis of the divinity.

The seventh of these preliminary steps, that of enhancing the disciple, entails placing the spiritual aspirants within the (pledges of) six Tathagata Families, invoking Vajrasattva, and so forth.

The actual initiation process is constituted of three phases: the seven called 'entering like a child'; the four higher initiations; and the four higher-than-higher initiations.

(As for the first of these three sets), when one is born as a child into this world one undergoes seven experiences: being washed; having one's hair cut; having one's ears pierced; learning to laugh and speak; using the sensory objects; being given a name; and learning to read and write, etc.

Accordingly the Kalachakra initiation begins with seven processes that are likened to these seven steps in childhood.

To receive these the disciple stands before each of the four faces of Kalachakra in turn—white, red, black and yellow in color—and is given the seven initiations: water, headdress, silk ribbon, vajra and bell, activity, name, and permission.

By means of these initiations the disciple experiences purification of the five aggregates, ten energies, right and left energy channels, ten sensory powers and their objects, the activities of the five bodily functions, the three doors, and the element of wisdom.

As for the pledges taken during this process, seven of the (fourteen) root precepts have interpretations common to the other highest yoga tantra systems; the remaining seven have interpretations exclusive to the Kalachakra system.

In addition, there are the twenty-five special precepts of the Kalachakra tradition. These are comprised of five each relating to the five topics of negativity, secondary negativity, killing, thought and desire.

During this phase of the initiation ceremony these are introduced and one is advised to guard them well.

Next one receives the four conventional higher initiations, also known as the four worldly initiations. Here the disciple is established in the path of the four joys by means of the vase waters, tasting the secret substances, experiencing the melting of the drops and the resultant bliss, and being introduced to the bliss and void.

Finally there are the four higher-than-higher initiations, also known as the four beyond-worldly initiations. Here the disciple is introduced to the consciousness which directly perceives emptiness while abiding in supreme unchanging great bliss, a consciousness that is of one taste with the empty body arising in the form of Kalachakra and Consort in sexual union.

By gaining these initiations the disciple is introduced to the real meaning of being a layman, a novice, a fully ordained monk, a sangha elder, and a leader of living beings.

Also, during the rite the significance of each of the steps in initiation is pointed out. In this way the disciples receive the empowerments of the three vajras, are shown the disciplines, and gain the initiation of a great vajra master, thus ripening their mindstreams and preparing them for entrance into the actual yogic practices of the Kalachakra tradition.

As for the various mandalas that can be used as the basis of the generation stage yogas, *The Kalachakra Root Tantra* speaks of the mandala of glorious moving stars containing one thousand, six hundred and twenty mandala deities. *The Abbreviated Tantra* speaks of seven hundred and twenty-two divinities in the mandalas of body, speech and mind. Other optional traditions are the mind mandala of thirty-six divinities and the mind mandala of thirty-two divinities. Then there are the smaller mandalas of twenty-five, twenty-three, nineteen, thirteen and nine divinities. Finally, there is the mandala with only Kalachakra and Consort, and also the mandala of Solitary Kalachakra.[2]

In the generation stage practice the yogi contemplates one of these various mandalas by means of the three samadhis, engaging in the four-branched propitiation, maintaining the four vajra points, and cultivating the four enlightenments.

In the completion stage the meditator engages in the six yogas: individual withdrawal, dhyana, energy control, retention, subsequent mindfulness and samadhi.

These six yogas abbreviate into the four branches: the branch producing form, the branch producing energy, the branch producing bliss, and the branch of great accomplishment.

Here the first branch is linked to the first two yogas, and the second branch to the third and fourth yogas. Finally, the third and fourth branches are linked to the fifth and sixth yogas.

By means of these six yogas the disciple gains the great seal of an empty body. The energies enter the central channel, and the drops of red and white sexual forces respectively flow down from the crown chakra above and flow up from the chakra at the secret place below. 21,600 of each of the two sexual drops [male and female] are gathered together in this way, giving rise to an experience of great bliss focused (in meditation) upon emptiness. Each occasion of experience of this great bliss dissolves an according amount of karmic energy and atomic bodily matter. The obscurations of the drops of the four occasions—the waking state, the dream state, deep sleep and sexual climax—are thus eliminated, and one travels to the twelfth stage of attainment, the enlightenment state of Kalachakra's unchanging great bliss.

This is the system of the Kalachakra initiations, generation stage yogas, and completion stage yogas that produce the four kayas of a fully enlightened being.

Buddha Shakyamuni originally taught this tradition at the Dhanyakataka Stupa in South India. The teaching had been requested by King Suchandra of Shambala, who was an actual emanation of the bodhisattva Vajrapani. Emissaries from six different kingdoms were also present.

On that occasion Buddha transmitted *The Kalachakra Root Tantra* in twelve thousand lines, and shortly thereafter Suchandra composed his extensive commentary in sixty thousand lines. However, the only section of *The Kalachakra Root Tantra* to come down to us is the chapter known as *The Treatise on the Initiations*.

Later, Manju Yashas, who was the first of the twenty-five kalkin masters of Shambala, wrote a summary of *The Kalachakra Root Tantra* that is known by the title *The Abbreviated Kalachakra Tantra*, which is in five chapters. Two different versions of an early summary of this, *Essence of the Abbreviated Tantra*, exists in the Tibetan canon.

Another important text is *The Great Commentary: A Stainless Light*, which is an extensive elucidation of *The Abbreviated Kalachakra Tantra*. This work is perhaps better known in connection with the threefold collection *Trilogy of the Bodhisattvas*. It was written by the second of the Shambala lineage holders,

Pundarika.

Also of significance is the bodhisattva Vajragarbha's commentary known simply as *The Vajragarbha Commentary*. This work unpacks the themes of *The Tantra of Two Forms,* which is the root tantra in the Hevajra system. However, it comments upon Hevajra in a manner consistent with the Kalachakra presentation of the path, so it is often read in conjunction with a study of the Kalachakra tradition.

Also important is Bodhisattva Vajrapani's commentary, again known simply as *The Vajrapani Commentary,* which explains the essential points of the root tantra of Heruka Chakrasamvara in terms compatible with the Kalachakra system.[3]

The Subsequent Tantra of Guhyasamaja presents the path in a manner consistent with the Kalachakra structure. A study of it is therefore considered helpful to a study of Kalachakra.

In addition, Kalachakrapada's extensive and abbreviated commentaries to the Kalachakra generation stage yogas are fundamental reading, as are the writings of the Dro masters.

The trilogy of Acharya Abhayakara [Abhayakaragupta, an important disciple of Naropa] known as *The Three Rosaries* also contains a number of important early Kalachakra works: *The Vajra Rosary,* which contains forty-two mandala rites from all four classes of tantras; *The Rosary of Complete Yoga,* which is a sadhana collection; and *A Rosary of Sunbeams,* which is a collection of fire rite practices.

Finally, there is *A Compendium of Purification Practices* by Acharya Jagaddarpana.

This is the principal Kalachakra literature that was translated (from Sanskrit) into Tibetan and that serves as the basis of the Kalachakra transmission in Tibet.

It is often said that in order to successfully practice the tantric path one should train under the guidance of a qualified tantric master, avoid wrong attitudes toward him or her, cultivate positive attitudes, and remain within the framework of the pledges and commitments of the tantric path. This is even more crucial in the resultant Vajrayana than in the causal Sutrayana.

To generate effective attitudes toward the spiritual master it is useful to know the beneficial effects of doing so and the shortcomings of not. One should also know how to regard the guru's entourage and environment, the nature of correct and incorrect practice, and so forth.

The general tantric teachings concerning how to correctly rely upon the vajra guru were gleaned from early source works and collected into fifty quintessential verses, entitled *Fifty Verses on the Guru* by Acharya Vira.

As for the precepts to be maintained by a practitioner of highest yoga tantra, some of the unique features of Kalachakra in this regard were mentioned above.

The general trainings of the highest yoga tantras include subjects like the commitment of consumption, i.e., the pledge to rely upon the use of the five meats and five drinks, etc.; the commitments to keep the sacred tantric materials, such as vajra, bell, the six tantric ornaments[4] and so forth; the commitment of protection, meaning the pledge to guard the root and branch trainings; and so forth.

The root pledges are said to be fourteen in number, and transgressions of them are known as 'root downfalls.' By understanding their individual natures, what constitutes each, and being apprehensive of the shortcomings of transgression, one guards against failure in the disciplines. Should a root downfall occur, there are numerous methods of restoring the strength of it.

(As for how the code of fourteen root and eight secondary tantric pledges arose), based on numerous early canonical works Acharya Ashvaghosha compiled the list of fourteen root tantric downfalls, and Acharya Nagarjuna compiled the list of the eight secondary precepts.

In addition to these, practitioners of the female highest yoga tantras (the division to which Kalachakra belongs) are instructed to observe a number of additional precepts, such as initiating all activities with the left side of the body, performing a tantric feast (*tsok*) on the tenth day of each lunar cycle, and so forth.

Should either the root or secondary tantric precepts be transgressed, the strength of the disciplines can be restored by means of taking the initiation again, or else by means of performing the self-initiation practice.

To prevent negative effects arising from any downfalls that have been created it is useful to practice the meditations and mantric recitations associated with the tantric systems of Vajrasattva or Samayavajra, and also to perform the Vajradaka fire rite. These methods of purifying transgressions of the tantric precepts are taught in numerous scriptures.

(I would like to conclude by saying that) the omniscient master Buton Rinchen Druppa, who understood and elucidated all the central teachings of Buddha Shakyamuni, greatly contributed to the preservation and dissemination of the buddhist tantras here in Tibet.[5] Lama Tsongkhapa and his immediate disciples continued his legacy.

My own guru, Purchokpa Rinpochey, received the complete tradition coming from them, analyzed it with pure reason, and internalized its meaning through intense meditation. He thus crossed the vast ocean of study, contemplation and meditation in the tantric tradition.

It was under his kind guidance that I myself ventured into the Vajrayana. And although I cannot boast of spectacular personal accomplishments, I must say that I feel very honored to have trained in this vast and profound system under the guidance of such an accomplished master.

17 Notes on the Two Yogic Stages of Glorious Kalachakra

To Entice the Minds of the Wise

by Gyalwa Gendun Druppa,
the First Dalai Lama (1391-1474/5)

Homage to the feet of the Lama
Inseparably one with Primordial Kalachakra

Here the explanation of the two yogic stages in the practice of the Kalachakra path will be presented under two headings: a presentation of the general nature of the paths and practices leading to enlightenment, and an explanation of the individual paths and stages.

THE GENERAL NATURE OF THE PATHS AND PRACTICES

One should first refine the mind by means of the ordinary Sutrayana methods. In specific, cultivate a definite understanding of the pure view of emptiness. Then seek out the complete initiations that ripen the mind and permit one to enter into the extraordinary Vajrayana path. Thereafter as intensely

as one cherishes one's life one should cherish the disciplines and commitments of the tantric path, as elucidated at the time of initiation.

With this as the basis one engages in the coarse and subtle yogas of the generation stage, which mature one's being for practice of the completion stage. Finally, when these generation stage yogas have been taken to fulfillment one enters into meditation upon the completion stage, together with its six yogic branches.[1]

The result is the attainment of complete buddhahood in the form of Kalachakra and Consort.

THE INDIVIDUAL PATHS AND PRACTICES

This will be presented under two headings: the initiations which make one into a proper vessel for tantric practice; and, having become a proper vessel, the paths upon which one is to meditate.

The first of these involves four subjects: the mandala into which initiation is given; the number and stages of initiation; the nature of the individual initiations; and the purpose of initiation.

The Mandala into which Initiation is Given

The (Indian) mahasiddha Tilbupa[2] (Skt., Gandhapada) writes,

> There are three types of mandalas used as the basis of initiation: those made from colored particles, those painted on canvas and those visualized in the body.

The Guhyasamaja Tantra and also (Acharya Abhayakaragupta's) *The Vajra Rosary of Initiation Rites*[3] mention the mandala of dhyana, or meditative application as a fourth alternative.

The Kalachakra tradition differs somewhat from these

mainstream traditions, as is explained in *The Treatise on the Initiations:*

> There are seven initiations. The mandala should be constructed and these should be given. The basis is a mandala made from colored particles.

As clearly stated (by Naropa) in *A Commentary to the Treatise on the Initiations,* the Kalachakra empowerments are to be given solely on the basis of a mandala made of colored powders. Moreover, it is sufficient to use solely one of the mind mandalas. Accordingly, in (the master's preliminary activity of) generating the mandala by means of the propitiatory recitation, it is sufficient to use a text of only the mind mandala. There is no need to perform the (extensive) invocations of all three mandalas (i.e., of body, speech and mind).

The Number and Stages of Initiation

Generally it is said that there are eleven initiations: the seven of entering like a child, together with the four standard highest yoga tantra initiations—vase, secret, wisdom, and fourth.

These latter four are given twice, the two phases being called the 'higher' and the 'higher-than-higher' initiations. However, as the names and nature of these are the same in both phases, they are grouped together. That is, both vase initiations are counted as one, and both secret as one. Both wisdom initiations, together with the fourth initiation of the first set, are also counted as one, as they all share the same nature. Finally, the fourth initiation of the higher-than-higher phase is counted by itself as the fourth initiation (for it alone reveals the full meaning of enlightenment).

These two phases (of four initiations) are preceded by the seven initiations of entering the mandala like a child enters the world. This process of spiritual rebirth is likened to the birth and stages in the growth of a child, such as washing, piercing the ears, giving earrings, encouraging the child to laugh and smile, and so forth. Thus are their names derived.

The initiation ceremony begins with the usual preliminaries (of taking refuge, generating the bodhimind, etc.), analyzing the disciple, and so forth. One is then brought to the mandala and given the seven initiations of a child. These are followed by the four higher and then the four higher-than-higher initiations.

During the initiation ceremony one assumes the pledge of secrecy and thereafter if one reveals the secrets of Vajrayana to the uninitiated or to the spiritually immature, one's mystic link with the Vajrayana is broken.

Similarly, if the guru confuses the stages of initiation he creates the root downfall of speaking the higher secrets to the uninitiated; for the ceremony will be invalid and consequently even though the disciples hear the procedures they remain without initiation.

The Nature and Purpose of the Initiations

The seven initiations of entering like a child are each followed by the sprinkling of vase waters. Therefore they are also called the water initiations. The four faces of Kalachakra, which represent the vajra body, speech, mind, and wisdom, reveal the nature of these initiations.

Firstly the disciples are shown the white face of vajra body, which is in the north. This causes them to generate the vajra body. The four consorts residing in the mandala that has been produced from colored powders bestow the water initiation, and the five Tathagatas bestow the initiation of the vajra crown.[4]

Next they are shown the red face of vajra speech, which is in the south. This causes them to generate vajra speech. The ten powerful goddesses then bestow the initiation of the silk headdress, and Kalachakra and Consort bestow the initiation of vajra and bell.

The disciples are now shown the black face of vajra mind, which is in the east. This causes them to generate the vajra mind. The heroes and heroines of the mandala then give the initiation of discipline, and the male and female Wrathful Ones give the initiation of the name.

Finally the disciples are shown the yellow face of wisdom, which is in the west. This causes the vajra wisdom to be generated within them. Vajrasattva and Consort give the initiation of permissions.

Anyone who attains these seven initiations and takes the practice of the generation stage to fulfillment shall become a master of the seven stages[5] in this very life. Even if one is not able to complete these generation stage yogas before death strikes, this attainment will definitely be achieved within seven lifetimes.

The main purpose of these seven initiations is to transform the spiritual aspirant into a vessel suitable for practice of the generation stage yogas, and to provide a path for the cultivation of meditative stability. However, the initiations of the silk headdress and of the vajra and bell also have the function of transforming the disciple into a vessel capable of successfully practicing the completion stage yogas, which gain control over the ten energies flowing through the secondary channels of the body and redirect them into the dhuti, the central channel.

The next set of initiations, known as the four higher initiations, have both generation and completion stage associations.

For example, the nature of the vase initiation is as follows. The disciple is (symbolically) given a mudra possessing the appropriate characteristics. He (visualizes) holding her in his arms, stroking her breasts, and so forth.

The great bliss that arises confers the vase initiation. Thus it is associated with the initiation of a master and is explained as the yoga of transforming ordinary lust into a force of enlightenment.

The reason it is given the name 'the master's initiation' is revealed by the following scriptural passage (from *The Abbreviated Kalachakra Tantra*),

The masters regard sensuality as (a potential path of) purification.[6]

The four phases of the first set of four initiations that follow are much the same as their counterparts in the mainstream highest yoga tantras, although there are a few exceptions. For example, even though the secret initiation in the first set (of four) is much the same as in other highest yoga tantra systems, there is the distinction that here in Kalachakra when the blindfold is removed from the disciple's eyes he is told to look at the outspread vulva of a knowledge dakini. This arouses fierce passion, that in turn gives rise to great bliss. This bliss introduces the nature of the secret initiation. (In other words, the initiation is not bestowed by the power of the red and white substances, as they are in the mainstream tantras.)

Also, the fourth initiation (of the first set of four) differs from the fourth initiation given in the mainstream tantric systems. Here it is called by the name of a fourth initiation, but in fact is closer in nature to the third, that of wisdom awareness. The disciple (visualizes being) given a knowledge dakini and entering into sexual union with her. The sexual substances come to the tip of the jewel, and the bliss thus aroused confers this fourth initiation. (As this bliss is in the nature of the wisdom initiation), this fourth initiation is called 'the worldly fourth initiation' (for it does not reveal the final meaning of enlightenment).

The first three of the higher-than-higher initiations that follow are as in the previous set, with the exception that on each occasion the visualized sexual union is performed with nine consorts rather than only one. The manner of inducing (the bliss that confers) the initiations is much the same. However, here the fourth initiation, which reveals the full meaning of what is to be accomplished and what transcended, possesses the full characteristics of a fourth initiation and thus is called 'the non-worldly fourth initiation.'

THE PATH TO BE MEDITATED UPON

This will be presented under three headings: the vows, commitments and disciplines to be maintained by a Kalachakra initiate; on the basis of this training, how to meditate on the generation stage yogas; and, having thus ripened one's stream of being, how to meditate upon the completion stage yogas.

The Disciplines and Commitments to be Maintained

These should be known from either the long or short versions of *A Treatise on the Root Downfalls*.[7]

The Generation Stage Yogas

The degree to which one accomplishes the generation stage yogas is the degree to which one prepares the basis to be purified and ripens one's mindstream for the higher yogas (of the completion stage). The meditator who has accomplished the generation stage yogas will have little difficulty in mastering the yogas of the completion stage. Thus its purpose is one of speed in the attainment of enlightenment.

However, meditation upon Solitary Kalachakra alone is not enough to bring about the desired purification, even on the coarse level. Taking a complete mandala [of body, speech and mind], or one such as the mind mandala, which uses symbolism revealing all stages of evolution and dissolution of the world, the basis to be purified, we should apply ourselves to the three Kalachakras to be understood—outer, inner, and alternative—and meditate upon the four stages of the Kalachakra generation stage yoga,[8] which uses spiritual symbolism based on the natural processes of evolution and dissolution [i.e., how the world comes into existence and then disintegrates, and how sentient beings enter the world and then leave it].

Of the three Kalachakras mentioned above, outer and inner Kalachakras are the bases to be purified, whereas alternative Kalachakra refers to the yogic practices that effect this purification and produce the three purified results.

External Kalachakra is comprised of the outer world which is the vessel supporting the living beings. Thus it includes the planets of this solar system, as well as the sun, moon, stars, and so on.

Inner Kalachakra refers to the living beings of the world,

such as human beings, who are born from a womb, and who possess the six elements. Here the basis to be purified includes the aggregates, spheres of perception, channels, mystic drops, and so forth of these beings. These are all incorporated into the symbolism of the path.

One meditates upon these two Kalachakras in order to free them from obscurations.

These are the outer and inner Kalachakras, the bases to be purified. Because they are thus associated with the path and its results, they may be subsumed under the classification of alternative Kalachakra.

In this context, alternative Kalachakra has three aspects: the methods of purifying the internal bases, those for purifying the external bases, and the methods of proceeding in the generation stage yogas as a means to prepare the mind for the completion stage.

(A characteristic of the Kalachakra generation stage practice is that) the wheel of protection is not applied to the basis of purification. Instead one begins by paying homage to the visualized Field of Merit. This is a spiritual metaphor for how sentient beings generate the positive karma that produces rebirth with a special form in future lives.

One then recites the passage, "Because there is no inherent existence there is no inherent meditation. Meditation that grasps at inherent existence [of meditation] is not real meditation. Similarly, the things that we perceive are all non-existent." Having pronounced this, one meditates on the stages of dissolution of the dual appearance of the world and its inhabitants, and then concentrates directly on the four doors of liberation [emptiness, signlessness, wishlessness, and non-activity].

This is a spiritual metaphor for the dissolution of the physical elements during the death of someone who has created much positive karma and whose death is followed by the conscious experience of clear light.

One then proceeds with the five purifications, or 'enlightenments.' This begins with the visualization of the space-like *dharmodaya,* or 'source of phenomena,' which symbolizes the basis of existence. In Kalachakra, this is represented by empty space, and is symbolized by the sexual organ of a woman. (Just as we humans issue forth from the sexual organ of our mother, all phenomena manifest from within empty space, and the mandala of Kalachakra issues forth from the blissful wisdom of emptiness.)

Inside of this is the air mandala, which is related to the area between the crown and forehead of the consort. Above the air mandala is the mandala of fire, associated with the area from the forehead to the throat. Above this is the water mandala, associated with the area from the throat to the heart. Above this is the mandala of earth, associated with the area between the heart and navel of the consort. Above this is Mount Meru, associated with the area from the navel to the anus. Above this is a lotus, associated with the area between the secret place and secret lotus of the consort.

Above this is a moon, sun, and kalagni disc.[9] These are associated with the three energy channels leading to the lotus of the consort, called 'the conch,' and which direct the energies causing solid and liquid wastes, as well as the sexual substances, to move. Then above this is the vajra tent, symbolic of the father's act of placing his vajra in the secret place of the consort.

Inside the vajra tent is the inconceivable mansion, the secret place of the consort; and inside this the vowels and consonants of the Sanskrit alphabet stand upright upon cushions of moon and sun discs. From the moon(s) and sun(s) arise the white and red bodhimind substances, symbolic of the mixing of sperm and ovum in the secret place of the consort.[10]

Between the moon and sun appears the letter *hūm,* like the outline of the hare in the moon, symbolic of the entrance of a bardo being into the newly fertilized ovum mixture. This is marked by a black letter *hih,* symbolizing the vital energies [produced by the fusion of sperm and ovum] which act as the vehicle of consciousness [symbolized by the syllable *hūm*]. These all merge together and transform into the letter *ham,* symbolic of the growth of the body in the womb of the consort. The letter *ham* then transforms into light and re-emerges as complete Glorious Kalachakra.

This process, until the complete generation of the deities of the supremely victorious mandala [i.e., first of the four generation stage meditations], symbolizes the complete evolution of the fetus, including the five aggregates, five elements, six sensory powers, six spheres of perception, five powers of action, and their five functions. This process is given a spiritual context by the twenty stages called 'the twenty enlightenments.'

When the meditation enters the phase known as victorious activity [i.e., second of the four generation stage meditations], Vajravega arises from the wisdom-energies at one's heart and emanates forth. Instantly the wisdom-winds stir, summoning the Wisdom Beings, who merge with the previously visualized Symbolic Beings, becoming of one taste with them.

This stage of meditation until the completion of the victorious activities practice represents the growth of the body and the experience of sexuality.

One then engages in 'the yoga of the drop.' Here one focuses on the multicolored consort, consecrates the vajra of the male and the lotus of the female, and meditates that they enter into sexual union.

This causes the letter *ham* to melt and fall from its abode at the crown. Gradually it descends [through the energy centers of the body], inducing the four joys successively. Finally it arrives at the tip of the jewel, where it is retained.

This is the yoga of the drop of simultaneously arising bliss and (primordial wisdom of) emptiness [i.e., third of the four generation stage meditations].

The drop is then drawn back up to the crown, and one meditates within the sphere of bliss and emptiness. This is 'the subtle yoga' [i.e., the fourth generation stage meditation].

Having generated the mandala and completed the four generation stage meditations in this way, one then proceeds to recite the mantras and so forth.

The conventional symbol for these experiences is a sixteen-year-old maiden with a special sensitivity for sensual ecstasy.

The Completion Stage Yogas

The explanation of the completion stage yogas will be given under three headings: the characteristics of the vajra body upon which the yogas are concentrated; a general explanation of how these six yogas are used in this application; and an explanation of each yoga individually.

The Characteristics of the Vajra Body

The first of these involves three subjects: the abiding channels, the flowing energies, and the bodhimind substances that are to be directed.

The discussion of the energy channels involves three subjects: the nature of the six main channels and the six main chakras (energy centers) at which these converge, how these energy centers are stimulated through the six-branched yoga, and an outline of which of the six yogas is applied to which of the six energy centers.

The Six Channels and Six Energy Centers

The three main energy channels are called *roma, kyangma,* and *dhuti.* These begin at the tip of the sexual organ, proceed back to the anus, and then run straight up the center of the body with an occasional slight bend. Eventually they come to the inside of the cranium and then curve down, terminating respectively at the top of the nostril passages and at the pillar between these.

These three are divided into upper and lower portions.

The upper central channel, called (the planet) *rahu,* and also *nyipang* and *abadhuti,* begins just above the navel. Associated with the element space, it is greenish in color, and its main function is to cause the descent of vital energy in the body.

To the right of this is *roma,* also called *rasana* and *nyima* [the sun]. Red in color, it is associated with the element fire, and its main function is to cause female sexual fluids [i.e., hormones] and blood [ovum] to descend.

To the left of this is *kyangma,* which is also called *lalana* and *dawa* [the moon]. White in color, it is associated with the element water and its main function is to cause the male fluids to descend.

All three of these energy channels are dominated by the life-supporting energies flowing within them.

Below the navel, the central channel curves to the right and comes to the tip of the sexual organ. Here it is called (the flower) *kundarma, dungchen* (the conch) and (the planet) *kalagni.* Associated with the element of primordial wisdom, its color is blue and its main function is to cause male hormones and sperm to descend.

The left channel also curves to the center and comes to the tip of the organ. Called *lug* (the sheep), it is black in color and is associated with the air element. Its main function is to cause waste fluids to descend.

The right channel curves to the left and comes to the anus. Its name is *marser* (crimson), and it is associated with the earth element. Yellow in color, its main function is to cause feces and wastes to descend.

All three of these channels are conditioned by the downward moving energies flowing within them.

Sometimes through incorrect meditation the downward-moving energies (that reside in the lower channels) are caused to flow into the upper channels, and the life-supporting energies (that reside above) are forced to flow down into the lower, giving rise to many unpleasant and dangerous conditions, such as violent disease.

If such dramatic effects can be produced through [incorrect] meditation, then why should correct application not have similarly powerful results in the opposite direction—results such as eliminating physical diseases and destroying the causes of death?

In the Kalachakra system, the six energy centers, or chakras, are as follows.

The first is located just below the crown aperture of the skull and has four petals of energy channels. The second is at the forehead and has sixteen petals. The third is located at the throat and has thirty-two petals. The fourth, which has eight petals, is at the heart. The fifth has sixty-four petals and is located at the navel. The sixth has two branches: the first at the anus, with thirty-two petals, and the second at the center of the sexual jewel, with eight petals.[11]

At the energy centers, the left channel coils clockwise around the central channel, and the right counterclockwise, thus forming two knots that obstruct the free flow of vital energies.

One should also know how these channels converge at the centers and how they influence the flow of vital energies. This may be studied in larger commentaries.

The nature and binding effect of these knots upon the subtle energies of the body, and the consequent repercussions on consciousness, is explained in detail in the "Chapter on Wisdom" of *The Abbreviated Kalachakra Tantra*.

In other tantric systems it is often said that when the side channels form knots around the central channel, they do so very tightly, leaving no space whatsoever in the coils. In Kalachakra, however, one visualizes the knots as being loose and as having space between the coils.

How the Energy Centers are Stimulated

There are many different methods for generating tantric experience by means of drawing the male and female substances as well as the vital energies through the center of the chakras as explained above and for opening the central channel from top to bottom. These may be learned in detail from larger commentaries. The essence is as follows.

The Six Yogas and the Six Energy Centers

When practicing the first two yogas—those of individual withdrawal and dhyana[12]—one successively concentrates the drops and energies at the upper aperture of the central channel. During the yogas of energy control and subsequent mindfulness one focuses these at the navel. The yoga of retention brings them into the central channel running through the center of all six energy centers. Finally, by means of the yogas of samadhi the energies are concentrated from the base to the top of the central channel.

The Flowing Energies

The Kalachakra literature does not speak of five root and five secondary energies [as do the mainstream tantras such as Guhyasamaja and so forth]. Yet it too speaks of ten subtle bodily energies, and these share the same nature [as the ten in the mainstream systems]. In fact the ten [in both systems] are actually subsumed under the five root energies. In this tradition [i.e., Kalachakra] it is said that the all-pervading energy flows mainly through the gates of the nostrils.

Where are these first energies generated and where do they abide?

Ten energy channels converge at the heart. The two apertures of the central channel, above and below the knots at the heart, are the respective sites where the life-sustaining and downward-moving energies first arise and then abide.

As for the pathways of their flow, the life-sustaining energy mostly flows in the three upper channels and the downward-moving through the three lower channels.

Similarly, the petals to the east and southeast of the heart are the sites of the equally abiding and 'turtle' energies. The south and southwest are the sites of the upward moving and pristine energies. The north and northeast petals are the sites of the all-pervading and divinely predisposed energies. The western and northwestern petals are the sites of the *lu* and *norlegyal* energies. These are the sites where they first arise and where they abide.

These then flow through the major ten channels. The channels themselves subdivide into many smaller passageways, which pervade the entire body like a fine network of interconnected tunnels.

The Bodhimind Substances to be Directed

This involves three subjects: how at the time of conception the body is formed from the white and red bodhimind substances, or white and red drops; how these evolve during one's life; and how they move at the time of death.

The Kalachakra tradition speaks of the drop-like substances in three ways: the drops generated on the four occasions [waking, dreaming, deep sleep, and sexual excitation]; the drops of body, speech, mind, and wisdom; and the drops of form, sound, thought, and primordial wisdom. These terms have the same referents, and an understanding of their basis, nature, and functions is indispensable to the completion stage practices. Therefore the topic is usually introduced at this point in the presentation.

The site of the drop of the waking state occasion, the body, and form is at the forehead. The site of the drop of the dream state, speech, and sound is at the throat. The site of the drop of deep sleep, mind, and thought is at the heart. Finally, the site of the drop of sexual ecstasy, wisdom, and primordial wisdom is at the navel.

Again, the procedure of working with these drops is to bring them down from above through the central channel to the center of the tip of the jewel, beginning with the waking state drop and eventually uniting with the drop of primordial wisdom.

Moreover, when the drop of the fourth occasion melts [i.e., sexual ecstasy] and the collective substances are brought through the energy centers at the navel and jewel, one experiences an especially intense great bliss. The reason for this is that the drop of the fourth occasion is first generated at these two points.

The forehead and the jewel are the main sites of the white bodhimind substances, and here the red substances are weaker. The actual abode of the white substances, which act as the basis increasing the male energies, is the chakra at the forehead.

The main sites of the red bodhimind substances are the energy centers of the navel, secret place and throat. Here the force of the red substance dominates, and the white is weaker.

At the energy center located at the heart the two substances (white and red) abide with equal strength.

As explained in *The Vajra Rosary Tantra*, the drops formed

from the white and red droplets that abide in each of these energy centers are visualized as being the size of a sesame seed.

In the Kalachakra tradition all obscurations are categorized within the drops of the four occasions. As for how the obscurations are linked to the drops, here it is said that the drops are focal points for the extremely subtle energies and states of consciousness, and the instincts of the obscurations actually abide upon them. These instincts give rise to both the obscurations to liberation [or the host of 84,000 delusions] and the obscurations to knowledge.

Thus although the drops are composed of atoms [and therefore cannot actually function as a basis of obscuration, in that they act as focal points of the subtle energies and states of consciousness which carry the instincts of obscurations], to speak of them in this way is reasonable.

The drops of both the waking and fourth occasion states are at the navel. Through generating either or both of them one stimulates the according instincts and experiences the according occasion [i.e., wakefulness and/or sexual ecstasy].

Concerning the drop at the heart, it is said to represent the basis of the body in which one experiences deep sleep.

The way in which the drops of deep sleep, dream and waking occasions cause us to experience these three events is as follows.

When the coarse energies absorb into the chakras of the central channel at the jewel and heart, one experiences deep sleep. When these energies arise and enter into both the throat and secret place, one experiences very clear dreams for a prolonged period of time. Should these energies move to the navel and forehead, one awakens from sleep and is able to perceive the manifest objects of the external world.

Thus in the course of our day-to-day experience our mindset arises in synchronicity with these inner changes. This suggests that control of these energies and drops has a great effect on our stream of being, and that if one is able to apply the skillful yogas of the tantric path one can control one's states of consciousness on this primordial level and transform them

into qualities of buddhahood. This powerful technique of working with the subtle energies and energy centers is found exclusively in the highest yoga tantra systems.

For ordinary beings the drops of the four occasions—waking,
dream, deep sleep and sexual ecstasy—carry the potencies that
induce perception of the impure objects of the world, the
potencies that cause confused appearances and sound, the
potencies giving rise to obscurity of mind and ignorance, and
the potencies arousing dissipating bliss.

These potencies are purified by the Kalachakra yogas. To
be specific, they are transformed into the empty body, unconfused sound, non-conceptual wisdom and unchanging bliss.
These are cultivated to perfection, giving rise to the vajra body,
speech, and mind of a buddha, and to fully manifest primordial wisdom.

How do the six yogas purify the bases?

The stains generated on the occasion of the waking state are
purified and transformed into a similitude of the path by a
concentrated application of the combined yogas of individual
withdrawal, dhyana, and subsequent mindfulness. The drop
of sleep is purified and transformed into the path through the
yoga of energy control and retention. The drops of sleep and
sexual climax are purified through the combined yogas of subsequent mindfulness and samadhi, and are thus turned into
the nature of the path.

The first of these purifications—the yoga of individual
withdrawal—eliminates the stains of the drop generated in the
waking state of the forehead and transforms it into the nature
of the path. The yoga of subsequent mindfulness eliminates
the stains of the waking drop at the navel, and, used in another way, also purifies the stains of the drop of sexual ecstasy.
As explained earlier, the drop at the navel carries the potencies of generating both waking state and sexual ecstasy experiences [so this combined yogic approach is necessary].

A General Explanation of How the Six Yogas are to be Applied

Upon what original tantric texts and later Indian commentaries do we base the Kalachakra doctrines of the six yogas and the manner in which they work with the drops, energies, channels, and so forth?

It seems that the extensive version of *The Kalachakra Root Tantra*[13] [that Buddha taught to Suchandra] remained in Shambala and never appeared in either India or Tibet. Only that section of *The Kalachakra Root Tantra* entitled *The Treatise on the Initiations* has come down to us today. Naropa wrote an important commentary to this, and the two are often studied together.

Other important early Kalachakra texts (written in Shambala and India) are *The Abbreviated Kalachakra Tantra* (by Manju Yashas (of Shambala); the threefold collection known as *Trilogy of the Bodhisattvas*[14] [i.e., *The Great Commentary: A Stainless Light, The Vajragarbha Commentary,* and *The Vajrapani Commentary*]; the treatise on the six yogas by the mahasiddha Anupamarakshita, whom we Tibetans call Pemetso; and the commentary to that by Suryashri.[15] There are also the (four) works of Shavari: one on the six yogas, one on his personal insights, his summary, and his approach to the ultimate.[16]

The opening discussion of the six yogas will address three topics: a general introduction to the six yogas; the certainty of their number; and the certainty of their order in practice.

How the Six Yogas are Introduced

The first of these subjects involves four topics: the names of the six yogas; how these six yogas function as the four branches of approach and accomplishment; how they are grouped into the threefold vajra yoga and the threefold virtue; and how they are grouped into the three branches (of attainment).

The names of the six yogas are: individual withdrawal, dhyana, energy control, retention, subsequent mindfulness, and samadhi or absorption.

As for the second topic [of how the yogas function as ap-

proach and accomplishment] here the yogas of individual withdrawal and dhyana are the approach. The yogas of energy control and retention serve as the proximate accomplishment. The
yoga of subsequent mindfulness serves as the accomplishment;
and the yoga of samadhi is linked to the great accomplishment,
the attainment of the state of a mahasiddha, a mighty tantric
adept.

The third topic involves the threefold vajra yoga and the
threefold virtue. These are explained as follows. In the beginning of practice the yogas of individual withdrawal and dhyana
serve as the virtuous vajra body yoga. In the middle, the yogas
of energy control and retention serve as the virtuous vajra
speech yoga. Finally, the yogas of subsequent mindfulness and
samadhi serve as the virtuous vajra mind yoga.

When these are spoken of as four rather than the three vajras,
this is effected by subdividing the last category into two, at
which time the yoga of subsequent mindfulness is associated
with the vajra mind, and the yoga of samadhi is linked to
primordial vajra wisdom.

The six yogas can also be otherwise arranged into three
branches, wherein the yogas of individual withdrawal and
dhyana combine as the branch that accomplishes form; the
yogas of energy control and retention combine as the branch
that accomplishes higher energy; and the yogas of subsequent
mindfulness and samadhi combine as the branch that accomplishes bliss.

To explain what this means in easily understood terms, the
idea is that we apply the yogas of individual withdrawal and
dhyana in order to produce a previously unknown form, and
then by means of making this accomplishment firm, we stabilize the (substitute) empty body. Therefore these two yogas
are said to be branches accomplishing form.

We then engage the yoga of energy control and apply the
special techniques in order to direct the life-sustaining and
downward-moving energies to the navel energy center, where
they are brought together and used to gain control over the
other energies. After this, the yoga of retention is applied to

bring the energies of all the six centers to the navel as before. Therefore these two yogas serve as branches producing higher energy. They are also therefore sometimes referred to as the branch establishing control over the vital energies.

Thus the yogas of individual withdrawal and dhyana reveal the empty body, and the yogas of energy control and retention bring the vital energies under control. That uncontrived yogi applies subsequent mindfulness to his own empty body, and attains the ability to arise in the form of Kalachakra and Consort. At that time there appear the forms of the various empty body shaktis. This is known as 'empty body mahamudra.' The yogi, who has arisen in the form of the empty body deity, then sexually unites with these goddesses, giving rise to the extraordinary, supreme, unchanging bliss. This is the fruition and final experience of the yoga of samadhi, and it is for this reason that the fifth and sixth yogas are grouped together as the branch producing bliss.

The Number of the Yogas

As we can see from the above description, by accomplishing the first four yogas one engages the fifth (the yoga of subsequent mindfulness) and gains the ability to arise in a qualified empty body. The strength of that attainment in turn provides the basis for success in the sixth and final yoga, that of samadhi.

Thus (the six yogas by themselves have the power to generate the attainment of full enlightenment, and so) there is no need to supplement them with various assortments of other practices, nor to practice anything on top of them. On the other hand, to omit any of them will impair the system's potency (to produce enlightenment).

Their Order in Practice

The six yogas are practiced in the order listed above. That is, one gains proficiency in the first before proceeding to the second, and so forth. To practice the later yogas before accomplishing the earlier ones will not produce the desired results.

It is the impact of each one that carries the yogi successively across the stages of the path, and that prepares one for the next yoga to be approached. It is important to understand how this process works, and to engage in the training accordingly.

The Kalachakra doctrine of the extraordinary empty body is somewhat similar to the illusory body doctrine of the mainstream yoga tantra systems, although the basis of this accomplishment must be effected by means of the first of the six yogas, that of individual withdrawal. The second yoga, that of dhyana, then makes this attainment firm. The empty body which has thus been produced by these two yogas, which are categorized as the branch accomplishing form, becomes one's extraordinary body (used as the basis supporting the mind in meditation). The third and fourth yogas—those of energy control and retention—are then applied in order to gain control over the subtle energies. Next, in reliance upon the external condition of a mudra, one applies subsequent mindfulness to one's own attainment and arises in the empty body form of Kalachakra and Consort. This gives rise to the bliss that is the yoga of samadhi abiding in union.

Here the empty body produced by the yoga of subsequent mindfulness is similar to the third stage illusory body attainment of the completion stage yogas of mainstream tantric paths such as Guhyasamaja [i.e., the 'impure' illusory body].

Moreover, the yoga of samadhi is similar to the yoga of great union in the other systems, although there are significant differences within the boundaries of the stages and how they are said to be accomplished. For instance, (in Guhyasamaja and so forth) the yoga of great union is associated solely with the arya stages, whereas in the Kalachakra tradition the yoga of samadhi also includes non-arya stages. From the time one first engages the yoga of samadhi until the time this yoga is fulfilled, one experiences the twelve levels as a result of the 1,800 dissolutions produced by the 21,600 moments of unchanging bliss. The first of these levels begins on the ordinary [i.e., non-arya] stage.

According to the illusory body doctrine in systems like Guhyasamaja, the basis of the accomplishment is established by the very first yoga, namely, that of body isolation. This is then gradually intensified by means of the yoga of speech isolation, until eventually one comes to the third stage and arises within an illusory body.

If we compare this to the process of the empty body discussed in the Kalachakra tradition, here a stabilized similitude of this special body is first produced by the second yoga, that of dhyana. This accomplishment is gradually intensified from that point until the yoga of retention; but the empty body itself is not actually produced until the fifth yoga is applied, that of subsequent mindfulness. The empty body produced here has very little equivalent on the stage of the yoga of individual withdrawal (for this one is utterly non-material).

Having applied the yoga of subsequent mindfulness, in the occasions that follow one relinquishes all physical attributes and arises solely on the basis of the Kalachakra empty body.

An Explanation of Each of the Yogas

Here each of the six yogas will be explained in turn, beginning with the yoga of individual withdrawal.

1. The Yoga of Individual Withdrawal. This will be explained under seven headings: (a) the meaning of the name of the yoga, (b) the place for performing the meditation, (c) the time for the meditation, (d) ascertaining the position of the body, (e) the manner of glancing, (f) entering the suchness of mind, and (g) the signs of progress.

(a) The yoga of individual withdrawal is so called because its main function is to cut off the individual activity of vital energies in the six sensory organs and the six spheres of sensory perception, and to withdraw these energies into utter stillness, and then individually release them.

As is said in the "Chapter of Accomplishment" (of *The Abbreviated Kalachakra Tantra*), "In the yoga of individual withdrawal, the vital energies are not allowed to divert into the objects or object perceivers." The meaning is that the currents of energies to the diverse sites of sensory perception and to their objects are severed.

This is also stated in *The Treatise on Severing the Connections:*

> The method is not the simple application of attentive mindfulness [as is the case of the Sutrayana path]. Merely holding the mind in one-pointed concentration upon a mental object is not enough to withdraw the subtle energies from the organs of sensory awareness. Holding the mind on a second object does not have the power to cause (the energies) to withdraw from other activity.

The reason is that a mere mental application is not strong enough to eliminate the activity of the subtle energies in the sensory spheres and so forth.

Therefore in the Kalachakra yogas it is said that one should stimulate the points of the vajra body, causing the vital energies upon which consciousness rides to be diverted into the central channel. Here they enter, abide and dissolve, giving rise to a yogic experience wherein sensory consciousness is turned back from moving toward the sensory objects, and the connections to the individual subjects are severed.

(b) The place for practicing this meditation is an extremely dark room.

(c) As for the time of the practice, it is said that the yoga is to be applied when the earth energies course more strongly in the right nostril. This is a period when one's system is in a natural posture of withdrawal, so to apply the yogas of individual withdrawal at this time easily produces results.

(d) The position in which one should sit to perform the yoga of individual withdrawal is either the vajra or sattva positions. The hands are formed into vajra fists, with the finger knuckles facing upwards and the back of the hands pressed tightly against the two major arteries of the thighs. The elbows are kept tightly against the body and the back totally straight.

One should sit in this position without moving for the entire session, regardless of what pains come into the limbs, eyes, and so forth.

(e) Progress in the yoga of individual withdrawal is accompanied by the ten signs. These must arise inside the abadhuti, the central channel.

As is said in "The Chapter on Wisdom" [of *The Abbreviated Kalachakra Tantra*, by the Shambala kalkin Manju Yashas],

> ...until one sees a black outline emanating stainless light inside the channel of time.

Also *The Great Commentary: A Stainless Light* [by Kalkin Pundarika of Shambala] states, "...until the signs appear in the abadhuti, the channel of time."

Also, the "Chapter on Wisdom" [from *The Abbreviated Kalachakra Tantra*] states, "The signs do not appear externally, such as in the sky. The eyes are partially closed, a glance cast upward, and the signs observed in the central channel."

The Great Commentary adds,

> One glances at the vajra path. When the vital energies enter into the center of this and only emptiness is experienced, one beholds the signs, such as smoke.

The meaning (of this passage) is that by bringing the vital energies into the central channel, holding them there, and then dissolving them, one gradually attains the ten signs of progress, such as smoke.

As said above, the eyes and the mind should focus upon the central channel at the point where it passes through the energy center of the forehead. This is pointed out in the "Chapter on Accomplishment" [of *The Abbreviated Kalachakra Tantra*],

> In the first of the ten yogic applications the yogi performing the propitiation casts the wrathful glance of the wheel bearer. This glance, the destroyer of demons,

enters into the path of nectar and reveals the signs of progress in the six-branched yoga.

The Great Commentary: A Stainless Light adds,

> The (words) 'wheel bearer' refer to the wrathful glance (that the yogi casts) toward the crown protrusion, his eyes partially closed and looking upward. This causes the signs to appear.

Thus during the yogas of individual withdrawal and dhyana the casting of the upward glance is said to be crucial to the practice.

The Great Commentary: A Stainless Light continues,

> . . . in the expression 'the glance that destroys demons,' the destroyer of demons is the (drop of) swirling nectar. The glance moves to the place of the nectar, meaning that it moves toward the forehead chakra.

What this is talking about is the droplet of bodhimind substance, likened to *kunda* nectar, that resides in the central channel at the chakra of the forehead. Casting the glance there means focusing on the site of the droplet of nectar.

The reason for casting the glance at this spot is that by the yogas of individual withdrawal and dhyana one newly produces the empty body and then makes this attainment firm. As said earlier, the drop of the waking state is located at the energy center at the crown, and it is this drop that carries the potencies that give rise to the appearances that characterize the waking state. By focusing on this and entering into meditation, the experiences of the various objects that manifest to the mind on the basis of this drop are severed. When this occurs, images of empty body deities begin to arise at this site.

As for the signs themselves, *The Guhyasamaja Tantra* states,

> The first is like a mirage, the second like smoke, the

third like the flickering of fireflies, the fourth like a
butterlamp and the fifth like the space of clouds. These
are the five signs that appear.

In Kalachakra, the first two signs arise in reversed order.
Also the *Arali Tantra* states,

The eyes are held half closed and a glance cast upward at the point between the eyebrows.

The meaning is that the yogi casts a glance up to the center
of the eyebrows and focuses the mind one-pointedly on the
empty space of the upper aperture of the central channel, thus
concentrating the vital energies.

Here the expression 'mind focused on space' is used. This
'space' refers to that inside the upper aperture of the central
channel. Awareness should not be allowed to wander elsewhere.
The word 'space' here does not suggest that we place the awareness on the nature of external space; it is suggesting something altogether different. This is 'the space inside the upper
aperture.'

(f) (At a later stage in the practice,) when we apply the yogas
of energy control and retention [i.e., the third and fourth of
the Kalachakra six yogas], the vital energies are brought under control and directed into the central channel. This causes
the fires of the mystic heat to blaze upward and to melt the
bodhimind substances, giving rise to great bliss. This consciousness of great bliss then becomes the subjective mind that
is directed into meditation upon the object of suchness.

However, here when we are still in the stages of the first two
yogas—those of individual withdrawal and dhyana—our purpose is solely to newly create a substitute of an empty body,
and then to make that accomplishment firm. It is not to establish a meditation upon suchness as a cause sharing the nature of the dharmakaya, but rather simply to establish a similitude of the empty body.

(g) Many stages of signs appear during the yogas of individual withdrawal and dhyana, beginning with those that arise when one concentrates the energies at the doors of the organs and so forth. At this point in practice, the signs seem to arise in one's meditation hut.

Next one brings the energies into the central channel for the first time. The signs of this experience seem to appear at various places throughout the body, but not inside the central channel itself.

The signs that seem to arise inside the upper aperture itself are those that indicate (progress in the production of) the empty body at the site of the upper aperture.

The scriptures state that four signs arise during the day and six during the night, elucidating the manner of their appearance with certainty. The signs appear consecutively, and the third must arise before the fourth, etc., (for their appearance to be significant). Each stage of yogic experience must be made clear and firm before proceeding to the next.

In the Guhyasamaja yogas the first sign to appear is that like a mirage. In the Kalachakra yogas, however, the first to appear is the smoke-like apparition. There are a number of reasons for this, linked to the place, time and manner in which the specific yogic techniques are applied, and the manner in which the observation (for signs) is made.

In the Kalachakra system, the signs such as smoke and so forth that arise when the yogi begins to newly create the special empty body, arise in the order they do because they signify the successive diversions of the ten energies that flow through the 'petals' of channels that converge at the heart.

First the vital energies passing through the four petals of the four intermediate directions at the heart chakra—the *rupel, tsangpa, lhachin,* and *norlegyal* energies—are successively arrested, beginning with those of the southeast channel and moving around to the northwest 'petal.' From this one experiences the four signs: those of smoke, a mirage, flickering (like that of) fireflies, and a butterlamp. Then beginning in the east and moving around to the west, the energies flowing through the channels of the cardinal directions are arrested. These are the equally abiding, upward-flowing, all-pervading, and lu energies. One perceives the signs that are like (the appearance in the sky of the planet) kalagni, the moon, the sun and (the planet) rahu.

One then cuts off the flow of the life-sustaining and downward-moving energies that course above and below, thus experiencing the signs of lightning and the drop.

This phase of the completion stage yogas, which gives rise to the experience of these signs of controlling the ten energies in the production of the (substitute) empty body, is made possible by the foundations that were laid earlier in the generation stage yoga. This involved the meditation on the eight shaktis, who were contemplated as being in the nature of the knots in the channels at the heart and navel, together with the petals of the chakra of bliss at the navel. In the generation stage yogas (these eight become ten by counting them together with) Kalachakra and Consort, (thus symbolizing the control over all ten energies). Here Kalachakra represents the element of space, and the Consort symbolizes primordial awareness. Their sexual union is the joining of the upper and lower apertures, and the union of the two principal energies.

In this way the generation stage yogas make one into a vessel for the completion stage practices. This meditation upon the ten vital energies of the student as the powerful goddesses is also linked with the initiation of the silk headdress.

At the end of appearance of the ten signs there arises the image of a shimmering black outline, the thickness of a hair, in the drop. This signifies the production of (the basis of) a sambhogakaya form possessed of the five certainties. Here the certain time is at the end of the completion of the arisal of the ten signs, and the certain place is inside the central channel. The certain nature is that this body is not based upon either coarse or subtle atoms but is produced purely by the appearance arising in the mind. The certain body is that of Vajrasattva, the Diamond Being. Finally, the certain aspect is the blissful kiss of the inner male and female forces. Thus the five certainties achieved here are not the same as those discussed in other scriptures.

The form that is created at this level of practice, which gives rise to the ten signs, can be perceived [i.e., the experience of it generated] at any time one so desires. This brings the powers of the yoga to their full capacity, and prepares the yogi for entering into the yoga of dhyana, second of the six completion stage branches.

The reason for practicing the yoga of individual withdrawal in both daily and nightly yogic sessions is that different signs are more easily attained at different times. In the actual stages of practice, for instance, the empty body is said to be more easily attained in darkness and difficult to generate in brightness.

To explain the stages in simple terms, if (the sensory organs of the practitioner are stimulated by) vivid appearances (from the environment) at the time the glance is cast and the observation for signs made, that yogi will not be able to cut off the interfering effects of those appearances. As a result, it is difficult at those times to arise in an empty body form. This interference does not occur in times of darkness.

The measure of accomplishment in this [the yoga of individual withdrawal] is well known from the descriptions found in *The Abbreviated Kalachakra Tantra* and in *The Trilogy of the Bodhisattvas.*

The scripture *The Vajragarbha Commentary* comments that the experience is like a direct sensory perception. At that time the appearance of the five (types of sensory) objects arises directly within the mental consciousness.

2. *The Yoga of Dhyana.* The physical position for performing the yoga of dhyana is as previously explained.

At the time of actual application of this yoga one fills the skies with 'certainties,' such as the various empty body forms that previously appeared in the drop, as well as with 'uncertainties,' such as the symbols and so forth. These are then dissolved into one another, until eventually they all are absorbed by into the sambhogakaya form described above. One establishes special divine pride within this sphere of meditation, until it arises effortlessly. The strength of this is increased, until eventually one's mind spontaneously projects the divine pride marked by complete certainty.

When this achievement has been made firm, the yoga of dhyana is fulfilled and one is ready to enter into the third of the six yogas, that of energy control.

The yoga of dhyana is comprised of five limbs. These are called conceptualization, experience, joy, bliss and one-pointedness.

The meaning of these is given in Naropa's *Commentary to the Treatise on the Initiations:*

> Seeing merely the nature of the coarse empty body
> is conceptualization; seeing deeply into the nature of
> the subtle empty body is experience. The feelings as-
> sociated with the mental consciousness which arises
> from the pliancy of mind thus effected give rise to joy.
> The feelings associated with the physical conscious-
> ness arising from the pliancy of body give rise to bliss.
> Finally, the images of mind that arise in the form of
> Vajrasattva possessing the five certainties are insepara-
> bly mixed with the inner nature of one's own mind,
> giving rise to a consciousness which is an inseparable
> unity of form and consciousness. This is the branch
> of one-pointedness.

The first two of these five branches combine as the practice of vipashyana, or special insight meditation. The last three combine as shamatha, or meditative tranquility. Thus the yoga of dhyana essentially is the samadhi which is the inseparable unity of vipashyana and shamatha, or insight and tranquility.

3. The Yoga of Energy Control. The yoga of energy control is associated with the branch that accomplishes higher energy. In this context the term 'energy' refers to the subtle winds. The meaning of the words 'energy control' is that one arrests the flow of energies moving in the right and left channels.

The reason for engaging in this yoga is that although previously one generated the divine pride of the inseparable nature of one's own mind and the empty bodies beheld in the central channel, the interference of the peripheral energies sustained a sense of distance (between the two). By arresting the movement of these energies one gains the ability to dwell firmly in the unfeigned pride of Vajrasattva's form. Moreover, in addition to the methods previously taught for stimulating the energy centers, here in the yoga of energy control we especially focus on the center of the navel chakra and apply the techniques that ignite the mystic heat, causing it to blaze forth with special strength. It flares up the central channel, melts the substances of bodhimind, and gives rise to an experience of unprecedented great bliss.

A second need for the yoga of energy control is in the work with the life-sustaining and downward-moving energies, and in specific with the process of bringing them to the navel chakra and blending them. This was not accomplished by the earlier yogas. Here we meditate on these two energies, apply the yoga of energy control to them, and effect the blending.

The two main techniques used in the yoga of energy control are the vajra recitation and the vase breathing methods.

The first of these, the technique known as the vajra recitation, which includes the methods for concentrating, retaining and dissolving the vital energies, is as explained in *The Vajrapani Commentary* and so forth.

As for the order (of the two, vajra recitation and vase breathing), one begins by applying the vajra recitation technique until one's essential nature becomes clear and the bodily elements relaxed. This causes the vital energies to flow especially smoothly. One then changes to the meditation upon vase breathing.

Concerning the manner of application of the vajra recitation technique, some Tibetan yogis have said that when the breath energies flow evenly through both nostrils it should be visualized as entering into the two side channels and also the central channel. They advise that it should then be visualized as entering, abiding, and dissolving in the form of the three letters *oṃ, hūṃ* and *āḥ*. There is also talk of how vajra recitation focused successively on each of the three main energy channels are the vajra recitations of vajra body, vajra speech, and vajra mind. None of this is particularly meaningful.

In our tradition, the vajra recitation of the three mantric syllables is as explained in *The Commentary to the Praise of Chakrasamvara* and also in (Naropa's) *A Commentary to the Treatise on the Initiations*. Here when one meditates upon the yoga of energy control one casts the glance eliminating demons, and watches for the metaphoric and certain signs as explained previously in the yoga of individual withdrawal. One observes the empty body images unified with the vital energies.

At the time the energies enter inside (i.e., as you inhale), meditate that the energies arise with the vibrance of the syllable *oṃ*. This is brought to the chakra at the forehead, at the center of which abides the empty body that was previously produced through the first two yogas. These are then brought down to the navel chakra, at the center of the dhuti.

At the time the energies abide [that is, when the breath pauses between inhalation and exhalation], meditate that the energies arise with the vibrance of *hūṃ*. This and the empty body together are brought to rest at the center of the navel chakra.

Then as the energies are released [i.e., when you exhale] meditate that the energies arise with the vibrance of the syllable *āḥ*. The strength of the flowing energies causes the empty body to move up the path of the central channel to the upper aperture.

If one meditates repeatedly in this way, the inhalation and exhalation periods gradually decrease in length and the periods of retention increase until one eventually is able to retain the application of the empty body and the vital energies inside the dhuti at the navel chakra for prolonged periods of time. Finally one gains the power of completely cutting off the flow of energy [i.e., breath] passing through the nostrils, and is able to abide unwaveringly in meditation at the center of the navel. This marks the boundary wherein the yoga of energy control has been taken to fulfillment. One is now ready to proceed to the vase breathing technique. From this point onward, whenever the energies (and breath) move, one should see them as flowing inside the central channel itself.

As for the method of applying the vase breathing technique, this is as follows. The life-sustaining and downward-moving energies are brought to the lower aperture of the central channel, and to the center of the navel chakra. Here with the force of the mind they enter the drop that carries the potencies inducing the experience of sexual ecstasy. These two energies, together with one's own mind and the special empty body, are blended into one taste, and this state of consciousness is carefully maintained. One then meditates on vase breathing. This is what is meant by the scriptural passage,

> The energies that course above and below
> Are brought together in a kiss of the mind.

Meditating in this way, one forms a vase with the energies and ignites the fires of mystic heat inside the central channel at the navel chakra. This gives rise to the four joys descending from above (induced by the descent of the drop through the four principal chakras). When one has achieved the power to generate this experience at will, the yoga of energy control has been fulfilled. One should then engage the yoga of retention.

4. The Yoga of Retention. The meditations that constitute the yoga of retention employ the vase breathing technique in much the same way as it was utilized in the previous yoga.

As for the place and the stages of the practice, firstly the place is explained.

Here it is said (that to establish the environment of the practice) one begins with the meditation of dissolving the elements in the manner they dissolve at death. Firstly inside the central channel or dhuti at the heart chakra, as the earth element dissolves into water; then inside the throat chakra, as water dissolves into fire; next inside the forehead chakra, as fire dissolves into air; then inside the crown chakra, as air dissolves into the space element; and finally inside the center of the chakra at the secret place, as space dissolves into wisdom. At each of these sites one meditates within the framework of the experience of the inseparable nature of two principal energies, the mind, and the empty body, as was done in the previous yoga. Practicing in this way one eventually achieves the ability to move the vase-like collection (of energies, mind and the empty body) to each of the chakras, and to retain it at these sites. One also achieves the ability to induce the four joys of (the drop) ascending from below. At this time one should focus in meditation upon bliss and emptiness in inseparable union.

As a preliminary to this stage of endeavor one generates the strong thought, "I myself will arise in the form of Kalachakra and Consort." The force of this determination activates the predispositions on the mind for arising in an empty body form or its similitude.

The presentation of the Kalachakra yoga of retention is similar to that of the clear light yoga as found in other tantric systems such as Guhyasamaja. However, its unique features here involve the extraordinary methods of separating the drop of the four occasions from obscurations. One should understand these well.

When one has achieved the ability to blend at one time the two main energies, one's mind and the empty body, into an inseparable entity inside each of the six chakras, and to retain the object of meditation [i.e., the threefold collection] at will, the yoga of retention has been carried to fulfillment. One is now ready to engage in the yoga of subsequent mindfulness.

5. *The Yoga of Subsequent Mindfulness.* The yoga of subsequent mindfulness, also known as 'vajra mind yoga,' is associated with the branch for producing bliss.

The etymology of its name is given in *The Great Commentary: A Stainless Light,*

The scripture [*The Abbreviated Kalachakra Tantra*] states, "One first recollects the image of the form, and then secondly applies a mindfulness to it. Thus there are said to be two." The meaning of this passage is that there are two mindfulnesses, one applied first to the image of the empty body previously accomplished, and then a second kind that comes later.

(To say something about each of these two:) Earlier when practicing the yoga of dhyana we produced a similitude of the empty body; this was the first (object of) mindfulness to be cultivated. After that one achieves a more qualified empty body; this is the second (object of) mindfulness.

In the latter phase of the yoga of retention one arose in the form of a sensual empty body deity in union with consort, and achieved the power to effortlessly establish divine pride. The sensual empty body 'Male and Consort' deities filled the universe with luminosity emanated forth from their pore apertures, and then entered into union. However, this did not give rise to the unchanging bliss. Therefore the attainment remained on the level of a similitude of an empty body.

One persists in the meditation until the mind spontaneously arises in the empty body form of Kalachakra and Consort. This causes lights to emanate forth from one's pores, arousing the desire of the empty body mahamudra deities, such as the multicolored consort and the ten powerful goddesses. One then practices sexual union with these mahamudra empty body deities and achieves the unchanging great bliss. When one has achieved the full power of this mudra inducing the unchanging bliss, the yoga of subsequent mindfulness has been fulfilled.

As for this practice, *The Abbreviated Kalachakra Tantra* [by Manju Yashas of Shambala] and also (its principal commentary) *The Great Commentary: A Stainless Light* [by Pundarika of Shambala] lists four types of mudras: karmamudra (action seal), jnanamudra (wisdom seal), mahamudra (great seal) and samayamudra (commitment seal).

The first three of these give rise to the unchanging bliss; the fourth mudra is explained as the bliss that arises in dependence on what was accomplished by the former three.

Karmamudra is explained as the practice performed with a maiden possessing the physical attributes of a woman, such as beautiful hair and so forth, with whom one has a strong karmic link. Here the maiden herself has the ability to induce the full experience by means of her skillful embrace, without reliance on the powers of meditation.

Jnanamudra is a maiden created through the power of one's own mental projection.

As for the mahamudra, this refers to the empty bodies that actually arise as consorts from the appearances within one's own mind.

One relies upon (one of) these three types of mudra, and when the experience of bliss arises it causes the bodhimind substances abiding in the upper sites to descend. They come to the tip of the jewel, where they are retained and are not allowed to slip away, change or to move (to other sites).

Concerning these terms (of falling, moving and changing bliss arising from the movement of the drops), *The Great Commentary: A Stainless Light* states,

> Karmamudra is the maiden who gives the falling bliss.
> Jnanamudra is the maiden who gives the moving bliss.
> Mahamudra is the maiden who gives the unchanging bliss.

How is this so? If the yogi is unable to control the movement of the drops solely through the power of meditation, he takes up the practice of karmamudra. Because the karmamudra gives him the power to direct the vital substances to the tip of the jewel, she is called 'the maiden who bestows the falling bliss.'

Union with the jnanamudra causes the drops to fall from the upper energy centers to the tip of the jewel; but as they cannot be retained motionlessly, they are directed through various other points of the body. Thus she is called 'the maiden who brings the moving bliss.'

One sits in union with the mahamudra, which causes the substances to melt and come to the tip of the jewel. Not only are these to be prevented from slipping; they must also be prevented from flowing into other sites. Thus it is said, 'the maiden who brings unchanging bliss.'

The yogis who actually arise within the empty body of Kalachakra and Consort are of three types: sharp, middling, and dull.

The first of these rely exclusively upon mahamudra. They are able to experience the unchanging great bliss solely through union with her. The second must first rely upon jnanamudra to generate a basis of bliss through which they are able to enter into mahamudra.

Practitioners in the third category, i.e., those of dull capacity, must first rely upon a karmamudra, or actual physical consort, in order to induce the experience of bliss. Only then can they proceed to the mahamudra.

In this way, all three types of yogis eventually come to the mahamudra. They enter into sexual union directly with the mahamudra; the drop of white substances that abides in the crown in the form of a syllable *ham* is caused to melt and fall to the chakra at the tip of the jewel. Simultaneously, the red drop moves to the energy center at the crown. The two substances are then retained and are not allowed to change to other sites [i.e., to move to other chakras]. The presence of the two drops in the two chakras is made firm until the supremely unchanging bliss is experienced. The first time this unchanging bliss arises from the stabilized presence (of the two drops in the two chakras, in reverse placement), is the border demarcating the fulfillment of the yoga of subsequent mindfulness. One is now ready to move on to the sixth yoga, that of samadhi.

6. *The Yoga of Samadhi.* When one thus simultaneously brings the white and red substances to the tip of the jewel and chakras of the crown protrusion [i.e., one brings the white drop down to the tip of the sexual organ and the red drop up to

the crown], and retains them there with stability, this gives rise to a momentary flash of stabilized bliss. Of the 21,600 factors which make up our coarse form, one is dissolved. Simultaneously, of the 21,600 karmic energies coursing through the nostrils, one part of (one of the twelve sets of) 1,800 are halted.

When (in the first set) 1,800 experiences of bliss have been fulfilled and 1,799 of the vital drops piled up, one attains to the 'great supreme dharma' stage of the path of application [i.e., the fourth and final stage of the second level of the path to enlightenment]. A further one part of the 1,800 such moments places one on the stage of an arya, the path of direct vision [third level of the five paths to enlightenment].

If in this way one can draw 21,600 (white) male drops, the supports of bliss, to the tip of the jewel, and stack them in a stable column that extends up to the crown chakra, and if one also can bring 21,600 red drops up and form them into a red column beginning at the crown (chakra) and extending down to the tip of the jewel, on the basis of each of the (21,600 sets of red and white drops) one experiences a moment of stabilized bliss. In this way 21,600 moments of 'supported' unchanging bliss arise. Each of these cuts off one part of the 21,600 karmic winds, and this in turn causes the utter dissolution of one of the 21,600 factors of the physical body.

One's form aggregate, together with the elements and objects connected with it, becomes freed from obscuration. One transcends all obscurations to knowledge and simultaneously in this very lifetime attains the state of enlightenment in the aspect of the Primordial Buddha Kalachakra.

The Abbreviated Kalachakra Tantra states,

> When one realizes the body, speech and mind produced by the path of the Kalachakra yogas, one's body transcends ordinary substantiality, becomes as clear and lucent as the sky, and manifests all the major and minor signs of perfection. One's mind fills with supreme bliss and enters into an eternal embrace with the innately unmoving wisdom.

The meaning here is that the Kalachakra yogi accomplishes enlightenment in one lifetime in such a way that his or her body attains the characteristics of the form of Kalachakra and Consort, a vast empty body adorned with all the marks and signs of perfection, a body similar to space itself. It is 'clear and lucent' because it is intangible and immaterial, being empty of a mundane atomic structure.

This is the bodily attainment. As for the mental attainment, its essential nature is compassion arising as the supreme, unmoving, unchanging bliss locked in eternal union with the one taste of wisdom perceiving the emptiness of non-inherent existence, the 'emptiness without characteristics.'

When in this way the body and mind are experienced as an inseparable entity based on the supporting empty body and the supported wisdom of unchanging bliss, this is what is meant by 'Primordial Kalachakra.' From amongst the branches of the six-branched yoga of the Kalachakra system, it represents the sixth yoga, that of samadhi.

In the Kalachakra literature one sees a lot of discussion focused on the topics of 'emptiness with characteristics,' and 'true emptiness without characteristics.'

In the first of these, the mind directly perceiving the empty body arises within an appreciation of a subtle light of dual appearance. It is nonetheless called 'emptiness' because in it the object of negation, the coarse and subtle atomic structure of the body, has been eliminated, and is altogether empty of physical matter.

In the second case [i.e., emptiness without characteristics], this refers to the mind directly perceiving the emptiness of its object of negation, namely, the emptiness of inherent existence. Because that mind has reversed all dual appearance, it is called 'without characteristics.'

Thus (in the Kalachakra tradition) the discussion of the empty body as explained above, wherein the wisdom of emptiness is brought into one taste with supreme, unchanging great bliss, is a substitute for the clear light and illusory body doctrines found in the other highest yoga tantra systems [that is, the empty body substitutes for the illusory body doctrine, and the one-tasteness of unchanging bliss and wisdom substitutes for the clear light doctrine]. The assembling of these two [i.e., the empty body and the unchanging bliss absorbed in the wisdom of emptiness] within the stream of one's body and mind, substitutes for the Great Union (of the clear light and illusory body) spoken of in the other highest yoga tantras.

In Kalachakra, however, the yogi goes through twelve successive levels [Tib., *sa*], known as the 'twelve Kalachakra stages,' each of which is comprised of a series of extraordinary events. On each of these twelve stages one undergoes 1,800 (moments of) the wisdom of bliss and emptiness, which arise from 1,800 experiences of unchanging bliss. These arrest 1,800 subtle energy currents, cause 1,800 (of the 21,600) factors of the physical body to dematerialize, and eliminate 1,800 delusions [i.e., the 'share' of that particular 'level']. At the same time one stacks 1,800 drops.

The complete presence of one set of 1,800 factors constitutes one of the twelve Kalachakra stages [*sa*] leading to enlightenment. Traversing all twelve of the stages means that 21,600 of each of the factors have been experienced.

In brief, first one establishes the empty body of male and consort at the (chakra of) the secret place, and then stage by stage brings it up through the other chakras, from the navel to the crown.

With the exception of the doctrine of the empty body, the Kalachakra presentation of the manner of traversing the paranormal stages of the path is quite like the presentation found in the *Lam Drey*[17] teaching [of the Sakya school of Tibetan Buddhism].

> O hark!
> This brief treatise on the six yogas
> Of Primordial Buddha Kalachakra's completion stage
> Draws from the ancient Indian scriptures
> And presents their thought without error.

Requested by several of my disciples,
I, Gendun Druppa, wrote it to stimulate my mind;
And to express my respect for the practice
And teachings of the great yogis of old.
May it benefit those of a similar predisposition.

May any small merits that it has
Cause living beings to enter the Diamond Vehicle;
That they may be filled with the glory
Of supreme bliss and the wisdom of emptiness, and
Attain to the state of Primordial Buddha Kalachakra.

The Colophon: Written by Gendun Druppa, a minor disciple
of the omniscient master Pakpa Yonten Gyatso.

18 A Kalachakra Guruyoga Method

by Kyabjey Khangsar Dorjey Chang (1888-1941)[1]

Namo guru kālachakra bhyah

Herein lies a spiritual method capable of inspiring every happiness and spiritual quality, a guruyoga meditation focusing upon glorious Kalachakra.

(The Preliminaries)

Begin by constructing a clear visualization of the objects of refuge. Then as a preliminary to the actual meditation upon the spiritual master as inseparably one in nature with glorious Kalachakra, recite the verse for turning the mind to refuge and for arousing the compassionate bodhimind, and the verse of the four boundless thoughts [of compassion, love, joy and equaminity]:

> To the Buddhas, the Dharma, and the Sangha
> I turn for refuge until enlightenment is gained.
> By the merits of my practices, such as the six
>   perfections,
> May buddhahood be attained for the sake of all. *(3x)*

May all sentient beings have happiness and its causes;
May they be free of suffering and its causes;
May they never be separated from that happiness which
is without suffering;
And may they be free from attraction to the near and
aversion to the far. *(3x)*

(The Actual Meditation)

In the sky before me
Is a lion-throne of precious substances.
There, on cushions of lotus, sun, moon,
And the planets rahu and kalagni,
Is the embodiment of all refuge objects,
My root guru in the form of glorious Kalachakra,
Body blue in color, having one face,
His two hands holding a vajra and a bell.

Sexually embracing his consort Vishvamata,
He stands in the posture of haughtiness,
His two feet trampling a white and a red deity.
White *om* marks his crown, red *āh* his throat
And blue *hūm* his heart.

Lights emanate from *hūm* at his heart.
They invite all objects of refuge: Gurus,
Meditational Deities, Buddhas, Bodhisattvas,
Shravaka Arhants, Pratyekabuddhas,
Dakas, Dakinis and Dharma Protectors.
These are absorbed into the two, and they become
In nature all three objects of refuge
Collected into one entity.

In deep respect I pay homage with all three doors;
All material and mentally created things I offer;
I acknowledge every negativity and failing
Accumulated since beginninglessness;

And in the goodness of both ordinary beings
And transcended masters I rejoice.
O masters, remain in samsara until it is emptied
And turn the wheel of knowledge.
Pray, firmly stay until the end of the world.
All goodness I dedicate to the peerless enlightenment.

The body, speech and mind of both myself and others,
Our wealth and our masses of goodness
Of the past, present and future,
And the precious mandala of Mount Meru and so
    forth,
Together with Samantabhadra's peerless offerings,
I mentally claim and offer (as a mandala)
To the Gurus, Meditational Deities and Three Precious
    Gems;
Out of compassion please accept them
And bestow upon me your transforming powers.

Now recite the name mantra [in this case, of His Holiness
the Dalai Lama] as many times as possible: *oṃ āḥ guru vajradhara vāgindra sumati śhāsanadhara samudra shrībhadra sarva
siddhi hūṃ hūṃ.*[2]

O rain of benefits and spiritual happiness,
King of jewels, *chittamani*, fulfiller of wishes,
To you, teacher and meditational deity,
All sources of power combined,
I make this request.
Inspire the stream of my being
With your transforming powers and blessings.

By the strength of this single-pointed request,
The constantly sympathetic one
Comes to the crown of my head
And dissolves into me. I myself become glorious
    Kalachakra,
With all faces and arms.

(The Kalachakra Mantric Recitation)

At your heart visualize either a sun-disc bearing the letter *hūm,* or else a moon-disc bearing the syllable 'Possessed of Ten Powers.' In either case these are encircled by the *mantramala.*

As you recite the mantra, visualize that light-rays go out from these, accomplish the two purposes (of self and others), and then collect together and dissolve back into the mantramala.

The mantra to be recited is as follows: *oṃ āḥ hūṃ hoḥ hamkshahmalavaraya hūṃ phaṭ.*[3]

(The Concluding Prayer)

> By the meritorious energy of this practice,
> May I never become separated from
> But in life after life be cared for by
> The spiritual masters and meditational deities,
> And have the fortune to attain the supreme path.
>
> By having full confidence in the kind masters,
> The foundation of all joy and goodness,
> Source of every spiritual attainment,
> May I delight them with the offerings
> Of respect, service, and effective practice.
>
> The opportunities of a human form—
> So meaningful, hard to gain and easily lost;
> The sufferings of the lower realms—
> So intense and long-lasting:
> Knowing this may I live in accord
> With karmic law and the precepts of refuge
> By constantly living within the guideline
> Of transcending the negative and cultivating the good.
>
> No need to speak of the misery of the lower realms,
> Even the pleasures of the higher worlds

262 *The Practice of Kalachakra*

Are little more than honey on a razor's edge.
In order to gain liberation from this round of
    becoming,
May I establish within myself the three higher trainings
Of discipline, meditative concentration and wisdom,
And then increase their forces evermore.

May I always dwell within the compassionate
    bodhimind,
The aspiration for enlightenment to benefit the world,
And diligently train in the bodhisattva ways—
The six perfections and four means of benefiting—
And quickly complete the collections of merit and
    wisdom.

Having thus trained the mind
In the fundamental practices of exoteric Mahayana
And properly entered into the gateway of the peerless
    Vajrayana
By receiving the appropriate initiations,
May I honor the tantric precepts and commitments
As deeply as I cherish my very life.

Whenever preconceptions of mundane appearance
    arise,
They should be transformed into the wisdom of bliss
    and emptiness.
May I single-pointedly practice to fulfillment
The central concept of tantra's two yogic stages,
This ear-whispered lineage of the great mystery.

May I come before the sublime countenance
Of the illustrious Lord of Shambala in the
Wondrous land of purity, and quickly actualize
The state of great union, the inseparability
Of the empty body male-and-consort
And the unchanging great bliss.

In the future, during the ripened era of
Raudra Chakri, 'The Wrathful Holder of the Wheel,'
May I take birth amongst the foremost disciples
And complete the sublime path of the Primordial
    Kalachakra,
Becoming a supreme adept, a friend to all.

May I never ever be separated from the spiritual
    masters;
May I always have access to their enlightenment
    teachings;
May I accomplish the ten stages and five paths
And quickly attain the state of Buddha Vajradhara.

The merits of having engaged in this practice
I turn into causes for the fulfillment of the deeds
And prayers of the buddhas and bodhisattvas,
And to the upholding of Dharma, scriptural and
    insight.

The colophon: This [Tibetan] text is one of ten thousand printed for free distribution at the Kalachakra initiation given by His Holiness the Dalai Lama in Ladakh in 1976, and was adapted from the short guruyoga method composed by Kyabjey Khangsar Dorjey Chang.

19 The Best of Jewels
A Sadhana Focusing on Glorious Kalachakra
by the Buddhist Monk
Buton Rinchen Druppa (1290-1364)

Homage to Kalachakra, glorious Wheel of Time.

With body, speech and mind, I signal respect
To the masters inseparable from Kalachakra,
Who have transcended all imperfections.
To repay their kindness I herein will compose
A brief summary of the Kalachakra sadhana,
The meditation methods of the generation stage yogas.

The practitioner of this sadhana (should be someone who has) received the Kalachakra initiation, and who has managed to maintain the major precepts and commitments. He or she should place a comfortable meditation cushion in an appropriate place of practice, one having all the recommended conditions.

Before commencing the practice, rinse the mouth with a sip of water infused with a sacred *dutsi rilbu* pill.[1] Then sit on your meditation seat and contemplate as follows.

Visualize that you instantly appear as glorious Kalachakra, a lotus and moon seat at your heart, the syllable *hūṃ* standing upon it. *Hūṃ* becomes a vajra that radiates with blazing lights.

These lights summon forth the buddhas and bodhisattvas of the ten directions. They come in the form of Kalachakra mandala deities.

Contemplate that you bow to them in respect. Then from your heart there emanate forth the twelve offering goddesses, who hold up the various offering substances to the assembly of holy beings. They sing the following verse:

> Homage to the supreme Kalachakra mandala,
> Which is beyond qualification and preconceptions,
> An object of refuge to the greatest of beings.

Offer prostrations; send forth vast offerings; acknowledge all personal failings and shortcomings; and without any feelings of envy rejoice in the creative energies and enlightened ways of the buddhas, bodhisattvas and host of transcended beings.

Next offer the following thought, and reflect on its meaning:

> In order personally to achieve sublime
>   enlightenment
> I turn for refuge to the Buddhas, the Dharma and
>   the Sangha.
> In order to benefit all living beings
> I myself will achieve their most exalted state.

Recite the mantra of emptiness. Recollect how both the world as vessel and the living beings as inhabitants of that vessel, and in fact all phenomena, have the nature of emptiness. That emptiness possesses the quality of being beyond the limits of coarse or subtle matter.

Oṃ śhūnyatā jñāna vajra svabhāvātmako 'ham. Everything becomes a vast expanse of emptiness. From within emptiness appears a vast *dharmodaya*, a reality source, in nature space.

Inside this appears the syllable *yaṃ*. It transforms into an air mandala, black in color, shaped like a bow, and marked by victory banners. Above this is the syllable *raṃ*. It becomes a fire mandala, red in color, triangular, marked by the auspicious signs (svastikas). Above this is the syllable *vaṃ*. It becomes a water mandala, white in color, marked by lotuses. Finally, above this the syllable *laṃ* transforms into an earth mandala, yellow, square in shape, marked by vajras.

Above and below everything, from syllables of *hūṃ*, appear two crossed vajras. Above this appears the syllable *maṃ*. It transforms into Mount Meru, its width sixteen thousand yojanas at the base and fifty thousand at the top. At the center, half that size, stands the syllable *kṣhaṃ*. It becomes a lotus, its stamen marked by *haṃ*. This becomes a moon disc. The *tsek drak* (*visarga*)[2] becomes a sun disc, and the drop becomes (the planet) Rahu.

These all mix together, emerging as the mantric sounds *haṃ-kṣha-ma-la-va-ra-ya*.

One then repeats the above process, from the generation of the air mandala until "the drop becomes (the planet) Rahu."

Above all of these visualized objects the syllable *hūṃ* becomes a vajra tent, inside of which stands the syllable *bhrūṃ*. This transforms into the inconceivable celestial mansion, square in shape, having four entrances, four archways, and possessing all the features in their completeness.

At the center of the inconceivable mansion stands the syllable *oṃ*. It becomes a variegated lotus, the syllables *aṃ, aḥ* and *a* standing upon it. These become the moon, sun and Rahu discs, stacked one above the other.

The thirty-two vowels appear, and become moon discs marked by the thirty-two vowels.[3]

Also, the eighty consonants appear and become sun discs marked by the eighty consonants.[3]

At the center of the moon disc is a syllable *hūm*, like the mark (i.e., outline) in the moon.

These three all merge into one, and there emerges life-sustaining energy, possessing a syllable *hī*. From this there emerges consciousness, possessing a syllable *ham*.

From this appears glorious Kalachakra, complete in all features, radiating with the five lights.

His body is blue in color, and he has three necks: the center one blue, the right red, and the left white.

His main face is black. It is ferocious and reveals bared fangs. The right face is red and has a lustful expression. The face behind is yellow, and is in the gaze of meditation. The face on the left is white and is utterly peaceful.

All four faces have three eyes. They wear headdresses having a crossed vajra, a half moon and Vajrasattva as crown ornament.

Kalachakra is adorned with vajra jewels, vajra earrings, a vajra necklace, vajra bracelets, a vajra belt, vajra anklets, a vajra shawl, and a vajra chain. A tiger skin hangs freely as his loin cloth.

The first shoulder on both the right and left is blue, the second red, and the third white. Thus he has six shoulders. These branch out to become twelve upper arms. Each of these then branches out to become two arms and hands.

Thus he has twenty-four arms. Of these, the first set of four on both right and left are black; the next set of four is red; and the third set of four is white.

As for the fingers, on each hand the thumb is yellow, the index finger white, the middle finger red, the ring finger black, and the little finger green. The [skin on the inside of the fingers between] the joints is black, red and white, respectively [from base to tip]. His hands are also adorned with numerous rings, and he radiates with light.

In the first of the four black hands on the right is a vajra; in the second a sword; in the third a trident; and in the fourth a curved knife.

In the first of the four red hands are three arrows; in

the second a vajra hook; in the third a damaru drum reverberant with sound; and in the fourth a hammer.

In the first of the four white hands is a wheel; in the second a spear; in the third a club; and in the fourth a battle axe.

In the first of the four black hands on the left is a bell with a vajra handle; in the second a shield; in the third a katvanga; and in the fourth a skull cup filled with blood.

In the first of the four red hands is a bow; in the second a vajra noose; in the third a jewel; and in the fourth a white lotus.

In the first of the four white hands is a conch shell; in the second a mirror; in the third vajra chains; and in the fourth the head of Brahma, with four faces and adorned by flowers.

He stands dramatically on a seat made of (cushions representing the celestial bodies of) the sun, moon, rahu [and kalagni], with his right leg outstretched.

With his right foot, which is red, he presses down on red Kamadeva, who has one face and four arms, and holds five flower arrows, a bow, a noose and a hook.

Kalachakra's left foot, white in color, presses down on white Rudra, who has one face, three eyes, and four arms. He holds a trident, a damaru hand-drum, a skull cup, and a katvanga. Rati and Uma, Mara's (or Kamadeva's) and Rudra's devis, gaze plaintively as they pull up on (Kalachakra's) feet.

Then visualize Kalachakra's consort, Vishvamata, who is sexually embracing him from in front. She is yellow in color, and has four faces. These are yellow, white, blue and red in color, respectively. Each head has three eyes.

She has eight hands, of which the four on the right hold a curved knife, a hook, a damaru resounding rhythmically, and a counting mala. The four on the left hold a skull cup, a noose, a white lotus in ful! bloom, and a jewel.

Vajrasattva is her crown ornament, and she is adorned with the five mudras. Standing with her left leg outstretched, she sexually embraces Kalachakra with great passion. Meditate in that way.

The sounds of joy of the male and female in sexual union summon the buddhas and bodhisattvas, together with their consorts. They dissolve into your body [into you as Kalachakra], and reappear as drops.

They enter the womb of the consort, and then are issued forth. These become the mandala deities, with Akshobhya Buddha as principal figure. Akshobhya remains as the principal figure, and the others take their respective places in the mandala. Meditate like that.

One then summons all sentient beings to the mandala. The initiation of the bodhimind substances transforms them into divinities, transmuting their aggregates, elements, sensory powers and essential nature into those of a tantric deity. They become the thirty-two symbols, and are sent to their respective sites (in the mandala).

One concludes by reciting the following mantra: *oṃ suviśhuddha dharmadhātu svabhāvātmako 'haṃ.*

This is the phase of the generation stage practice known as 'the supremely victorious mandala.'

One then establishes the mantric syllables at their appropriate bodily sites: *oṃ* at the forehead; *āḥ* at the throat; *hūṃ* at the heart; and *hoḥ* at both the navel and the crown of the head.

The sexual union of Male and Consort causes the mystic heat at the navel, represented by the syllable *hoḥ*, to blaze forth. The Male and Consort themselves are dissolved, and become drops.

The devis, such as Lochana and so forth, then call out to them, "You who have transcended all faults and possess every perfection, you hold the power to benefit limitless sentient beings. I request you, come forth and work your benefits for the world. O great vajra master, fulfill the wishes of the spiritual aspirants."

When this request has been heard, the drop transforms into a [blue] *hūṃ,* which then transforms into a vajra. From that there emerges glorious Kalachakra and Consort. Visualize them here as was described earlier, but in particular with Akshobhya as the crown ornament.

The joyous sounds of their sexual union summon the buddhas, bodhisattvas and their retinues. These dissolve into one's body [visualized as Kalachakra] and melt into drops. As before the mantric seed syllables of the deities appear, transform into symbols, and eventually become the mandala deities, who are sent to their appropriate abodes in the mandala.

One makes the hooking mudra; utters *jah*, and Vajra Force manifests. The wisdom beings are summoned in front and offerings made to them. *Hūṃ*: one makes the vajra mudra, and the Devourer effects entering; *vaṃ*: one makes the noose mudra, and the Petrifier effects the binding; *hoh*: one makes the bell mudra, and the Uplifter effects utter fulfillment. *Hī*: one makes the club mudra, and Great Strength causes the symbolic beings and the wisdom beings to become of one taste.[4] Buddha Akshobhya appears as a crown above Kalachakra's head. The consort's crown becomes adorned with Vajrasattva.

The syllables *oṃ, āh, hūṃ* and *hoh* seal the sites at the forehead, throat, heart and navel.

The syllable *a* at the forehead becomes a moon disc marked by the syllable *oṃ*. This becomes a wheel, which becomes white Vajra Form, in union with his consort. His body is white in color, with a white, a black and a red face. He has six arms, and in the three hands on the right he holds a wheel, a vajra and a lotus. In the three on the left he holds a sword, a bell and a jewel.

He teaches the Dharma to the trainees of vajra body nature, and then returns and comes in front. "Oh Vajra Form, please bestow initiation upon me."

When this request has been heard, the devis of bodily nature pronounce the mantra *oṃ ā ī ṛi ū ḷi pañchadhātu viśhodhani svāhā* and bestow initiation with waters from

their vases. All vajra form is absorbed into the moon disc
at my forehead.

The holder of the glorious Vajra Form
Meditated on the three inseparable vajras
Hence through the Holder of Vajra Form
May I receive transforming blessings.

The buddhas abiding in the ten directions
Meditated on the inseparable three vajras.
Hence through the Buddha of Vajra Form
May I receive transforming blessings.

Meditate that in this way your body becomes in nature
the holy Vajra Form.

Now at the throat the syllable *ra* becomes a sun disc
marked by *āḥ*. This becomes a lotus, which transforms into
red Vajra Speech, with a red, a white and a black face.
He has six arms, of which the three on the right hold a lotus,
a vajra and a wheel, and the three on the left hold a jewel,
a bell and a sword.

He is emanated forth, together with his wisdom lady.

He teaches to the trainees of Vajra Speech, and so forth
(as with Vajra Body); until the phase of receiving the
initiation. Then all of vajra speech is absorbed into the
sun disc at one's throat.

One then repeats the same two verses as above, merely
replacing the words Vajra Form with Vajra Speech. Think
that your speech has become of one nature with the holy
Vajra Speech.

Then at the heart appears a drop. It becomes a disc
(representing the planet) Rahu, the syllable *hūṃ* standing
above it. This becomes a five-spoked vajra, which in turn
becomes black Vajra Mind. His three faces are black, red
and white in color, and he has six arms. In his three right
hands he holds a vajra, a wheel and a lotus. In his three
left he holds a bell, a sword and a jewel.

He emanates forth, together with his knowledge lady.

One continues as earlier, in the section on Vajra Form, simply exchanging the word "mind" for "form."

Conclude by meditating that your mind has become of one nature with the holy Vajra Mind.

Now especially turn your attention to the syllable *hoḥ* at the navel, *svā* at the secret place, and *hā* at the crown of the head. Consecrate the sites, and hold the pride of being the three vajras brought into one. Recite the following mantra: *oṃ sarva tathāgata kāya vāk chitta svabhāvātmako 'haṃ*. One then recites the lines revealing the pure nature symbolized by the mandala and its inhabitants, and reflects upon these pristine qualities symbolized by the mandala:

> The pure nature of time is (symbolized by) the glorious Vajra Holder, lord of men, with the divisions of years, months and so forth;
>
> The pure nature of the enlightened mind is (symbolized by) Vishvamata, who represents not the sun itself, but (the sun's) effect of daily cycles.
>
> (To symbolize) the purifications of delusions, Rudra and consort bow at the feet of all-pervading Kalachakra, as do the hosts of maras.
>
> Those (suchness natures), symbolized by the implements of the master, by the power of natural perfection mark the spheres of perception as external mudras.
>
> The [three] vajras (symbolize) the inner mudras abiding on a moon at the heart of the Vajra Holder.
>
> Finally, the three existential qualities of the glorious Vajra Holder and Vishvamata in union (symbolize) the unchanging wisdom.

This completes the phase of the generation stage meditation known as 'the supreme activity practice.'

Next one visualizes mantric syllables on the bodies of both Male and Consort: *oṃ* at the forehead, *āḥ* at the throat, *hūṃ* at the heart, *hoḥ* at the navel, *svā* at the secret place, and *hā* at the crown.

The Male's sexual organ, the syllable *hūṃ*, becomes a vajra. This is marked by a lotus transformed from the syllable *āḥ*.

In the sexual space of the Consort appears the syllable *āḥ* which becomes a lotus. This is marked by a vajra transformed from the syllable *hūṃ*.

Visualize that the Male and Consort enter into sexual union. The fires of mystic heat at the navel ignite. From the syllable *haṃ* the bodhichitta substances melt and fall. The droplet comes downward (through the four chakras), giving rise to the experience of the four downward-moving joys.

Meditating in this way is the yoga of the drop [i.e., third of the four generation stage yogas].

This droplet then moves back up the course by which it had descended, beginning at the secret center and then ascending up to the navel, heart and throat; the drops of body, speech, mind and primordial wisdom.

At the crown as the stainless drop it emanates the mandala of tantric deities.

Light rays radiate forth from the drops of body, speech, mind and primordial wisdom. They purify the body, speech and mind of all the living beings, who then manifest as deities of the mandala.

Meditating like this is the practice of subtle yoga [i.e., fourth of the four generation stage yogas].

Now from the drop at the heart there emanates forth the mantras. These possess the five light rays. They descend to the vajra of the male and enter into the lotus of the consort, rising up inside her body and eventually coming to her mouth. They pass into the mouth of the male and dissolve into the drop.

Now one recites the essence and near-essence mantras of Kalachakra, and the principal mantra of the consort. Firstly, those of Kalachakra:

oṃ āḥ hūṃ hoḥ haṃ-kṣha-ma-la-va-ra-ya hūṃ phaṭ.
oṃ hrāṃ hrīṃ hṛīṃ hrūṃ hṛīṃ hraḥ hūṃ phaṭ.

The mantra of Vishvamata:

om phrem viśhvamātā hūm phaṭ.

One should recite each of these three mantras in turn as much as possible. When this recitation has been completed one visualizes that from one's heart there emanate forth the twelve offering devis. They make their individual offerings.[5]

The offering devis hold up their individual offerings, and maidens offer unchanging bliss. One then sends forth the verse of praise:

I bow to the glorious Kalachakra,
Whose nature is compassion and emptiness,
Without birth or death in the three worlds,
In one form both mind and objects of the mind.

I bow to the consort Vishvamata,
Who has transcended birth and destruction,
The source giving rise to all buddhas,
She of ways always sublime.

At this point it is appropriate to use alcohol if you have it. If you do not, visualize that you do. First cleanse and purify the substance with the usual mantras. Then visualize that everything becomes emptiness. From within the sphere of emptiness the syllable *yam* appears and becomes an air mandala; *ram* becomes a fire mandala; *kam* becomes three human heads, upon which the syllable *a* becomes a skull cup. Inside of this are the five meats and five liquids.

Contemplating in this way, show your left hand. As you recite the syllable *om*, a moon disc marked by *om* appears. It sends forth waves of light-rays, which draw back all the nectars of vajra body. These melt and flow into (the alcohol), causing it to be purified of all impurities and faults.

Show your right hand and utter *āh*. A sun disc marked by *āh* appears. Light rays from it draw back the nectars of vajra speech. This melts and flows into the liquid, causing it to be infused with every sensual flavor.

Then covering with both hands one utters *hūṃ*. A rahu disc marked by *hūṃ* appears and emits lights. These draw back the essence of vajra mind, which melts and flows into the liquid, causing it to flare up and greatly increase.

One shows the garuda mudra and utters *hoḥ*. A kalagni disc marked by *hoḥ* appears and radiates forth lights. These draw back the essence of wisdom, which melts and flows into the liquid, causing it to become in nature the essence of infallible primordial wisdom.

One offers the consecrated liquid to the gurus and meditational deities, and then drinks some oneself, meditating that one's mindstream becomes infused with great bliss. One then offers to the dakas, dakinis and dharma protectors.

Finally one dissolves the emanated mandala into oneself.

[If there is time] then at the end of the session [before dissolving the mandala into oneself] take some of the alcohol on the tip of your ring finger. Clearly and radiantly imagine the mandala in front. Inside the triangular Reality Source, at the center of a circle, is the Wisdom Wheel [i.e., Kalachakra]. Make offerings by means of emanating the twelve offering devis. Then offer the consecrated nectar to the lineage and present masters, as well as to the mandala deities, and so forth. Also offer verses of praise. Conclude with a ritual *torma* offering as follows:

Purify (the torma) with the mantra *oṃ āḥ hūṃ hrāḥ phaṭ*. Follow with the shunyata mantra of emptiness, and then transform it as the amrita was consecrated earlier. Make the vajra mudra and recite the mantra:

> *oṃ āḥ hūṃ hoḥ ham-kṣha-ma-la-va-ra-ya kāla-*
> *chakra saparivārebhya idaṃ baliṃ gandhaṃ*
> *puṣhpaṃ dhūpaṃ dīpaṃ akṣhataṃ dadāmahe*
> *te chāgatya saparivārāḥ śhīghram idaṃ baliṃ*

*grihnantu khādantu pibantu jah hūṃ vaṃ hoh
saṃtṛiptāh sarva sattvānāṃ śāntiṃ puṣhṭiṃ
rakṣhāvaraṇa guptiṃ kurvantu hūṃ hūṃ phaṭ /
vajradhara ājñāpayati svāhā.*

Perform this brief torma rite in each of the three between-session periods.

Also, when you eat a meal, transform it in the way the amrita was consecrated, and offer it to the Lord of Sensuality [i.e., Kalachakra] and to the torma [that represents Kalachakra]. Then, reciting the mantra *oṃ hārīti piṇḍake pratīchchha svāhā*, offer two *changbu* [food offerings made of squeezing dough in the clenched hand until it forms a small bar bearing the outline of hand and fingers] to the inspirational forces (*'phrog-ma*). One also recites the mantra *oṃ dūtike agrāgra sampratīchchha svāhā oṃ āh hūṃ* and offers changbu of the first portion of the food to the female messengers (*pho-nya-mo*). Place this on the earth until the meal is complete. Within the framework of deity yoga, one eats and enjoys the meal.

One also recites the mantra *oṃ kha kha khā hi khā hi uchchhiṣhṭa baliṃ bhakṣha bhakṣhaka svāhā* and offers leftovers to the spirits (*'byung-po*) and sends forth the prayer of generosity, "By the meritorious energy of this activity, may all sentient beings residing in the three worlds evolve towards highest enlightenment."

Then focus on the mandala in front. Send forth offerings and praises (as earlier to oneself as the deity). Recite the 100-syllable mantra (of Vajrasattva), and request patience for any errors in practice made during the meditation. Thus one collects whatever spiritual attainments and powers that one seeks.

Next one dedicates the meritorious energy generated by the practice: "Just as all past Buddhas, lords of the sun, arose from the attainment of this knowledge and wisdom, similarly may all sentient beings found in the three dimensions of the world know the kindness of Kalachakra, 'the

Wheel of Time,' and gain that same level of illumination and knowledge."

One now dissolves the mandala. As you inhale, visualize that the Wisdom Wheel[6] [Kalachakra] is absorbed into your heart. With the backs of your hands facing outward, snap the fingers three times. The samsaric beings return to their natural abodes. One recites the following auspicious verse:

> In the heavens above this earth, a host of bodhi-
> sattvas who easily can intimidate the forces of
> evil;
> On the face of this world of humans, the Kings of
> Fury and their Queens, who reside in all places
> and directions;
> And below the earth, the King of Nagas, who binds
> the forces of negativity and harm—
> May these (three) sources of power work day and
> night to protect the beings of the world who are
> lost in unknowing.

After this auspicious verse has been recited, one dons the mantric armor by visualizing the appropriate mantric syllables at the various sites: *oṃ hrḷiṃ namaḥ* at the heart; *oṃ hrūṃ svāhā* at the forehead; *oṃ hrr̄iṃ vauṣhaṭ* at the crown; *oṃ hrīṃ hūṃ* at the limbs; *oṃ hrāṃ vaṣhaṭ* at the eyes; and *oṃ hraḥ phaṭ* in the appropriate directions. One arises in the aspect of the tantric divinity, and within the sphere of having established firm deity pride, goes about the four types of daily activities (i.e., moving, sitting, etc.).

When going to bed at night establish clear visualization of the six chakras and their mantric syllables: *hrāṃ* at the crown protrusion, *hrīṃ* at the forehead, *hrr̄iṃ* at the throat, *hrūṃ* at the heart, *hrḷiṃ* at the navel, and *hraḥ* at the secret center. Establish these, and also the mantric seeds of the six Buddha Families, *ā ī ṛi ū ḷi aḥ*. Lie in the lion posture, and revert into sleep from within this contemplation.

In the morning visualize that you are awakened by the sound of damaru hand drums played by the dakas and yoginis, who hover in the space above your bed. As an aid to meditation, bathe in the manner of taking tantric initiation.

Practicing in this way one soon gains the conventional spiritual powers, and these in turn eventually bring one to the highest primordial wisdom.

The colophon: This sadhana, entitled *The Best of Jewels*, was written by the Buddhist monk Rinchen Drup. May any meritorious energy that it generates cause the living beings to evolve toward the enlightenment state of glorious Kalachakra.

20 An Aspiration to Fulfill the Stages of the Glorious Kalachakra Path

by Lobzang Chokyi Gyaltsen,
the First Panchen Lama (1567-1662)

Namo guru shrī kālachakra ye

(The Homage)

From within the sportive play
Of profound, radiant bliss united with the wisdom of
    emptiness,
The mandala of glorious Kalachakra manifests.
By meditating upon it may I delight the enlightened
    beings
And amass a mighty ocean of positive energy.

(The 'Shared' Sutrayana Vehicle)

Through that vast force of white goodness,
May I constantly be cared for by the spiritual masters
Inseparable in nature from Kalachakra, the Primordial
    Buddha,

And quickly fill my mind's vase with the nectars
Of inner experience of the shared path.

(Receiving Initiation)

Having received the tantric initiations
Of entering like a child, as well as the worldly and non-
   worldly initiations
That purify one's continuum of stains
And plant the seeds of the four kayas, may I dwell
Gracefully within the tantric disciplines and trainings.

(The Generation Stage Yogas)

Through the yoga of donning the armor of the four
   conventional vajras
And invoking Vajravega, lord of terrific furies,
Surrounded by the sixty protectors,
May I achieve the power to overcome
All negativities and hindrances.

May I learn to integrate great bliss inseparable
From the emptiness of the four doors of liberation,
And thus purify ordinary death, transmigration and
   rebirth;
Through meditation on the sphere of space,
The four elements, the King of Mountains, and so
   forth,
May I realize the abiding nature of the diamond body.

By invoking the samadhi focused on the mystical
   palace,
At its center the Great Hero, with aspects and without,
Born from the five enlightenments, embracing a
   Consort,
May uncontrolled transmigration and rebirth be made
   pure.

Called forth by the sounds of love-making,
The tantric deities melt into the lotus (of the Consort)
And then emanate in their mandala forms.
Through meditating upon the supremely victorious
    mandala, the branch of approach,
May the obscurations, such as those of the aggregates,
    be removed.

May I accomplish the meditations of the twenty phases
    of enlightenment—
Male and Consort entering into union, the fires
Of their passion causing a great melting,
The invocation, the re-emerging,
The emanation of the circle of deities,
Becoming of one taste, the empowerment, and so forth—
And thus fulfill the supremely victorious activities, the
    proximate accomplishment.

Chandali melts the drop, giving rise to the four joys
    that descend from above:
May I quickly fulfill this branch of accomplishment,
    the yoga of the drop.
The substance moves upward, giving rise to the four
    joys that ascend from below:
May I quickly fulfill this subtle yoga, the great
    acomplishment.

(The Completion Stage: The First Four Yogas)

Through practice of the yogas of individual withdrawal
    and dhyana that accomplish form,
And the yogas of energy control and retention that ac-
    complish higher energy,
May I arise in the actual form of a wisdom deity,
Male and Consort, master of the wheel of the empty
    body
At the lotus garden of the navel.

(The Completion Stage: The Fifth and Sixth Yogas)

Then may I accomplish the yoga of subsequent mind-
fulness
And through joyous interplay with a mudra
Give rise to a series of 21,600 experiences of bliss
From the place of union of the sun and moon
In the middle of the central channel,
Thus taking to perfection the yoga of samadhi.

(The Mandala Activities)

The tantric deities of the glorious Kalachakra mandala
Fill the myriad world systems of the ten directions;
And by means of the magical activities of pacification,
   increase, power and wrath
They are working even now for your success and en-
lightenment.
Know that this is so; take joy in that knowledge,
And I will sing an auspicious song.

(An Auspicious Song to the Kalachakra Lineage Masters)

Hail to (Buddha as) Kalachakra and Consort, in nature
Indestructible compassion and wisdom of emptiness
Made manifest in a form radiant with the marks and
   signs of perfection,
Like an entrancing painting of an exquisite rainbow.
I call out to you, and to all lineage masters past and
   present,
Especially the original seven Shambala masters,
And the twenty-five kalkins of Shambala.
Especially I call to Suchandra, who first received
This king of tantras (from the Buddha),
And to Pundarika, who wrote the extensive
   commentary.

By the power of the auspicious qualities of these
masters,
May all of our hindrances and imperfections fade away
And goodness and joy increase like the waxing moon,
Giving rise to a festival of wonder and glory.

(Auspicious Song of the Kalachakra Practice)

Recollecting merely a toenail of the tantric divinities
Who dance over the heads of gods and demons alike,
Kalachakra and Consort, the mystical lord and lady
Who abide in the mandala palace of vajra jewels,
Gives rise to a measureless surge of positive karma.
By the power of the auspicious qualities of this force
May all of our hindrances and imperfections fade away
And goodness and joy increase like the waxing moon,
Giving rise to a festival of wonder and glory.

(Auspicious Song of the Kalachakra Legacy)

The highest and foremost of all tantric systems
Taught by the glorious Buddha, lord of all mandalas,
Is none other than the Kalachakra transmission.
By the power of the auspicious qualities of this legacy
May all of our hindrances and imperfections fade away
And goodness and joy increase like the waxing moon,
Giving rise to a festival of wonder and glory.

(Auspicious Song of the Kalachakra Adepts)

By the power of the auspicious qualities that exist
In the men and women who have found supreme
realization
Through the path of this glorious Primordial Buddha,
And in the masters who uphold the scriptural
knowledge
And the inner realizations of this tantric tradition,

May all of our hindrances and imperfections fade away
And goodness and joy increase like the waxing moon,
Giving rise to a festival of wonder and glory.

The colophon: Composed in an unbroken stream by the
Kalachakra yogi and Buddhist Monk Lobzang Chokyi Gyalt-
sen [the First Panchen Lama], in the temple of Tashi Lhunpo
Monastery.

Notes

CHAPTER ONE

1. I once saw a map of a proposal for the development of Bodh Gaya as a place of pilgrimage, signed by the late Prime Minister Mrs. Indira Gandhi as early as 1963, that envisioned dedicating an area of a mile or two in radius around the Great Stupa to the creation of an international buddhist park. Unfortunately she was never able to accomplish the dream, and Bodh Gaya has fallen instead to the chaotic clutches of crass entrepreneurialism. Hopefully one day that early blueprint will re-surface and receive a second reading.

2. At the 1973 initiation, the line of those seeking the 'hand empowerment,' or *chakwang* (Phyag-dbang), as the Tibetans call it, continued for two full days. As we neared the temple the pressure from the pushing and shoving of the crowd increased, and on a number of occasions I found myself floating in a sea of bodies, my feet several inches off the ground. Carried along in a current of humanity on the move, we all flowed along an approach to the temple designed for crowd safety and management; around buildings and corridors, through alleyways, up the stairs, and then finally into the temple.

The *chakwang* only lasts a few seconds, and comes after many hours of intense work on the part of the participant. But His Holiness easily makes it all worthwhile, creating a sense of intimacy and contact with each and every pilgrim who comes before him. I had decided to pass in the line with eyes cast downward, a traditional Tibetan sign of respect. As I passed before him he reached under my chin and gave my tiny beard a sharp twist. Rather startled, I looked up to see His Holiness laughing mischievously. Time stood still, and the two-second 'hand initiation' transformed into a feeling of a quiet afternoon in the house of a friend.

CHAPTER TWO

1. His Holiness the Dalai Lama quotes this verse in *Toward Universal Responsibility* (Dharamsala: Library of Tibetan Works and Archives, 1980). It is an early Kadampa expression, probably from Geshey Potowa. His Holiness gives it (in translation) as follows:

> Outward conduct is practiced in accordance with Vinaya (Hinayana);
> Inwardly, mental activity is practiced with the bodhimind (Mahayana);
> Practiced in secrecy is the Tantra (Vajrayana).

In recent years some buddhist scholars have objected to the use of the terms Hinayana and Mahayana on the grounds that the former, which translates as 'the Small Vehicle,' may be offensive to certain sects. There is no doubt that it had something of a negative connotation in its usage by some of the early Indian buddhist masters, such as Nagarjuna and Asanga.

The Tibetans, however, transformed and resurrected it, giving it a more personal flavor that perhaps would be better translated as 'the Compact Vehicle,' or 'the Way of Simplicity,' which seems to me to be a more useful and appropriate application.

2. There are numerous accounts of these Indian masters available in English. A simple but pleasantly readable presentation of the classical Tibetan understanding of their lives and deeds is Lobsang Tsonawa's translation of the history prepared by the Gegen Ojung (dGe-gan-os-'byung), or Teachers Training College, for the Tibetan high schools in India. The Gegen Ojung drew from the traditional Tibetan sources, such as Taranatha, Go Lotsawa, and so forth.

Lobsang Tsonawa's rendition, published under the title *Lives of the Indian Pandits* (Dharamsala: LTWA, 1985), is supplemented by an extensive bibliography listing the works by each of these masters that are to be found in the Tibetan *Tengyur*, or canon of translated Indian shastras.

3. The difficulty of establishing dates for these tantric saints is pointed out by Prof. Alex Wayman in his article ''Early Literary History of the Buddhist Tantras, Especially the Guhyasamaja-tantra,'' *Annals of the Bhandarkar Oriental Research Institute*, 1968, pp.48-49.

4. I paraphrase this passage from a translation I prepared with Lobsang Tsonawa, published in *Dreloma*, Mundgod, India, 1982.

5. One of the better portraits of buddhist life in eleventh-century India can be found in *Atisha and Tibet*, by A. Chattopadhya and Lama Chinpa (Calcutta: 1967). This work, a study of the life and activities of Lama Atisha, also reveals the part that Atisha played in the Kalachakra transmission in Tibet.

CHAPTER THREE

1. As we will see later, each of the four classes of tantra uses a unique terminology to describe this concept. Again, even within the same tantra class a different focus can be found in literature dealing with the various levels of yogic application.

Compare, for example, the presentation found in the generation stage application of the highest yoga tantras with the presentation found in the completion stage. In the generation stage of the mainstream tantras the link to the resultant stage of the form body is forged by means of the visualization of particular forms and qualities; in the completion stage, the link is forged on the basis of the subtle and extremely subtle bodily energies.

2. This quote is taken from the Seventh Dalai Lama's *The Prerequisites of Receiving Tantric Initiation*, included as Chapter Fifteen of this volume.

3. The Seventh Dalai Lama's Kalachakra teacher Trichen Ngawang Chokden writes in his Guhyasamaja commentary entitled *A Lamp Elucidating the Meaning of the Generation Stage Yogas of Glorious Guhyasamaja (dPal-gsang-'dus-skyed-rim-gyi-don-gsal-bar-byed-pai-sgron-me)*, folio 4b,

What type of prior training is required for entering into

the generation stage practices of highest yoga tantra?

Firstly we should train ourselves in the basics of the small and medium stages in spiritual perspective, in order to give rise within the mindstream to an unfabricated aspiration to achieve liberation from samsara for oneself. After that one cultivates the mind of love and compassion, and gives rise to the thought of universal responsibility, and to the aspiration to highest enlightenment as a means of benefiting the world. Then one adopts the disciplines and trainings of the six perfections, and cultivates stability in the bodhisattva ways.

Finally, when these general preliminaries have been completed one has to receive the appropriate initiations from a qualified lineage holder.

4. *Lam Rim*, or 'Stages on the Path,' is an abbreviation of a longer phrase, *Jangchup Lamrim*, or 'Stages on the Enlightenment Path.' In one sense the Lam Rim was and is Atisha Dipamkara's version of buddhism, in that it was born from his explanations on how the 84,000 teachings given by the Buddha are to be integrated into a single practice by an individual.

Tibetans liked the idea, and Atisha's lineage rapidly became one of the largest schools of Tibetan buddhism. Its influence upon the other schools was so vast that eventually it became absorbed by them, and is now enshrined as a cornerstone in all Tibetan spiritual orders. In particular, it is the principal foundation upon which the Gelukpa school is built.

CHAPTER FOUR

1. All of these masters and texts are particularly important in the Kadampa school inspired by Lama Atisha. Two of them in particular, Nagarjuna and Shantideva, are fundamental to Atisha's presentation of the path to enlightenment. Both of these men were great authors, and their spiritual writings continue to inspire millions of buddhists throughout Asia and around the world.

2. A number of Ashvaghosha's poetic writings have been translated into English. The most famous of these in the buddhist countries of Asia remains his *Buddhacharita*, published in English as *The Deeds of the Buddha*, translated by E.H Johnson (Lahore: 1936).

The identification of Ashvaghosha, Vira and Aryasura as one and the same person is a well-supported theory; but, as with all historical statements concerning buddhist India, it remains an open question.

3. The best translation of this brief verse work by Lama Tsongkhapa is, in my estimation, that of the late Mongolian lama Geshe Wangyal, first published in *The Door of Liberation* (New York: Lotsawa, 1978).

4. The Seventh Dalai Lama's guru Ngawang Chokden, in his *A Lamp Elucidating the Meaning of the Generation Stage Yogas of Glorious Guhyasamaja (dPal-gsang-'dus-skyed-rim-gyi-don-gsal-bar-byed-pai-sgron-me)*, folio 37b, lists six reasons for beginning every tantric sadhana with the recitation and contemplation of an emptiness mantra:

> Why meditate on emptiness (with the emptiness mantra) at the very beginning of the practice?
>
> The Venerable Atisha gives the purpose in his commentary to Luipa's [Skt., Luipada] sadhana, where he provides six reasons....
>
> Firstly, this practice strengthens the karmic seeds of insight into emptiness. Secondly, it heightens our awareness of emptiness in general. Thirdly, contemplating emptiness causes the mind to become stabilized, and this is useful to any contemplative endeavor. Fourthly, it augments our forces of merit and wisdom. Fifthly, it causes us to transcend the concepts of ordinary appearances of body, speech and mind.
>
> Finally, from it [i.e., reciting the emptiness mantra and meditating on its meaning] we are encouraged to view the supporting and supported mandala that we are about to visualize (in the sadhana practice) as arising from within the sphere of emptiness.

CHAPTER FIVE

1. This and the other verses by Lama Tsongkhapa used in later chapters of Part One are taken from his concise spiritual autobiography entitled *Song of Spiritual Experience (rTogs-brjod-mdun-legs-ma)*, a brief but exceptionally inspired song by this important mas-

ter. In it Tsongkhapa presents a guide to all the sutra and tantra traditions that he studied while a young monk in training, pointing out the spiritual relevance and essence of each. This autobiographical poem has come to be regarded as a map to the Gelukpa training system. The Thirteenth Dalai Lama's *Guide to the Buddhist Tantras* is in fact a commentary to the tantric section of it.

2. In *A Rite of Medicinal Consecration* (included in *Path of the Bodhisattva Warrior*), the Thirteenth Dalai Lama quotes a verse spoken by Guru Padma Sambhava, the eighth-century Indian teacher of Oddiyana who was so instrumental in bringing buddhism to Tibet:

> The buddhas, fully understanding
> The different stages of the mind,
> Taught the Secret Mantra Vehicle.
> Of all the various doctrines,
> This vehicle is supreme,
> For it contains all the essential points
> And produces quick enlightenment.

3. One of the great classics of Tibetan literature dealing with the nature of the four tantra divisions is Lama Tsongkhapa's *Ngakrim Chenmo (sNgags-rim-chen-mo)*, or 'Great (Exposition of the) Stages on the Tantric Path,' which is in fourteen chapters.

The eighteenth-century Amdo master Longdol Lama presents the distilled essence of the contents of this work in his *Notes on the Structure of the Great Stages on the Mantra Path (sNgags-rim-chenmoi-sa-bcad)*.

Khedrupjey's *Gyudey Namshak (rGyud-sde-rnam-gshags)*, translated by F. Lessing and Alex Wayman as *Fundamentals of the Buddhist Tantras* (The Hague: 1968), is another Tibetan classic on the subject. Although Prof. Wayman has produced numerous volumes on Tibetan buddhism during his long and illustrious career, this probably stands as his most important contribution. In fact, it could be said that this rendition of Khedrupjey's *Fundamentals of the Buddhist Tantras* was the first authoritative Western work on the Gelukpa understanding of the buddhist tantras.

CHAPTER SIX

1. Tib., *gZhi-lam-'bras-bu,* or 'basis, path and fruit.' This is a popular analytic application that can be contextualized to the appreciation of almost any buddhist concept. For this reason one repeatedly encounters it in Tibetan literature.

2. The term *dhyana* has found a number of interesting applications in the buddhist world. It is this Sanskrit word, for example, that became *Ch'an* in China and then *Zen* in Japan.

In the Sutrayana it is used firstly in the Shravaka context of a mind well established in meditation (hence often is translated as 'meditative stabilization'). Here it also denotes those meditative techniques that contribute to a 'stabilized meditation.'

Later in the Mahayana the same term appears as 'the *paramita* of meditation,' fifth of the six perfections. As such it can contribute to the accumulation of creative energy when focused on meditations connected with the conventional level of truth, and can contribute to the accumulation of wisdom when focused on meditations linked with the exploration of the theme of emptiness. It does not achieve its full 'perfection' until the meditator achieves the fifth arya bodhisattva level, or fifth of the ten levels of sainthood that precede the full enlightenment of buddhahood.

Dhyana is used slightly differently in each of the four tantra classes in general, but finds its highest expression in the Kalachakra doctrine, where it is used to connote the second of the six completion stage yogas. Here one dwells on a subtle level of consciousness, the peripheral energies of the body having been arrested by the first yoga, and 'stabilizes' the similtude of an empty body (also generated by the first yoga). This leads to utter stilling of the peripheral energies and the preparation for the third yoga, which causes the energies to enter into the central channel.

3. In *Notes on the Structure of the Great Stages on the Mantra Path (sNgags-rim-chen-moi-sa-bcad),* Longdol Lama presents the following breakdown of the kriya tantra methodology:

> (Lama Tsongkhapa's *The Great Stages*) teaches the kriya tantra system under the following topics.... Firstly there is a discussion of the initiation ceremony that makes one into a suitable vessel for the kriya tantra meditations, and then an analysis of the pledges and commitments that es-

tablish the basis of accomplishing the powers of the kriya path. Next there is a presentation of the actual methods of kriya propitiation (for benefiting oneself through accomplishing enlightenment), and then the manner in which the kriya technology is used to benefit other sentient beings....

As for the section on the methods of practice, or propitiation, this firstly discusses the reasoning behind the various techniques, and then introduces the actual procedures of the training. This latter subject involves the dhyana which is practiced in conjunction with mantric recitation, and the dhyana which is practiced without relying on mantric recitation.

The former of these, the dhyana practiced in conjunction with mantric recitation, touches upon three subjects: how one prepares to engage in the four branches of recitation; how one actually engages in these four; and then how one concludes the practice.

The first of these involves four topics: how to prepare one's meditation hut; the manner of washing oneself and entering the place of meditation; preparing the altar and offerings, and performing the consecration; and establishing the protective sphere for oneself and others.

As for the second topic, how one actually engages in the dhyana of the four types of recitation, this involves the dhyana of the branch of recitation, and the recitation itself.

The first of these begins with the self-generation of the mandala deity (or deities), and then proceeds with the invocation of the wisdom beings, the meditation of making offerings, and so forth.

This is accomplished in six stages: generating the supporting mandala; invoking the supported mandala deities; expressing the mudras; sending forth offerings and eulogies; the steps of acknowledging one's failings, etc.; and meditating upon the four immeasurable attitudes [i.e., compassion, love, joy and equaminity].

As for the mantric recitation itself, which is performed on the basis of the above (sixfold) process, this can be accomplished in (any of) three (different) ways: by arranging the visualized objects of recitation in the manner of

a counting rosary, and then doing the mantra count; focusing on various aspects of the mandala and doing the according mantric visualization; and thirdly, performing the
mantric recitation whenever a negative circumstance arises
(in order to overcome it).

The first of these three methods can be performed in
either of two ways: performing the recitation while visualizing the forms of the mantric syllables at the hearts of the
mandala deities; or doing so while visualizing the mantras at one's own heart.

The dhyana which does not utilize mantric recitation involves two practices: the dhyana of abiding in the sound
of fire; and the dhyana at the end of sound. This second
process also involves two practices: the steps of releasing
the experience of sound; and the actual dhyana of the end
of sound.

These are the points covered (by Lama Tsongkhapa) in
the elucidation of the kriya tantras, in his explanation of
the stages of the great Buddha Vajradhara.

In another of his tantric treatises, *A Guide to the Tantric Scriptures (gSang-snags-sde-snod-ming-grangs)*, which is written in verse
form, Longdol Lama says this of the kriya methods:

As for the tradition of accomplishing (the kriya path),
This involves the practice of the four dhyanas:
There is the dhyana of the four types of recitation;
The dhyana of abiding in fire; the dhyana of abiding in
    sound;
And the dhyana bestowing liberation at the end of sound.

In the dhyana of the four branches of recitation,
Firstly there is the branch focusing on oneself as the basis;
Secondly is the branch focusing on the alternate basis;
Thirdly there is the branch focusing on the mental basis;
And fourthly there is the branch focusing on the audial
    basis.

4. In *Notes on the Structure of the Great Stages of the Tantric Path
(sNags-rim-chen-moi-sa-bcad)* Longdol Lama speaks as follows of

the charya tantra methodology:

> The stages of the charya yoga path involve four subjects: becoming a suitable vessel for meditating upon this path; having become a suitable vessel (through receiving the initiations), the pledges and commitments to be observed; observing the commitments well, the preliminary methods that are to be applied; and by training in the actual charya methods, how the spiritual powers that are accomplished are to be utilized.
>
> The first of these can be known from the general treatises on charya tantra practice. The second is as explained in *The Treatise on the Root Downfalls (rTsa-ldung-rnam-bshad)* (by Lama Tsongkhapa). Here, however, special emphasis should be placed on the explanation as given in the *Vairochana Abhisambodhi Tantra*.
>
> The third point is taught in two headings: the divisions of the charya yogas; and the explanations of the procedures in those individual divisions. The second of these entails an understanding of the yoga with symbols and the yoga beyond symbols.
>
> The yoga with symbols involves mantric recitation in accordance with the four external branches, and also mantric recitation in accordance with the four internal branches.
>
> These are the points covered (by Lama Tsongkhapa) in the eluciadation of the charya tantras, in his explanation of the stages of the great Buddha Vajradhara.

5. The two Tibetan terms *sherab* (Shes-rab) and *yeshey* (Ye-shes) have overlapping meanings. Both are usually translated into English as 'wisdom,' although to do so undoubtedly blurs some of the shades of difference that the two terms hold. For example, *sherab* achieves fulfillment on the sixth bodhisattva level, whereas *yeshey* does not do so until the tenth, indicating a significantly different range of the wisdom.

The *ye* in *yeshey* is a syllabic root linked to the concept of primordiality. Its next most common appearance in Tibetan scriptures is in the idiom *yewa ney* (Ye-ba-nas), meaning 'from the beginning,' or 'from primordial time.' Therefore I have chosen to keep *sherab* as 'wisdom' and *yeshey* as 'primordial wisdom,' or as 'gnosis.' In certain passages where *yeshey* is repeatedly used, I drop off a few 'primordials' on the grounds that its inferred presence should be clear from the context. Where 'primordial wisdom' does not seem to work I translate it as 'primordial awareness.'

In highest yoga tantra the term *sherab* is used in the context of meditation upon emptiness. It is also used as *Sherabma*, the 'wisdom consorts' who inspire the bliss able to glimpse the clear light experience. *Yeshey*, on the other hand, is used as *yeshey nga* (Yeshes-lnga), the five 'primordial wisdoms' that are the positive poles of our five psychophysical aggregates (the five negative poles being the five delusions).

In highest yoga tantra, the five principal phases of the vase initiation (first of the four empowerments given in this tantra division) purify the mind of the five delusions and activate the seeds of the five 'primordial wisdoms.'

The second of the four initiations in highest yoga tantra is called 'the wisdom/primordial wisdom empowerment.' Here we see the two terms *sherab* and *yeshey* fused into one.

6. The nineteen pledges of the five tathagatas are taken for the first time in the yoga tantra division. In the kriya and charya tantra classes these pledges were not introduced. At those levels in training, the student is expected instead to maintain the refuge, individual liberation, and bodhisattva precepts.

The nineteen pledges of the five Tathagatas essentially are guidelines on how to integrate tantric meditation into daily life. They are divided between the five Tathagatas, who here symbolize the primordially pure nature of the psychophysical aggregates. These guidelines, which should be reviewed three times each day and three times each night, instruct us to maintain the primordially pure nature at the forefront of our awareness at all times.

As we will see later, in the highest yoga tantras practitioners are encouraged to recite daily a brief liturgical text, known as a 'six-session *guruyoga*,' that contains the essential sentiments of the nineteen pledges of the five Tathagathas. One such text is translated in Chapter Eighteen.

7. It is interesting to note that it was the yoga tantra class that attracted the greatest attention in both China and Japan. The latter country still maintains a strong tradition in this respect in the Shingon school of Japanese buddhism.

In *Notes on the Structure of the Great Stages of the Tantric Path* *(sNags-rim-chen-moi-sa-bcad)* Longdol Lama speaks as follows of the yoga tantra path:

> (Lama Tsongkhapa) discusses the yoga tantra path under two general headings: how the original tantric scriptures (of the yoga tantra class) present (the yoga tantra doctrines); and how one takes up the practices taught therein.
>
> This latter subject involves four topics: becoming a suitable vessel for meditating upon this path; having become a suitable vessel (through receiving the initiations), the pledges and commitments that are to be observed; the methods that are to be applied by one who observes these commitments; and by training in the actual yoga tantra methods, how the spiritual powers are to be accomplished. . . .
>
> The third of these topics involves both the yoga with symbols and the yoga beyond symbols. The yoga with symbols is comprised of the two processes: the yoga of four sessions of focusing upon oneself as the mandala deity (or deities); and the yoga of four sessions of focusing upon the deity symbols (or hand implements).
>
> The former of these involves the meditations in four sessions; and also what is to be done if this cannot be accomplished. Again, the former of these has two aspects: the yoga of four sessions as practiced by someone who has gained only the initiations of a disciple; and the yoga of four sessions as practiced by someone who has also gained the initiation of a master. In the second of these two cases there is a discussion of three subjects: the purpose of the subtle meditations; how to stabilize the mind by means of the subtle visualizations; and then, having stabilized the mind, the processes of emanation, reabsorption, and so forth.
>
> As for the meditations comprising the yoga beyond symbols, (Lama Tsongkhapa) discusses these from three perspectives: the methods as taught in the *Tattvasamgraha;* the methods as taught in the *Subsequent Tantra;* and a summary of the stages of this meditative process.
>
> The last of these topics involves four subjects, namely,

the manners of meditating in the Tathagata, Vajra, Ratna and Padma Families, respectively.

Fourthly there is a discussion of how someone who has accomplished the various yogic methods should utilize the various spiritual powers. This is accomplished in any of three ways: doing so by means of dhyana, doing so by means of mantric recitation, and doing so by means of fire rites.

These are the points covered (by Lama Tsongkhapa) in the elucidation of the yoga tantras, in his explanation of the stages of the great Buddha Vajradhara.

CHAPTER SEVEN

1. The initiations of the five Tathagata Families purify the disciples of the five delusions, causing these to arise in the nature of the five primordial wisdoms. The five psychophysical aggregates are purified and caused to arise in the nature of the five Tathagatas. This prepares the disciples for practice of the generation stage yogas.

2. There is in the Tibetan tradition a genre of liturgical text known as *dangjuk* (bDag-'jug), or 'self-initiation,' whereby the practitioner refreshes the strength of the four empowerments received at the time of initiation. Texts of this nature are generally utilized for recitation and meditation once a month.

3. This passage is taken from the Seventh Dalai Lama's *Songs of Spiritual Change* (Ithaca, N.Y.: Snow Lion Publications, 1981).

CHAPTER EIGHT

1. This work is included in my study of the life and works of the Thirteenth Dalai Lama, *Path of the Bodhisattva Warrior.*

2. The Tibetan term for the generation stage is *kyerim* (sKyes-rim), translated from the Sanskrit *utpattikrama*. It carries the sense of 'stage of visualization.' The completion stage, from the Sanskrit term *sampannakrama*, is *dzogrim* (rDzogs-rim) in Tibetan, and carries the sense of the fulfillment or realization of what was merely visualized in the generation stage. However, from this we should not assume that the generation stage is mere visualization. As well as intensifying the pace of our accumulation of merit and also radically transforming the sense of self (thus greatly enhancing wis-

dom), it also produces the accomplishment of meditative concentration, which in turn induces the eight great siddhis and various of the clairvoyant powers.

In Chapter Ten we will see the technical definitions of generation stage and completion stage as applied in the Kalachakra system.

3. Inner radiance and divine pride, or *selnang* (gSal-snang) and *lhai naljor* (hLai'-nal-'byor), are the two qualities most important to success in the generation stage yogas. The former empowers the meditation; the latter gives it its transformative quality.

4. This definition is taken from Trehor Kanjur Lama's (Tre-hor-bka'-'gyur-bla-ma) *A Moondrop Reflecting the Meaning of the Sutras and Tantras (mDo-snags-gnad-don-dril-bai-bza-bai-thig-le)*. The author continues, "It is called 'the generation stage' because in it the basis of purification is generated [i.e., visualized] as the resultant buddhahood."

5. The process of entering and leaving the bardo, as well as the links that this metaphysic has with generation stage tantric practice, is touched upon in one of my earlier books, *Death and Dying: The Tibetan Tradition* (New York: Arkana, 1986). It is also discussed in *Death, Intermediate State and Rebirth* by Lati Rinpochey and Jeffrey Hopkins (Ithaca: Snow Lion Publications, 1980).

6. The stage of transition from generation to completion stage overlaps into both yogas. Where precisely the line of demarcation lies has been a point of discussion and debate over the centuries.

For example, by the definition of the starting point of the completion stage yogas as practiced in the Guhyasamaja system, the first two Kalachakra completion stage yogas would not even qualify as completion stage practices. This is because the emphasis in Kalachakra is not on creating the illusory body, but rather on simply quieting the peripheral energies and generating a similitude of the empty body.

CHAPTER NINE

1. By this expression I mean the approach taken by the central monasteries of the Lhasa area, and in particular by the Lower and Upper Tantric Colleges, or Gyumey and Gyuto.

There is, however, no concrete trend in any of the Tibetan orders. Often two monasteries of the same sect in different parts of the country would differ more radically than would two monasteries of different sects in the same area. Every individual monastery essentially established its own training curriculum, based on the various lineages fused by the original monastic founders as well as upon the meditative experiences of later masters in the transmission.

An interesting project would be the comparison of spiritually inspired paintings, or *tangkhas*, from a given monastery at different periods in its history. Paintings of this nature tend to reflect the character of the tantric sentiment of the region under consideration in the period during which the painting was created.

For example, the best tangkha in my own collection comes from Dargyey Monastery, Eastern Tibet, and represents the Eighth Dalai Lama surrounded by various figures. Directly above the him are three tantric deities: the full form of Guhyasamaja; Kalachakra and Consort in their two-armed form; and Yamantaka in solitary form. The tangkha was painted during the Eighth's actual lifetime, and the tantric figures placed in this way indicate that the principal practices of the devotee who commissioned the painting was probably Guhyasamaja and Yamantaka as male tantras from the mainstream traditions of 'buried tantras'; and Kalachakra as a 'female tantra' and as a link to the 'clear tantras.'

2. For readers with a solid background in Tibetan studies, a useful account of the nature and structure of the six completion stage yogas of the Guhyasamaja system is Daniel Cozort's *Highest Yoga Tantra* (Ithaca: Snow Lion Publications, 1986). The final chapter includes a comparison of the Guhyasamaja approach with that of Kalachakra.

3. The buddhist concept of the illusory body is considerably different from the Western occult concept of the astral body. The latter is more akin to the Tibetan theory of a 'dream body,' something attainable at a more initial phase of spiritual development.

The 'dream body' can be developed early in one's practice, and then used to turn sleep into a period of meditation. For this reason in Tibet it was sometimes referred to as 'the lazy person's yoga,' a derogatory view that Lama Tsongkhapa scoffs at in his commentary to the six yogas of Naropa. Rather, as Tsongkhapa points out, the dream body yoga is a method to bring another aspect of our being into the enlightenment path.

The illusory body, on the other hand, is not generated until the point of transition of the path of preparation and the path of insight, i.e., the second and third of the five levels of the path to enlightenment. Before that time, practitioners only have access to it as a potential force; they cannot actually arise within it in their meditations.

By comparison, even practitioners on elementary stages can learn to work with the dream body.

The reason that dream and illusory bodies are often mentioned together is that in some respects they share the same nature. It could even be said that the former is an early proxy of the latter, for both dream and illusory bodies are formed from the subtle energies arising within one's being. The difference is that the dream body can arise on the basis of coarse energies by following and working with the natural process that arises in sleep and dream states; whereas the illusory body can only arise on the basis of the most subtle energies. For it to make its appearance, the coarse energies must have been quietened through yogic practices.

There is also a tradition of linking the dream, illusory and bardo bodies. Again, the reason is that they all arise on the basis of the subtle energies.

Untrained persons can experience only the dream and bardo bodies, and even these are undergone as uncontrolled processes arising from the forces of karma and delusion, that is, the natural processes of body and mind.

The tantric yogi masters the methods of working with the dream and bardo bodies by tuning in to the thread of 'clear light' consciousness that links our everyday waking consciousness with whichever of these two events arises (i.e., sleep or bardo). This 'foundation' clear light consciousness is the most subtle aspect of mind, and by retaining awareness of it when entering the dream or bardo states one becomes infused with freedom and power in one's experience of these events.

Working with the subtle consciousness of the sleep and dream states that arise naturally, and the experiences of death and the bardo, which are simulated in meditation by quietening and suspending the natural bodily functions, the yogi gains increasing familarity with the nature and flow of the body and mind complex on increasingly subtle levels. This later becomes very useful knowledge in preparing to work in meditation on the most subtle level with the illusory body and clear light mind.

Because of this intimate link between the nature of dreams, bardo, and illusory body, the yogi who has achieved the illusory body but has not yet achieved full enlightenment is nonetheless said to be assured of enlightenment in this lifetime, in the sense that at the very least he or she will be able to sublimate the natural tendency to arise in a bardo body at the time of death, and will be able instead to arise on the basis of the illusory body. The mind arising in this illusory body can then be held in focus on the clear light consciousness. Synchronizing with natural processes in this way, the slow yogi achieves enlightenment at the time of death.

Therefore in *The Tantric Yogas of Sister Niguma* the Second Dalai Lama states, quoting *The Vajra Verses*,

> Through practice of this supreme path
> The wisdom of blissful emptiness automatically arises
> And one attains enlightenment in this lifetime,
> Or, at the very least, in the bardo. . .

> Thus, as is stated here, the practitioners of highest capacity, who are likened to a precious jewel, attain enlightenment in this very lifetime. Lesser practitioners attain enlightenment in the bardo, or at least within seven or sixteen lifetimes.

4. The four empties and four joys become important topics in the completion stage yogas. Essentially, the 'joys' arise when the drops pass through the energy centers, or chakras, as they are being directed up or down the central channel by the meditator. The 'empties' are subtle states of consciousness that can be induced through yogic practice from the experience of the joys.

This joyous consciousness characterized by the subtleness sublimated by the four joys is then directed to meditation upon emptiness. Thus this stage of practice is really a forerunner to the illusory body and clear light yogas that are to follow.

5. Undoubtedly the best Western study of Naropa's six yogas is Herbert Guenther's *The Life and Teachings of Naropa* (London: Oxford University Press, 1967). It is perhaps distracting that his unique choice of translation terminology often seems to make these ancient buddhist masters sound suspiciously like early incarnations of nineteenth-century German existential philosophers; but nonetheless there are valid arguments for reading Tibetan buddhism in an existential light. The existentialists are perhaps the closest the West

gets to the buddhist view of things; however, they certainly differ in spiritual sentiment.

CHAPTER TEN

1. The Tibetan concept of *nyur lam* (Myur-lam), the 'quick path' that brings near-instant enlightenment, cuts nicely through the rather fruitless argument that trailed Far Eastern buddhism for centuries, namely, the 'instant versus gradual enlightenment' theories. This argument is perhaps best represented by the debate on this issue that continued in China. Rather than quibble over a speculative 'gradual or instant' enlightenment, the Tibetans preferred to think simply of 'quick enlightenment.'

As for Gelukpa attitudes toward gradual and instant enlightenment theories, it is quite safe to say that both are regarded as correct.

The former is correct because there is a difference between the inner state of a practitioner who has trained for twenty years and who will attain enlightenment ten minutes henceforth, and the inner state of that same practitioner twenty years earlier. That difference is the measure of the effects of the practice.

Nonetheless the latter is also correct, for there is a moment when there is an unenlightened being, and the next moment when there is an enlightened being.

This is illustrated in the life of Lama Tsongkhapa. He studied for many years in numerous monasteries and hermitages, and then performed a five-year retreat. One day during a break in his meditation he sat outside in the shade of a tree and read the Indian master Buddhapalita's treatise on the emptiness doctrine. During his reading session a fly alighted on one of the lines, and when Tsongkhapa's eyes fell on that line, drawn there by the fly, he achieved illumination. It is said that his understanding henceforth was completely transformed from what it previously had been. Thus he achieved 'instant enlightenment'; yet one could not discredit the value of the years he had put into study and meditation.

Sometimes it is said that this experience was not his final enlightenment, but rather was a slightly lesser attainment of sainthood. However, in all probability such talk is merely an evasive response to a monastic dilemma to do with the ostensible contradiction between the lifestyle of a buddhist monk and the tantric practice known as karmamudra.

2. In this context the term *mandala* refers to the device taken as the basis of the initiation ceremony. This may be one of four things: a painting on cloth, a sand painting, an assembly of tantric deities visualized in the body, or simply the power of meditative stability.

In any case, the device here is used as a symbol of the circle of tantric deities and their divine abode, of the tantric system into which initiation is being given, and the state of enlightenment one will achieve through the practice.

3. See Chapter Six, Note 6, above.

4. One of my own spiritual teachers, the inimitable Geshe Ngawang Dargyey, lists the special Kalachakra presentation of the fourteen root tantric precepts in *The Kalachakra Tantra* (Dharamsala: LTWA, 1988), pp.26-28.

5. In the Guhyasamaja system the names of the six yogas of Kalachakra are used to label the yogic applications in each of the six completion stage phases, i.e., body isolation and so forth. However, although they are used in a yogic context to describe completion stage experiences, the actual experiences they are speaking of seem altogether different from those of the six Kalachakra stages.

An example would be the Guhyasamaja yogic application of individual withdrawal, as compared to the Kalachakra yoga of individual withdrawal. In the former, the mystic heat is used to cause the energies of the side channels to enter into the central channel. In the Kalachakra yoga of individual withdrawal, the energies in the side channels are simply stilled; they are not caused to enter into the central channel, as they are in Guhyasamaja. Also, the mystic heat technique is not brought into this Kalachakra yoga, whereas it is a fundamental ingredient of the Guhyasamaja yoga of individual withdrawal.

Each of the succeeding Kalachakra yogas show equally significant differences from the Guhyasamaja yogic applications of the same name.

6. The Mongolian scholar Lobzang Tayang in his *Legacy of the Sun-like Masters* speaks of the Kalachakra generation stage yogas in this way (folio 3b):

> The generation stage yogas are twofold: the samadhi of the four doors of liberation; and the yoga of the four branches, i.e., the supremely victorious mandala, victorious activities, yoga of the drop, and the subtle drop. These involve

vajra body, speech, mind, and primordial wisdom, and also
the branches of propitiation, proximate accomplishment,
accomplishment, and great accomplishment. They are
practiced first as the coarse generation stage yoga, and then
as the subtle generation stage.

7. The yoga of energy withdrawal, which is *sordu* (Sor-sdud) in
Tibetan and *pratyahara* in Sanskrit, is defined as follows by Lobzang Tayang (folio 4b):

The yoga of individual withdrawal is defined as a completion stage yoga that is a branch accomplishing form wherein
(the essence of) body, subtle energies, and mind are
blended together and, by the powers of meditating upon
the empty body (as abiding) within the upper chakra, the
ten energies of apprehended and apprehending factors are
brought to that site, giving rise to the ten signs, arresting
the activity of the energies in the sense powers.

8. Lobzang Tayang defines this yoga, called *samten* (bSam-rtan)
in Tibetan and *dhyana* in Sanskrit, in the following terms (folio 4b):

The yoga of dhyana is a completion stage yoga stabilizing
form, wherein the mind is placed single-pointedly on the
empty body produced by the yoga of individual withdrawal
at the site of the drop of the body [i.e., the chakra]. Here
one generates an unfeigned divine pride of a sambhogakaya
form just as at the time of the result [i.e., buddhahood],
complete with the five factors [i.e., the five certainties].

9. The yoga of energy control, which is *soksol* (Srog-rtsol) in Tibetan and *pranayama* in Sanskrit, is defined as follows by Lobzang
Tayang (folio 5a):

The yoga of energy control is a completion stage yoga that
is a branch accomplishing higher energy, wherein by means
of meditating with either the vajra recitation or vase breathing techniques the vital energies coursing in the two side
channels are arrested and directed inside the middle of the
chakras at the central channel.

10. Lobzang Tayang defines the fourth yoga, which is *dzinpa* ('Dzin-pa) in Tibetan and *dharana* in Sanskrit, as follows (folio 5b):

The yoga of retention is a completion stage yoga that is a branch stabilizing higher energy, wherein the energies are brought to the center of various of the six chakras in the central channel; they are brought to the drops at these sites, and are retained there without moving, giving rise to the four joys descending from above and four joys ascending from below.

11. *Jedran* (rJes-dran), or *anusmriti* in Sanskrit, translated as the yoga of subsequent mindfulness, receives the following treatment in *Legacy of the Sun-like Masters* (folio 6b):

The yoga of subsequent mindfulness is a completion stage yoga that is a branch accomplishing bliss, wherein one meditates within the framework of relying on the outer condition of sexual union with whichever of the three mudras [i.e., types of consorts] are appropriate to the practitioner's faculties, and also relies upon the inner condition of the mind arising within the empty body in sexual union at the navel chakra. This causes one to arise in an actual empty body form at the navel chakra and bestows the power to fill the skies with emanated empty body forms like the one that one has attained, which are like images reflected in a mirror.

12. The sixth branch of the Kalachakra yogas, that known as *ting ngey dzin* (Ting-nge-'dzin) in Tibetan and *samadhi* in Sanskrit, is given the following definition by Lobzang Tayang (folio 7a):

The yoga of samadhi is defined as a completion stage yoga that is a branch stabilizing bliss, wherein one arises in the actual empty body form of Kalachakra and Consort at the time of the path; here by the power of dwelling one-pointedly in the great passion of union one enters into the experience of supreme unchanging bliss and the empty body embellished with the marks and signs of perfection, bringing the two kayas (of body and mind) into one essential nature.

13. It should be noted that the 'rainbow body' produced by the mainstream yogas is entirely different from the Kalachakra empty body that re-appears 'like a rainbow.' The former is created by the vital energies emanated in the lights of five colors; thus it is composed of subtle energy. In the Kalachakra empty body, which manifests like a rainbow, the energies have been dissolved into nothingness. What appears is something other than the radiance of the vital energies.

14. Unfortunately Khedrup Norzang Gyatso's original text was not available to me. My knowledge of it and statements concerning it are gleaned from references found in later Kalachakra literature. It seems that everyone likes to quote Khedrup Norzang Gyatso on Kalachakra, even when they do not agree with him on a given point. The original Kalachakra writings of this illustrious master remain rare. Only his Guhyasamaja commentary is to be found in Dharamsala.

The Mongolian master Lobzang Tayang brings up the uniqueness of Khedrup Norzang Gyatso's views several times in his *Legacy of the Sun-like Masters*. He especially delights in analyzing Norzang Gyatso's teachings on the methods of generating the twelve Kalachakra levels in one's mindstream. He points out that in Norzang Gyatso's tradition all twelve levels are induced as arya levels, which differs considerably from the general Kalachakra process, in which the first level is equivalent to the path of application. Lobzang Tayang points out that the consequence radically affects how the drops are counted as they are stacked into columns in the sixth yoga. Also in Khedrup Norzang Gyatso's tradition each experience of bliss and so forth has two stages, the first being the initial experience and the second being an effect induced by the first. Although seemingly a small point, there are far-reaching consequences to the metaphysics of the standard Kalachakra presentation. Thus it would seem that the Second Dalai Lama's guru purposely modified the Kalachakra yogas in a manner that would effect the sequence of events leading up to the experience of enlightenment.

This is all fairly obscure material, of course. But what shines through in every reference to Khedrup Norzang Gyatso is the sense of creative inventiveness in his approach to the ideas, and his willingness to rephrase concepts in ways that would challenge the established interpretations.

I very much hope to encounter a biography of this wild mountain yogi monk some day. He and the young Second Dalai Lama spent many years together as master and disciple, not long after the teenaged Dalai Lama had been kicked out of his hereditary monastery of Tashi Lhunpo for irritating the monastic administrators, especially the abbot Panchen Yeshey Tsemo (not one of the Panchen Lama incarnations, by the way). The two wandered from holy place to holy place, studying and practicing the Dharma in caves and hermitages throughout Central and Southern Tibet. Sometimes they were alone, just two wandering mendicants; at other times they would fail to hide their identities, and crowds of hundreds and even thousands would gather to hear them teach and to receive their blessings.

In later years, when their fame had made it impossible for them to live and practice quietly, they spent their time traveling from community to community, teaching and giving tantric initiations. They were also active at building, and numerous monasteries sprang up as a result of their activities. Included in these was Chokhorgyal, near the holy lake of Palden Lhamo, that (due to the Second Dalai Lama's empowerment) became the visionary lake in which lamas would come to look for clues in their searches for the reincarnations of the subsequent Dalai Lamas.

CHAPTER ELEVEN

1. The principal Tibetan source of popular knowledge of the Kalachakra history is Go Lotsawa's ('Gos-lo-tsa-ba) *The Blue Annals*, or *Tebter Ngopo (Thebs-ter-snon-po)*, written in the fourteenth century, in which an entire chapter is dedicated to a discussion of the different views on the history of Kalachakra. The English translation by George Roerich (Calcutta: 1946) remains a classic.

Two other popular Kalachakra histories are those of the seventeenth-century Jonangpa master Taranatha, and the eighteenth-century lexicographer Longdol Lama (kLang-rdol-bla-ma). These have both been published in India (in Tibetan) and are available from any U.S. Library of Congress lending facility around the world. Longdol Lama's important *Collected Works* was published as part of Lokesh Chandra's untiring efforts in New

Delhi, and is available in his Sata-Pitaka Series. To the best of my knowledge, neither of these has been published in English translation.

2. This version of the title, in Sanskrit the *Paramadibuddha* or 'Primordial Buddha,' is merely a variation of that so frequently seen as the *Dukor Tsagyu* (Dus-skor-rtsa-rgyud), or *The Kalachakra Root Tantra*. It has caused some confusion with translators, however, as this expression—'Paramadibuddha' or 'Primordial Buddha'—is often used as an epithet of Kalachakra.

3. As has been pointed out by a number of recent scholars, this misidentification (or rather, mis-reconstruction of the Tibetan name of 'Jam-dpal-grags-pa as Manjushrikirti instead of the correct Manju Yashas) was probably first made by the Hungarian explorer and tibetologist Csoma de Koros, in his article "Notes on the Origin of the Kalachakra and Adi-Buddha Systems," *Journal of the Asiatic Society of Bengal*, 1883.

His error has been imitated by succeeding generations of buddhologists. This unquestioning emulation would perhaps not be so unusual, but for the fact that the original Sanskrit text written by Manju Yashas still exists, and therefore there is no need to reconstruct the Sanskrit from its Tibetan counterpart.

Nevertheless, I should perhaps not say too much on the subject, since I myself made the same mistake in my earlier translation of the First Dalai Lama's *Notes on the Two Yogic Stages of Glorious Kalachakra*, published in *Selected Works of the Dalai Lama I: Bridging the Sutras and Tantras* (Ithaca, N.Y.: Snow Lion Publications, 1981).

4. This important work has been published in India in a trilingual edition including Sanskrit, Tibetan and Mongolian versions of Manju Yashas' text. The modern production was brought out by Prof. Raghu Vira and Dr. Lokesh Chandra at the International Academy of Indian Culture under the title *The Kalachakra Tantra and Other Texts*, Sata-Pitaka Series, Vol. 69, 1966.

5. Pundarika's *The Great Commentary: A Stainless Light*, has received far more attention in the Tibetan world than has its subject, *The Abbreviated Kalachakra Tantra*. Most important Tibetan lineage holders have written either an expansion or a summary of it. This text, in Sanskrit, Tibetan and Mongolian versions, is also published in Lokesh Chandra's Sata-Pitaka Series, 1966, as *The Shri Kalachakra*.

There were undoubtedly several hundred (if not thousand) commentaries to it composed in Tibet, many of which still exist. Yet amazingly, Westers scholarship knows almost nothing of its actual contents.

6. This title appears frequently in the Kalachakra literature as *kalki* as well as *kalkin*. The latter form seems to me to be the more attractive, and I have used it throughout.

7. Tibetan historians have had difficulty piecing together the many names and stories associated with the Indian Kalachakra lineage in the early eleventh century. Nowhere is their difficulty so obvious as in the case of Pindo Acharya. There seems to have been at least four Pindo Acharyas during that time period, if not more. In addition, Atisha had a guru in Indonesia by the same name, with whom he read certain Kalachakra scriptures. Atisha also had a disciple called Pindo.

Some Western scholars have identified Pindo Acharya as being the same person as Kalachakrapada the Elder. Not many Tibetans would agree. For example, the Seventh Dalai Lama mentions the two as being different people in the introductory prayer to the larger of his three Kalachakra sadhanas.

8. Again, numerous Western scholars have mistaken the Rva mentioned in 'the Rva Tradition' as referring to the earlier Rva Lotsawa, i.e., Rvalo Dorje Drak (Rva-lo-rdo-rje-grags). It does not. There is no doubt that the Rva mentioned here is Dorje Drak's disciple Rva Chorab, and not the guru.

9. The thirteenth-century traveler, scholar and explorer Manlung Guru (sMan-lung-gu-ru) seems to have thought so, as pointed out by the mid-twentieth-century Amdo scholar Gendun Chopel (dGe-'dun-chos-'phel) in his guide to the holy places in India and environs.

10. Buton Rinchen Druppa's collected works have been published in India by Proff. Raghu Vira and Lokesh Chandra, International Academy of Indian Culture, New Delhi, Satapitaka Series, Vols. 41-45, 1966.

11. It is sometimes said that Lama Tsongkhapa did not write extensively on Kalachakra. Be this as it may, his collected writings nonetheless contain half a dozen titles on the subject. One of these, the edited notes of an oral discourse that he gave on the key points of Pundarika's *The Great Commentary: A Stainless Light* is a wonderfully lucid presentation of the crucial themes of Pundarika's trea-

tise. Also, even though Lama Tsongkhapa's commentary to the Kalachakra six yogas is brief, it too shines with the brilliance that its author brings to so many of his literary creations.

Lama Tsongkhapa's two chief disciples—Gyaltsepjey and Khedrupjey—wrote extensively on Kalachakra, although the works of Khedrupje have proven to be the more popular over the centuries. His commentary to Pundarika's *The Great Commentary: A Stainless Light* is accorded the greatest respect throughout Central Asia. It is perhaps the single most popular Kalachakra treatise ever written by a Tibetan, and its prestige rivals in splendor that of even the great Kalachakra classics of Shambala and India.

12. These two monastic universities were to represent the established line of tantric studies in the Gelukpa School, for any monk graduating from one of the three high philosophical monastic universities of Ganden, Drepung, or Sera had to complete tantric studies in one of these two colleges in order to qualify for the highest position of the sect. The Ganden Tripas, or Holders of the Ganden Throne, the official heads of the Gelukpa order, are traditionally drawn exclusively from a list of former abbots of one of these two tantric institutions, on an alternating basis.

In the Gelukpa, the position of Ganden Tripa, or 'Holder of the Geluk Throne,' is given in rotation to former abbots of Gyuto and Gyumey. The two senior lamas on the two lists of ex-abbots (i.e., one from each list) are known as the Shartsey Chojey (i.e., the Dharma Master of Ganden Shartsey Monastery) and Jangtsey Chojey (i.e., the Dharma Master of Ganden Jangtsey Monastery). Shartsey (lit., the Western Peak) and Jangtsey (lit., the Eastern Peak) are the two main colleges of Ganden Monastery. These 'Dharma masters' are not drawn from Ganden Monastery, as the names may seem to suggest; nor need they even be Tibetans. (In fact, several Mongolians and Ladakhis have achieved the position.) However, they must have graduated from and served as abbot of one of the two tantric colleges, Gyuto and Gyumey.

13. This is one of the twenty-eight poems and songs in the collection *Mystical Verses of a Mad Dalai Lama* (see Bibliography).

14. My translation of his *Songs of Spiritual Change* was published by Snow Lion Publications in 1982.

15. I included a translation of this brief biography as an appendix to my study of the life and works of the Seventh Dalai Lama, *Songs of Spiritual Change*. I have slightly re-worked the passages

quoted here. The author, who was the Eighth Dalai Lama's guru Kachen Yeshey Gyaltsen (bKa'-chen-ye-shes-rgyal-mtshan), certainly ranks as one of the greatest writers of the eighteenth century. An extensive biography of his life was composed by the Eighth Dalai Lama himself.

16. Chandra Das is best known for his monumental *Tibetan English Dictionary*, first published in 1892. There is little doubt, however, that he subsidized his Tibetan studies with funds received from British intelligence. His 'scientific' (read 'map-making') expedition into Tibet in the late nineteenth century under documents secured from Tashi Lhunpo Monastery (then under British sponsorship) led to the senior tutor of the incumbent Panchen Lama being arrested on charges of treason. This created the initial friction between Tashi Lhunpo and the Lhasa aristocrats that eventually culminated in 1923 with the Panchen Lama leaving Tibet to live in exile in China.

Das barely escaped from Tibet with his life. Unable to return to complete his mission, he recruited a Japanese monk by the name of Ekai Kawaguchi to carry on in his place. Kawaguchi's hysterical reports from Lhasa played a prime role in the British decision of 1903 to invade Tibet. During that invasion the British were undoubtedly helped by the maps provided years earlier by Sarat Chandra Das.

How does all this tie in with Kalachakra? The subject introduces another interesting story that deserves a book in itself.

The reason for the British interest in Tibet was that the Russian Tsar was beginning to show an interest in Lhasa. Much of eastern Russia's Mongolian population was buddhist in the Tibetan tradition and regarded the Dalai Lama as their spiritual leader; and much of the Himalayan region of British India was Tibetan buddhist, also loyal principally to the Dalai Lama. Thus both superpowers were keen to have a say in things Tibetan.

At the time it so happened that one of the Thirteenth Dalai Lama's seven 'assistant tutors' was a Buriat monk. Dorjiev by name (from the Tibetan *dorjey*; rDo-rje), this monk had personal connections with the Tsar and had carried a number of communications from Lhasa to the Russian capital, St. Petersburg.

Kawaguchi reported that Dorjiev had published a book identifying Shambala with Russia and identifying the Tsar as the kalkin master. No trace of such a book has ever emerged; yet nonetheless the power of the Shambala legend struck apprehension into the British in India, and they set about with plans for an invasion.

The British conquest of Tibet was short-lived, and in the end may prove a political blessing in that it produced several international documents that could be used to support a case for Tibet's legal independence from China at the time. But it left the British uncomfortable about Kalachakra and Shambala for some decades to come.

This is perhaps one of the factors causing Sir Charles Bell, a British liaison officer to Tibet from 1910 onward, and in many ways a great friend of the Tibetans, to write derogatorily of the Kalachakra tradition in his accounts of Tibetan history and culture. For example, in his discussion of Atisha, a master whom he otherwise greatly admired, he almost apologized for Atisha's interest in the Kalachakra doctrines. He writes, "Atisha's teaching was largely based on the Kala Cakra (*sic*) system, one of the most debased forms of Tantric Buddhism. But it evidently met the needs of Tibet, and in him (Atisha) they had a man who had studied hard and gained a wide outlook... So whatever his own views may have been (concerning Kalachakra), he bowed to public opinion (and taught the Kalachakra). (*Tibet: Past and Present*, Oxford: 1926.)

There may, however, be some truth to the rumor that Dorjiev was attempting to build a Shambala myth in Russia, even if he never composed the book mentioned by Kawaguchi. The Kalachakra temple that he built in Leningrad (formerly St. Petersburg, home of the Tsar) still stands today in that city of near-forgotten glory. In fact, the Gorbachev government recently allowed it to re-open in a modest capacity. Who knows? It may still have a role to play.

17. This work has been translated by Edwin Bernbaum and was included in his excellent book, *The Way to Shambhala* (New York: Doubleday, 1980). Bernbaum provides the most comprehensive study of the Shambala myth to appear in English to date, including a survey of early Indian and Tibetan source materials, and extensive interviews on the subject with various contemporary lamas. The book is based on Bernbaum's doctoral thesis, but is brilliantly re-phrased for popular reading.

18. This prophecy is said to occur in some editions of the *Lankavatarasutra*.

Some early Tibetan historians, such as Sakya Pandita, who miscalculated the events of early Indian buddhist history by as much as five hundred years, took it to refer to the coming of buddhism to Tibet (for the Tibetans are of the red-faced race). This and many similar colossal historical errors were easily made by Tibetan writers due to the fact that the Tibetans did not adopt the sexantry system until the mid-eleventh century. Thus any given year simply stood as a name in a sea of thousands of names, and there was no way to link it to any particular century. After creating the sixty-year cycle system in the mid-eleventh century they had to work backwards in time through the historical evidence available to them, and locate specific events in the framework of the new conceptual system. Needless to say, the older an event the more difficult for the lamas to place it correctly. Many important events were miscalculated by numerous cycles of sixty years. The Buddha was placed almost five hundred years before his actual time. None of this, of course, particularly bothered the Tibetans. These events anyway were so long past that a minor historical misjudgement was of little significance.

However, after implementing their sexantry system the Tibetans became meticulous in their historical documentation, with everything being recorded down to the moment of the day.

As is evident in the Tibetan writings, for many centuries a large section of the lama community has thought of the above prophecy as speaking about Tibet. The fact that even after having put back the Buddha's life by five hundred years Sakya Pandita and the others were still five hundred years short of the 2,500 period stated in the prophecy, did not seem to daunt them in the least.

It is only in the last century, with knowledge of international standards in the dating of the life of the Buddha, that the Tibetans have begun to look for someone other than themselves as the subject of the prophecy. North America as the 'land of the red-faced people' quickly became a strong possibility in their minds, especially with the extent of interest shown in Tibetan buddhism over the last decades.

CHAPTER TWELVE

1. The buddhism of Tibet, particularly that propagated during the eighth to tenth centuries and today preserved in the Nyingma school, was perhaps more influenced by the buddhism of Oddiyana (Swat) than any other region of India, due to the work of Padma

Sambhava. This teacher was from Oddiyana, and it was under his guidance that the infrastructure was set in place for systematic translation of buddhist scriptures from Sanskrit into Tibetan.

2. Most scholars identify the Sita River with the Tanrim, of modern-day Eastern Turkestan. This, however, has never really been fully researched.

Tibetans tend to think of Shambala in allegorical terms. Consequently interest in the actual physical location of what once was the home of Suchandra, Manju Yashas, Pundarika and so many other Shambala masters has long faded. In addition, according to legend the secular plane of Shambala was conquered many centuries ago by Muslim armies and is temporarily under occupation and off-limits to buddhist pilgrims. Consequently although the Tibetan guidebooks to Shambala seem to speak in quite concrete terms, they usually fall short of providing information that could lead to a positive identification of the kingdom of Shambala.

3. "A History and Geography of Shambala," by Garjey Khamtrul Rinpochey, translated by Sharpa Tulku and Alex Berzin, *The Tibet Journal*, Vol. 3, No. 3 (1981).

4. The most extensive study of the names of Muslim places and people mentioned in the Kalachakra literature has been conducted by Helmut Hoffman. It is not an easy study, as tenth-century Sanskrit renditions of the buddhist names for these foreign labels are not always immediately recognizable. The Sanskrit phonetic rendition of a Shambalan mispronunciation of an Arabic name often produces ambiguous results. Nonetheless, the name of Mohammed is positively identified as 'the teacher (*guru swami*) of the la-los' in Manju Yashas' *The Abbreviated Kalachakra Tantra*.

Hoffman's "Manichaeism and Islam in the Buddhist Kalachakra System" (*Proceedings of the IXth International Congress for the History of Religions*, Tokyo, 1960) makes for interesting reading. So does his "Kalachakra Studies I: Manichaeism, Christianity, and Islam in the *Kalachakra Tantra*," *Central Asiatic Journal*, 1973. I agree with John Newman that Hoffman probably suspects a far bigger influence from the Middle East than actually was the case; but his thesis does demonstrate the extent of the international dialogue carried across the trade routes of tenth- and eleventh-century Asia.

5. I first noticed this comment linking the First Panchen Lama with Raudra, the twenty-fifth kalkin master of Shambala, in an article by the modern Mongolian scholar Ts. Damdinsuren, entitled

"Commentary on Kalachakra or the Wheel of Time," *The Tibet Journal*, Vol. IV, No. 1 (1981). I asked several lama friends about the story, and they confirmed that in fact there was a Tibetan legend to this effect.

6. This is taken from one of the seven Shambala prayers written by the Sixth Panchen Lama at the request of various disciples over the year or so following his giving of the Kalachakra initiation in Peking in the late 1920s. The complete *Collected Works* of the Sixth Panchen Lama has been published in India, and thus is available from any U.S. Library of Congress lending service.

CHAPTER THIRTEEN

1. The Sixth Panchen Lama directly lifts these two famous lines from Shantideva's *A Guide to the Bodhisattva Ways*, as a poetic salute to that illustrious eighth-century Indian buddhist master.

2. The Tibetan reads *Dangpo Sangyey* (Dang-poi-sangs-rgyas), literally 'the First Buddha.' This is an epithet of Kalachakra. It is the Tibetan equivalent of the Sanskrit word *Paramadibuddha*, which is also the name of the Kalachakra root tantra as redacted by Suchandra (and no longer extant).

3. Tib., Riwo Tsey Nga; Chinese, Wu-tai-shan. This is the only pilgrimage site in China held in high regard by the Tibetans. The Fifth, Seventh and Thirteenth Dalai Lamas all made pilgrimages there during their lives as part of their teaching tours of Eastern Tibet, Mongolia, and China.

CHAPTER FOURTEEN

1. I discussed these two types of tantras in Chapter Ten. As the Dalai Lama points out here, the principal difference between them is in how the fourth initiation is given.

2. Although karmic predispositions make a big difference in the effectiveness of a practice on the completion stage, this does not seem to be such an important factor on the generation stage.

For this reason the Tibetans often practice the generation stage of one tantric system, such as Yamantaka, and the completion stage of another, such as Kalachakra.

3. It seems that by the tenth and eleventh centuries the Tibetans had become very influential in the monastic hierarchies of India.

Several of these monasteries, including Nalanda and Vikramashila, even had special departments just for Tibetans, their numbers were so large. Nalanda also at the time had a department for Indonesians, and it seems that these were the two largest groups of foreigners in India at the time.

CHAPTER FIFTEEN

1. The Tibetan *Tengyur,* or collection of Indian buddhist works in translation contains several dozen works by Dipamkara Shrijnana. I have no idea in which of these this passage lies. The Seventh Dalai Lama gives no indication.

2. A characteristic of Tibetan spiritual writings is to quote a passage from one of the hundreds of sutras spoken by the Buddha, without giving the name of the specific sutra from which the passage is drawn. The Seventh Dalai Lama does this throughout his essay.

3. As was mentioned earlier, Vira is another name of the great Indian poet better known as Ashvaghosha.

4. These are classical verses, known by heart to most Tibetans, from Shantideva's *A Guide to the Bodhisattva Ways.*

5. Tokmey Zangpo is a renowned thirteenth-century Sakyapa master who is best known for two of his works: his commentary to Shantideva's *A Guide to the Bodhisattva Ways*, and a brief verse work known as *The Thirty-Seven Bodhisattva Practices (Byang-sems-yang-lag-so-bdun-ma).* I feel particularly indebted to Tokmey Zangpo: After two years of language studies in the Tibetan Library at Dharamsala I read the first of the above two works, both as a syllable-by-syllable reading and a general assessment survey. Tokmey Zangpo's lucid and personal style unfolded the multidimensional meanings of Shantideva's great classic, and reading him as a language study was a double boon.

His *Thirty-Seven Practices* has become more famous in recent years, as on a number of occasions His Holiness the Dalai Lama has chosen to teach it as a preliminary discourse to a large Kalachakra initiation. Jeffrey Hopkins includes a translation of it in *The Kalachakra Tantra: Rite of Initiation.*

Another rendition of it, with a brief commentary by His Holiness, is included in the collection *Four Buddhist Commentaries* (Dharamsala: LTWA, 1982).

6. I am delighted to include this text by the Seventh Dalai Lama in this collection. It places the process of tantric initiation and practice within the context of the bodhisattva ideals that tantric endeavor should aim to fulfill.

An interesting coincidence is that the Sixth Panchen Lama used this very text by the Seventh Dalai Lama as the basis of his preliminary discourse to the Kalachakra initiation that he gave in Peking in the late 1920s. His reading was recorded and transcribed, and published in Tibet together with his collected works. His collected works were later re-published in India, and thus became available to international tibetologists. I was delighted with his rephrasing of the Seventh Dalai Lama, and considered using it in this collection.

In the end I settled on the Seventh Dalai Lama's text, partly because of its more classical flavor, but also because the Seventh is such an important figure in the Kalachakra lineage of transmission.

7. The colophon to the Seventh Dalai Lama's text reads, "This brief account of the spiritual attitudes and qualities that must be cultivated as a preliminary to receiving the empowerments and initiations that render the mind fertile for tantric practice was written at the request of the Gyalak Khenpo Ertini Tsakhang Hutuktu, by the Buddhist Monk Lobzang Kalzang Gyatso Palzangpo, while residing in the Potala."

CHAPTER SIXTEEN

1. Again, this verse by Lama Tsongkhapa is drawn from his spiritual autobiography entitled *Song of Spiritual Experience (rTogs-brjod-mdun-legs-ma)*. See Chapter Five, Note 1, above.

2. In a private interview with His Holiness the Dalai Lama in Dharamsala during May of 1991, I asked him which of these various forms of the Kalachakra mandala he felt is most appropriate for beginning practitioners.

His Holiness replied, "This depends upon the individual practitioner, upon factors such as how much time he or she wishes to commit to a daily practice, how extensive is his or her background in the basic buddhist trainings, the individual predispositions of the practitioner, and so forth.

"However, it is generally said that the more extensive mandalas are more powerful if one is able to practice them properly. If not, it is better to begin with a simpler mandala form.''

3. All of the above texts, which were written in Shambala and India, were also recommended by the First Dalai Lama. Most of those to follow on the Thirteenth Dalai Lama's list, however, are not mentioned by the First Dalai Lama.

4. The samaya here is to keep a set of tantric implements, as well as a tantric costume of human bone. Tibetans found this impractical, and instead usually just kept a small woodblock print depicting the dozen or so principal tantric possessions.

5. The Thirteenth Dalai Lama was a great admirer of the life and writings of Buton Rinchen Druppa. Included in his collected works is a long biographical poem that he wrote on Buton which is highly emotional in its praise of him.

CHAPTER SEVENTEEN

1. The Tibetan term for these six yogas is *yang-lag-druk-gi nal-jor* (Yang-lag-drug-gi-rnal-'byor), or 'six-branched yoga.' The word 'branch' is used to stress the integral character of the six yogas. Therefore the First Dalai Lama comments,

> Thus (the six yogas by themselves have the power to generate the attainment of full enlightenment and so) there is no need to supplement them with various assortments of other practices, nor to practice anything on top of them. On the other hand, to omit any of them will impair the system's potency (to produce enlightenment).

2. We saw his name earlier in Part One; Tilbupa is one of the three major lineage masters in the Indian transmission of the Heruka Chakrasamvara tradition. Generally it is his lineage of Heruka that is used as the basis of the Six Yogas of Naropa.

Here Tilbupa is commenting on what mandalas can be used in the initiation ceremony. In this regard Ven. Lati Rinpochey provided the following oral comments:

> In the mainstream Vajrayana systems, such as Guhyasamaja, any of the above four 'mandalas' may be used. In Kalachakra, however, only the two-dimensional mandala made from colored powders is used.

As in the tantric tradition of Heruka Chakrasamvara, the Kalachakra system incorporates three principal mandalas: those of body, speech, and mind. In Kalachakra it is only necessary for the master to generate the last of these as a preliminary to the initiation ceremony, as it embodies the symbolism found in all three mandalas.

3. This is one of the three 'Rosaries' composed by Naropa's disciple Abhayakaragupta, as mentioned earlier in Chapter Sixteen by the Thirteenth Dalai Lama in his analysis of Indian literary sourceworks on Kalachakra.

4. During this phase of the initiation the disciples imagine that they come in turn before each of the four doors of the Kalachakra mandala mansion. At each door they see a different face of Kalachakra. They request and are given the according initiations. Here Lati Rinpochey commented,

Why is it necessary to receive initiation in order to practice the tantric path? Just as someone who wishes to undertake an important building project must first acquire the permission of the appropriate building authorities, the spiritual aspirant wishing to undertake the great task of the Vajrayana yoga must first gain the blessings of a qualified lineage master. Moreover, at the time of initiation the master plants the seeds of tantric attainment within the mind of the disciple, and without these seeds our practice of the two tantric stages will be unable to produce the tree, branches, and fruit of enlightenment.

5. The Tibetan reads *sa dun* (Sa-bdun), meaning 'seven levels.' It is not clear if this refers to the seventh arya bodhisattva level of the path to enlightenment, or the seventh level of the Kalachakra empty body yoga discussed later by the First Dalai Lama under the topic of the yoga of samadhi.

6. This passage could also be translated as, "The masters accept purified passion."

7. This important work (see Bibliography) by Lama Tsongkhapa outlines the structure of the Gelukpa interpretation of the tantric precepts and commitments.

Tsongkhapa describes the training in the maintenance of dis-

cipline as being threefold: that aspect related to individual liberation; that related to the bodhisattva aspiration; and that related to
the Vajrayana, and in specific to highest yoga tantra.

The first of these three refers to any of the eight types of *pratimok-
sha* precepts, such as those of a layman or laywoman, novice monk
and novice nun, etc. Because this level of commitment must be
based on refuge, the general guidelines of refuge are the basis of
'the vow of personal liberation.' Early in one's practice one should
attempt to adopt at least one of the five lay precepts, such as not
to kill humans, and so forth. Later one takes the bodhisattva precept to hold enlightenment as a priority and to treat living beings
with kindness. When stability in these disciplines has been gained
one enters into the Vajrayana and takes the precepts and commitments entailed by the specific tantric system being practiced.

The Thirteenth Dalai Lama provides a clear outline of the categories of these disciplines in the closing section of his *Summary of
the Kalachakra Tradition,* in the previous chapter of this volume.

The Ven. Lati Rinpochey here added the following oral
comments:

> Generally speaking, in the first two levels of the Mahayana
> tantras one takes refuge and the common Mahayana
> precepts, and in the yoga tantra division also takes the nine-
> teen precepts of the five Tathagatas. In highest yoga tantra
> one also takes the fourteen root and eight secondary
> precepts, as well as any precepts unique to the tantric sys-
> tem being imparted. For example, the Kalachakra tradi-
> tion also entails an additional twenty-five special com-
> mitments.
>
> It is said that if one guards the tantric precepts and in-
> tensely practices the yogas of the generation and comple-
> tion stages, enlightenment is easily attained in this very
> lifetime. Even should we not accomplish these two yogic
> stages, merely guarding the tantric precepts and practic-
> ing as well as we can guarantees enlightenment within seven
> lives. Finally, someone who receives an initiation into
> highest yoga tantra and guards the commitments well yet
> does not even engage in the yogas of the two stages will
> nonetheless gain enlightenment within seven lifetimes.

8. These four are discussed later by the First Dalai Lama. I also commented on them in Chapter Ten. The processes of the four should be clear by comparing these two sections with the sadhana of Buton Rinchen Druppa, to follow in Chapter Nineteen.

9. From this point of the First Dalai Lama's commentary, and also in the later chapters, we will see kalagni and rahu mentioned repeatedly.

These two represent the nodes of the sun and moon. It is they who play the fundamental role in solar and lunar eclipses. They are conceived here as heavenly bodies (i.e., planets), and are visualized as spherical, slightly flat discs, yellow and black in color, respectively, in the same manner as the sun and moon are visualized (these latter being red and white, respectively).

Kalachakra and Consort stand on disc-like cushions stacked one on top of another, representing the sun, moon, rahu, and kalagni (this last sometimes not being directly stated), to symbolize that they understand the processes of the external world. They bear an expression of power, for they are masters of the process.

In the completion stage these 'planets' symbolize specific levels of tantric attainment, as we will see later in the Kalachakra 'yoga of individual withdrawal.' They also symbolize the various levels of the emergence of the subtle minds, as likened to the stages experienced at the time of death.

10. This is all part of the sadhana process. It is presented in greater detail by Buton Rinchen Druppa in *The Best of Jewels*, to follow in Chapter Nineteen.

11. As we can see, the description of the chakras in the Kalachakra system differs considerably from that given in systems such as Guhyasamaja, Yamantaka and Heruka Chakrasamvara.

12. I have left the names of two of the six yogas in the original Sanskrit, namely, dhyana (the second yoga) and samadhi (the sixth). It seems futile to translate them, as there are no easy equivalents in English, nor even a meaningful and practical proxy term. Fortunately both Sanskrit words will already be familiar to most readers. The former term is most often rendered as meditation and the latter as meditative concentration; here neither term has that particular focus in meaning, as is evident by the First Dalai Lama's account of them in a section of his commentary to follow.

13. That is, the *Paramadibuddha*, or 'Primordial Buddha,' referred to in Chapter Thirteen, Note 2.

14. I have discussed this important trilogy in Chapter Eleven. I should confess that in my earlier translation of the First Dalai Lama's Kalachakra treatise, published in *Selected Works of the Dalai Lama I: Bridging the Sutras and Tantras*, I somewhat confused the relationship between the *Trilogy* and *The Great Commentary: A Stainless Light.*

See my note to *The Trilogy of the Bodhisattvas* in the first section of the Bibliography for more on this important collection. Also see Note 15 below.

15. Longdol Lama's *A Lexicon of Kalachakra Terms according to the Views of Lama Tsongkhapa* (see entry of this name in the Bibliography) throws light on the nature of several of these important source works of the Kalachakra tradition:

> As for the collection known as *The Trilogy of the Bodhisattvas*, this is comprised of *The Great Commentary: A Stainless Light*, which is in twelve thousand lines [i.e., verses]; *The Vajragarbha Commentary*, which is an elucidation of the *Hevajra Tantra* known as *The Tantra of Two Forms*, explained in terms of the Kalachakra path; and *The Vajrapani Commentary*, an elucidation of the *Heruka Chakrasamvara Tantra*, also expressed in terms compatible with the Kalachakra doctrine.
>
> As for the mahasiddha Naropa's *Commentary to the Treatise on the Initiations*, in composing this important work Naropa drew heavily from *The Guhyasamaja Tantra*, which is in eighteen chapters, doing so in terms consistent with the Kalachakra doctrine.

Longdol Lama then goes on to list other important Indian literature on the subject, such as the works of Kalachakrapada, and also the most important Gelukpa texts, such as those of Baso Chojey (Ba-so-chos-rje), Norzang Gyatso (Nor-bzang-brgya-'tsho), and so forth.

16. All of these works can be found in the Tibetan canon known as the *Tengyur*, the collection of buddhist works translated from Sanskrit, other than those spoken by Buddha himself. These latter scriptures are in the collection known as the *Kangyur*.

17. This refers to the special Sakyapa lineage originating with the Indian mahasiddha Virupa, a master who specialized in Hevajra

from the mainstream tantras and Kalachakra in the 'clear' tantras. He transmitted this fusion of ideas as understood in his personal meditational experience to a number of students, and eventually they became integral to the Sakya school of Tibetan Buddhism.

Virupa seems to have been the principal Indian teacher behind the cross-fertilizations that occurred with the Hevajra and Kalachakra traditions. The result has been that most thorough studies of the Kalachakra doctrine now incorporate several important texts from the Hevajra cycle. These are listed by the Thirteenth Dalai Lama in Chapter Sixteen.

CHAPTER EIGHTEEN

1. This important Kalachakra master transmitted the lineage to the tutors of the Dalai Lama. They in turn gave the lineage to His Holiness the present Dalai Lama. The senior tutor Ling Rinpochey was the principal transmission master amongst them.

Thus Kyabjey Khangsar Dorjey Chang is the spiritual grandfather of the Dalai Lama in the line of transmission.

Another important Kalachakra master of the same generation is the renowned Pabongkha Rinpochey, who also transmitted certain of the Kalachakra lineages to the two tutors.

2. Recitation of the name mantra of one's teacher is a common practice with Tibetan buddhists. Each school has a general way to present the name mantras of its masters; there are perhaps a dozen or so forms in vogue at the moment.

One popular mantric format is that given here for the Dalai Lama's name mantra. The first four words—*om āḥ guru vajradhara* —are part of the standard mantra, as are the last four words—*sarva siddhi hūṃ hūṃ*. The five words that are in the middle of the mantra as given here—*vāgindra sumati śhāsanadhara samudra shrībhadra*— are the personal ordination (monastic) names of His Holiness— Ngawang Lobzang Tenzin Gyatso, meaning Eloquent Wise Doctrine-Holder, He of Sublime Glory—translated into Sanskrit. These, by the way, are not flowery titles of the Dalai Lama; they are standard buddhist monastic names, no more grandiose than those received by the humblest novice at the time of ordination.

The name mantra is thus tailored to each specific teacher, by substituting the central part of the mantra with the Sanskrit equivalents of the names of one's personal teacher. For example, the way

I personally use the mantra sees the central section with the syllables *vāgindra maitri*. The first four and last four words of the mantra remain the same.

3. In *A Lexicon of Kalachakra Terms according to the Views of Lama Tsongkhapa* (see entry of this name in Section One of the Bibliography) Longdol Lama comments as follows:

> As for this mantra, known as 'Possessor of Ten Powers,' it can be explained either in terms of the form of (the syllables of) the mantra, or else in terms of the sound of the mantra.
>
> In the former case, the explanation can be given in terms of the external world (i.e., outer Kalachakra), the internal world (i.e., inner Kalackakra), the generation stage yogas, or the completion stage yogas (these last two being alternative Kalachakra)....
>
> In the latter case, when the mantra is explained in terms of sound, it is said that whenever there is sound there is energy, and whenever there is energy there is sound. The strength (or character) of that energy is one of three types. Male energy, which is aggressive, resounds with the resonance of *om;* female energy, which is delicate, resounds with the resonance of *āḥ;* and neutral energy, which is between these two in character, resounds with the resonance of *hūṃ.* Thus all subtle energies collect into these three mantric sounds. Moreover, the most subtle aspects of both energy and consciousness collect together into the resonance of these three mantric syllables, and therefore they are said to be the root of both samsara and nirvana.
>
> This is the meaning of the mantric syllables *e-vaṃ,* which most quintessentially carry the sense of the mantra "Possessor of Ten Powers."
>
> The manner in which the most subtle aspects of consciousness and the energies abide together is such that they cannot be differentiated from one another. For example, we can conventionally speak about the difference between the color, light and shape of the flame of a butterlamp; but other than giving them different names we cannot separate them as actual entities. In the same way, the subtle consciousness and the subtle energies upon which this con-

sciousness rides can be spoken of with different words, but in fact they are inseparable. Recitation of this mantra places us in communion with these subtle levels of energy and mind....

Thus the mantra can be used to explain everything in the external world (outer Kalachakra), everything in the internal world (inner Kalachakra), and all the yogic practices of both the generation and completion stages (alternative Kalachakra). In this way (the mantra) reveals the complete meaning of the entire Kalachakra doctrine.

As His Holiness the Dalai Lama explained at the Kalachakra initiation in Varanasi in January, 1991, the name 'Possessor of Ten Powers' is given in reference to the syllables at the middle of this mantra, i.e., *hamkshahmalavaraya*, which is the actual body of the mantra, and is composed of seven individual mantric syllables: *ham kshah ma la va ra ya*. These seven become eight because the vowel sound of *a* pervades each of them. They become ten by counting the visarga of the syllable *kshah* (represented by a moon sliver), and the anusvara of the syllable *ham* (depicted as a solar sphere). Sometimes to this is added an eleventh "power," symbolized by the nada, or zig-zag line that stands above the entire mantric composite.

There are various ways to link these ten (or eleven) mantric components to the outer, inner and alternative Kalachakras. The subject is too complex to outline here; it is perhaps best to content ourselves with the above comment of Longdol Lama, "...(the mantra) reveals the complete meaning of the entire Kalachakra doctrine."

CHAPTER NINETEEN

1. This type of tantric substance, which literally translates as 'ambrosia pill,' is used by lamas of all schools as a method of purification. The pills are first prepared from specific herbs, metals and sacred materials in accordance with a prescribed procedure, and then are consecrated by means of a tantric rite. After that they are slowly distributed among disciples as the need arises. These pills are used in most tantric retreats and in a large variety of rituals. They are also ingested as a medicine in times of illness.

2. The *tsek-drak* refers to the small double circle, one on the top

of another, that sometimes is placed after a mantric seed syllable. In some traditions the two circles are separated by a small hyphen-like line.

3. The thirty-two vowels are as follows:

a i ṛi u ḷi | a e ar o al | ha ya ra va la | aṃ
lā vā rā yā hā | āl au ār ai ā | Ḷi ū Ṛi ī ā | aḥ

The eighty consonants:

lla vva yya ḍḍa ḍhḍha | lla vva rra yya hha | ssa ḥpḥpa ṣhṣha
śhśha ḥkḥka | tta ththa dda dhdha nna | ppa phpha bba bhbha
mma | ṭṭa ṭhṭha ḍḍa ḍhḍha ṇṇa | chcha chhchha jja jhjha ñña |
kka khkha gga ghgha ṅṅa |
ṅa gha ga kha ka | ña jha ja chha cha | ṇa ḍha ḍa ṭha ṭa |
ma bha ba pha pa | na dha da tha ta | ḥka śha ṣha ḥpa sa |
ha ya ra va la | ḍha ḍa ya va la |

4. These four, Vajra Force and so forth, refer to the four divinities—Vajravega etc.—that establish the seal. It seemed appropriate to put their names in English.

5. If one wishes to recite the mantras of the offering devis, they are as follows:

oṃ cha-chha-ja-jha-ña vajra gandhe gandhārchanaṃ kuru kuru svāhā.
oṃ chā-chhā-jā-jhā-ñā vajra māle mālārchanaṃ kuru kuru svāhā.
oṃ ṭa-ṭha-ḍa-ḍha-ṇa vajra dhūpe dhūpārchanaṃ kuru kuru svāhā.
oṃ ṭa-ṭhā-ḍā-ḍhā-ṇā vajra pradīpe pradīpārchanaṃ kuru kuru svāhā.
oṃ pa-pha-ba-bha-ma vajrāmrite naivedya pūjāṃ kuru kuru svāhā.
oṃ pā-phā-bā-bhā-mā vajrākṣhate phalārchanaṃ kuru kuru svāhā.
oṃ ta-tha-da-dha-na vajra lāsye vastrābharaṇa pūjāṃ kuru kuru svāhā.
oṃ tā-thā-dā-dhā-nā vajra hāsye ghaṇṭādarśha pūjāṃ kuru kuru svāhā.
oṃ ka-kha-ga-gha-ṅa vajra vādye vādya pūjāṃ kuru kuru svāhā.
oṃ kā-khā-gā-ghā-ṅā vajra nritye nritya pūjāṃ kuru kuru svāhā.
oṃ sa-ḥpa-ṣha-śha-ḥka vajra gīte gīta pūjāṃ kuru kuru svāhā.
oṃ sā-ḥpā-ṣhā-śhā-ḥkā vajra kāme sarva buddha bodhisattvānāṃ
*   krodhādīnāṃ vajra surata pūjāṃ kuru kuru svāhā.*

6. The expression 'Wisdom Wheel' is here being used as an epithet of Kalachakra and Consort. The Sanskrit equivalent is *Jnanachakra.*

CHAPTER TWENTY

1. The full colophon to this text reads, "Composed in an unbroken stream by the Kalachakra yogi Lobzang Chokyi Gyaltsen [i.e., the First Panchen Lama] in the temple of Tashi Lhunpo Monastery. A monk disciple, Ngawang Lobzang by name, a practitioner with devotion, discipline and a marvellous proficiency in the yogas, had offered an extensive ritual [in Tashi Lhunpo] and then requested that I write him a song of spiritual aspirations that would summarize the essential points of the Kalachakra path in a few easily understandable words. This verse work was inspired by his sincere supplication."

Thus it would appear that the First Panchen Lama's brief verse work on Kalachakra was born of a humble origin. But as fate would have it, it became the most popular of his numerous Kalachakra writings, in spite of (or perhaps because of) its brevity.

Glossary

SPELLING GLOSS OF SANSKRIT NAMES AND WORDS USED IN THE TEXTS

ANGLICI-ZATION	FORMAL SPELLING
abadhuti	avadhūtī
Acharya	Ācārya
Aryadeva	Āryadeva
Acharya	Ācārya
Ashvaghosha	Aśvaghoṣa
Acharya Vira	Ācārya Vīra
Akshobhya	Akṣobhya
anuttara tantra	anuttara tantra
Asanga	Asaṅga
Ashoka	Aśoka
Ashvaghosha	Aśvaghoṣa
Atisha	Atīśa
Atisha	Atīśa
Dipamkara	Dīpaṃkara
Shrijnana	Śrījñāna
Avalokiteshvara	Avalokiteśvara
Bodh Gaya	Bodh Gayā
bodhichitta	bodhicitta
bodhisattva	bodhisattva
bodhisattvayana	bodhisattvayāna
buddha	buddha

ANGLICI-ZATION	FORMAL SPELLING
Buddha Shakyamuni	Buddha Śākyamuni
chakra	cakra
Chakrasamvara	Cakrasaṃvara
charya tantra	caryā tantra
Chilupa	Cilupa
chittamani	Cittamaṇi
Dhanyakataka	Dhānyakaṭaka
Stupa	Stūpa
Dharma	Dharma
dharmadhatu	dharmadhātu
dharmakaya	dharmakāya
dharmamudra	dharmamudrā
dharmodaya	dharmodaya
dhyana	dhyāna
Dipamkara	Dīpaṃkara
Shrijnana	Śrījñāna
Gandhapada	Gandhapāda
Guhyaman-trayana	Guhyaman-trayāna
Guhyasamaja	Guhyasamāja
guru	guru
guruyoga	guruyoga

Heruka	Heruka	rahu	rāhu
Heruka	Heruka	ratna	ratna
Chakrasamvara	Cakrasaṃvara	Raudra Chakri	Raudra Cakri
Hevajra	Hevajra	rupakaya	rūpakāya
Hinayana	Hīnayāna	sadhana	sādhana
Indrabhuti	Indrabhūti	samadhi	samādhi
Kalachakra	Kālacakra	Samanta	Samanta
Kalachakrapada	Kālacakrapāda	Shribhadra	Śrībhadra
Kalachakra	Kālacakra	samayamudra	samayamudrā
Tantra	Tantra	sambhogakaya	sambhogakāya
Kalagni	kālāgni	samsara	saṃsāra
kalkin	kalkin	Saraha	Saraha
karma	karma	shakti	śakti
karmamudra	karmamudrā	shamatha	śamatha
Krishnacharyin	Kṛṣṇacaryin	Shambala	Śambhala
kriya tantra	kriyā tantra	Shavari	Śabari
Lalitavajra	Lalitavajra	shravaka	śrāvaka
Luipada	Lūhipāda	shravaka arhant	śrāvaka arhat
maha anuttara	mahā anuttara	Shribhadra	Śrībhadra
tantra	tantra	Sitatapatra	Sitātapatra
Mahamaya	Mahāmāyā	Somanatha	Somanātha
mahamudra	mahāmudrā	stupa	stūpa
mahasiddha	mahāsiddha	Suchandra	Sucandra
Mahayana	Mahāyāna	Suryashri	Sūryaśrī
mandala	maṇḍala	sutra	sūtra
Manjukirti	Mañjukīrti	Sutrayana	Sūtrayāna
Manjushri	Mañjuśrī	svabhavikakaya	svābhāvikakāya
Manju Yashas	Mañju Yaśas	Tantrayana	Tantrayāna
mantra	mantra	Tara	Tārā
mantramala	mantramālā	tathagata	tathāgata
mantrayana	mantrayāna	Ushnishavijaya	Uṣṇīṣavijaya
naga	nāga	Vairochana	Vairocana
Nagarjuna	Nāgārjuna	vajra	vajra
Nalanda	Nālanda	Vajradhara	Vajradhara
Naropa	Nāropa	Vajrapani	Vajrapāṇi
nirmanakaya	nirmāṇakāya	Vajrasattva	Vajrasattva
nirvana	nirvāṇa	Vajravega	Vajravega
Odantapuri	Otantapura	Vajravidarana	Vajravidāraṇa
padma	padma	Vajrayana	Vajrayana
Pindo Acharya	Piṇḍo Ācārya	Vasubandhu	Vasubandhu
Prajnaparamita	Prajñāpāramitā	Vikramalashila	Vikramalaśīla
prajnaparamita	Prajñāpāramitā	vipashyana	vipaśyanā
sutras	sūtras	Vira	Vīra
Pratyekabuddha	Pratyekabuddha	yoga	yoga
Pundarika	Puṇḍarīka	yoga tantra	yoga tantra

SPELLING GLOSS OF TIBETAN NAMES AND WORDS USED IN THE TEXTS

ANGLICI-ZATION	*FORMAL SPELLING*
Amchok Tsennyi Gonpa	A-mchog-mtshan-nyid-dgon-pa
Amchok Tulku	A-mchog-sprul-sku
Amdo	A-mdo
bardo	bar-do
begyu	sbes-rgyud
Bodong Chokley Namgyal	Bo-dong-phyogs-las-rnam-rgyal
Buton	Bu-ston
Buton Rinchen Drubpa	Bus-ton-rin-chen-grub-pa
Chilupa	Tshil-lu-pa
Chimey Rinpochey	'Chi-med-rin-po-che
Chokyi Pel	Chos-kyi-dpal
Chomdzey Tashi Wangyal	Chos-mdzed-bkra-shis-dbang-rgyal
Dalai Lama	Ta-lai-bla-ma
dawa	zla-ba
dhuti	dhu-ti
Doboom Tulku	rDo-'bum-sprul-sku
Drepung	'Bres-spungs
Drepung Loseling	'Bras-spungs-blo-gsal-gling
Dro Lotsawa	'Bro-lo-tsa-ba
Drom Tonpa	'Brom-ston-pa
dungchen	dung-chen
dutsi rilbu	bDud-rtsi-ril-bu
Dvakpo Gomchen Ngawang Drakpa	Dvag-po-sgom-chen-ngag-dbang-grags-pa
Dzogchen Lam Rim	rDzogs-chen-lam-rim
Ganden	dGa'-ldan
Ganden Shartsey	dGa'-ldan-shar-brtse

ANGLICI-ZATION	*FORMAL SPELLING*
Garjey Khamtrul Tulku	Gar-byed-khams-sprul-sprul-sku
Geluk	dGe-lugs
Gelukpa	dGe-lugs-pa
Go Lotsawa	Gos-lo-tsa-ba
Gungru Gyaltsen Zangpo	Gung-ru-rGyal-mtshan-bzang-po
Gugey	Gu-ge
Gyaltsepjey	rGyal-tshab-rje
Gyalwa Gendun Druppa	rGyal-ba-dge-'dun-grub-pa
Gyalwa Gendun Gyatso	rGyal-ba-dge-'dun-brgya-mtsho
Gyalwa Kalzang Gyatso	rGyal-ba-bskal-bzang-brgya-mtsho
Gyalwa Sonam Gyatso	rGyal-ba-bsod-nams-brgya-mtsho
Gyalwa Tubten Gyatso	rGyal-ba-thub-bstan-brgya-mtsho
Jonang	Jo-nang
Jonangpa	Jo-nang-pa
jungpo	'Byung-po
Jyojo Dawai Ozer	Gyo-jo-zla-bai-od-zer
Kadam	bKa'-gdams
Kadampa	bKa'gdams-pa
Kargyu	bKa'-rgyud
Kargyupa	bKa-rgyud-pa
Kham	Khams
khamtsen	khang-tsan
Khedrup Norzang Gyatso	mKhas-grub-nor-bzang-brgya-mtsho
Khedrupjey	mKhas-grub-rje
Kumbum	sKu-'bum
kundarma	kun-dar-ma
Kyabjey Khangsar Dorjey Chang	sKyabs-rje-khang-sar-rdo-rje-chang

Kyabjey Ling Rinpochey	sKyabs-rje-gling-rin-po-che
kyangma	kyang-ma
lalana	la-la-na
lalo	kLa-klo
Lam Drey	lam-'bres
Lam Rim	lam-rim
Lama Drom Tonpa	bLa-ma-'brom-ston-pa
Lama Kalzang Tenzin	bLa-ma-bskal-bzang-bstan-'dzin
Lama Lobzang Chinpa	bLa-ma-slo-bzang-spyin-pa
Lama Tsongkhapa	bLa-ma-btsong-kha-pa
lam-tso-nam-sum	lam-gtso-rnam-gsum
Lati Rinpochey	bLa-ti-rin-po-che
Lhasa	lHa-sa
lhenkyey detong yeshey	lHan-skyes-bde-stong-ye-shes
Lobzang Chokyi Gyaltsen	bLo-bzang-chos-kyi-rgyal-mtshan
Lobzang Tayang	bLo-bzang-rta-dbyangs
Longdol Lama	kLong-rdol-bla-ma
lu	gLu
lug	lug
Luipa	Lui-pa
marser	mar-gser
Nakchopa	Nag-spyod-pa
Ngawang Chokden	Ngag-dbang-mchog-ldan
norlegyal	nor-las-rgyal
nyima	nyi-ma
Nyingma	rNying-ma
Nyingmapa	rNying-ma-pa
nyipang	gNyis-spang
Pakpa Yonden Gyatso	'Phags-pa-yon-tan-brgya-mtsho
Panchen Chokyi Gyaltsen	Pan-chen-chos-kyi-rgyal-mtshan
Panchen Chokyi Nyima	Pan-chen-chos-kyi-nyi-ma
Panchen Lama	Pan-chen-bla-ma
Pematso	Pad-ma-mtsho
Purchokpa Rinpochey	Phur-phyogs-pa-rin-po-che
rasana	ra-sa-na
Redeng	Rva-bsgreng
Redeng Rinpochey	Rva-bsgreng-rin-po-che
Rinchen Gang	Rin-chen-sgang
roma	ro-ma
rupel	rus-spal
Rva Chorab	Rva-chos-rab
Rva Dorjey Drak	Rva-rdo-rje-sgrags
Rva Lotsawa	Rva-lo-tsa-ba
Rva Yeshes Sengey	Rva-ye-shes-seng-ge
sa	sa
Sakya	Sa-skya
Sakyapa	Sa-skya-pa
selgyu	gSal-rgyud
Sera	Se-ra
sherab	Shes-rab
Shigatsey	Zhi-ga-brtse
Taktsang Lotsawa	sTag-tsang-lo-tsa-ba
Taranatha	Ta-ra-na-tha
Tashi Lhunpo	bKra-shis-lhun-po
Thepo Tulku	mTheb-bo-sprul-sku
tikley	thig-le
Tilbupa	Dril-bu-pa
Trichen Ngawang Chokden	Khri-chen-ngag-dbang-mchog-ldan
Trinley	'Phrin-las
tsa	rTsa
tsa lung tikley	rTsa-lung-thig-le
Tsechokling	Tse-mchog-gling
tsok	tshogs
Tsongkhapa	Tsong-kha-pa
yeshey	ye-shes
Zhalu	zha-lu

Bibliography

The bibliographical materials that follow have been arranged in three sections.

In the first of these I list the Sanskrit and Tibetan texts that I either quote or refer to in Part One of this volume, which is my own analysis of the Kalachakra yogic system and its contextual placement within the Vajrayana. Here I give a brief annotation to each entry, to provide the reader with a sense of the background of the particular sources from which I have chosen to draw.

Section Two lists the Tibetan titles and authors of the texts translated in Part Two of this volume. All of these are indigenous Tibetan writings.

Finally, Section Three contains a list of the Sanskrit and Tibetan texts quoted by the Tibetan authors in Part Two. Some of these are also quoted or referred to in my own analysis in Part One.

Tibetan literature generally gives the sources of a textual quotation by its title in Tibetan translation. It is not always clear whether a work being cited is a rendition from the Sanskrit, or an original Tibetan treatise. To further challenge the reader, the title is generally not presented in full form, but in an abbreviation of two or three syllables, and the author's name usually is not mentioned.

However, most Tibetan lamas are able to identify the origins of such quotations simply from familiarity with the material, and thus to discern if it is a translation or an original Tibetan text. Works in the former category are accompanied in the bibliography by both

Tibetan and Sanskrit versions of the title; those in the latter category are accompanied solely by a Tibetan title.

Another Tibetan literary tradition is simply to identify a quotation by giving the author's name, and not the title of the specific work being cited. I have not attempted to track down such quotations.

Tibetan translations from Sanskrit are preserved in two different canons. One of these is known as the *Kangyur (bKa-'gyur)*, or "Translations of the Words (of Buddha)," and is constituted of a hundred and eight volumes with more than a thousand titles; the second is known as the *Tengyur (bsTan-'gyur)*, or "Translations of the Treatises (of later Sanskrit writers)." This latter category is mostly comprised of works by later Indian Buddhist authors, but also contains numerous translated texts from other Buddhist countries with a Sanskrit tradition, such as Shambala, Oddiyana, Kashmir, and so forth. Many of these are now only extant as translations in the Tibetan canon.

SECTION ONE: TEXTS QUOTED IN PART ONE

An Aspiration to Fulfill the Stages of the Glorious Kalachakra Path
dPal-dus-'khor-rim-rdzogs-smon-lam
by the First Panchen Lama, Panchen Chokyi Gyaltsen (Pan-chen-chos-kyi-rgyal-mtshan)

> Included as Chapter Nineteen of the present volume.

The Abbreviated Kalachakra Tantra
dPal-dus-'khor-bsdus-rgyud; Skt., *Kālacakralaghutantrarāja*
by Manju Yashas

> Popularly known as the *Shri Kalachakra*, this is the summary of the Kalachakra system composed by Manju Yashas, the eighth Shambala lineage holder and first in the line of kalkin masters. As the original root tantra taught by the Buddha is no longer extant, this work serves as a proxy.

A Commentary to the Kalachakra Generation Stage Yogas
dPal-dus-'khor-skyed-rim-'khrid-yig
by Dvakpo Gomchen Ngawang Drakpa (Dvag-po-sgom-chen-ngag-dbang-grags-pa)

> A popular work attributed to the "Great Meditator of Dvakpa," although held by some Tibetan scholars to be not by him but

rather by one of his numerous disciples. Therefore the Tibetan text published in India has the words "yin-par-sung-pai" after the title and before the name of the author; i.e., the text "is said to be" the work of Dvakpa Gomchen. It nonetheless is esteemed as one of the finest generation-stage commentaries.

Commentary to the Treatise on the Initiations
dBang-dor-bstan-pai-'grel-pa; Skt., *Sekoddeśatīkā*
by Acharya Naropada

Naropa's commentary to *The Treatise on the Initiations,* the only section of *The Kalachakra Root Tantra* to have survived intact, is regarded as one of the most authoritative Indian texts on the nature of the Kalachakra path.

Concerning the Kalachakra Initiation
dPal-dus-'khor'-dbang-skor-gyi-skor
by the Fourteenth Dalai Lama, Gyalwa Tenzin Gyatso (rGyal-ba-bstan-'dzin-bya-mtsho)

A translation of this work is included as Chapter Fourteen of the present volume. In it H.H. the Dalai Lama discusses the background to receiving the Kalachakra initiation.

Cultivating A Daily Meditation
by H.H. the (Fourteenth) Dalai Lama, Gyalwa Tenzin Gyatso (rGyal-ba-bstan-'dzin-brgya-mtsho)

A commentary given in the English language by the present Dalai Lama on the basics of tantric meditation, published by the Library of Tibetan Works and Archives, Dharamsala, India, 1991.

Essence of Refined Gold
Lam-rim-gser-zhun-ma
by the Third Dalai Lama, Gyalwa Sonam Gyatso (rGyal-ba-bsod-nams-brgya-mtsho)

This text, together with a contemporary commentary to it by the present Dalai Lama, is included in my study of the life and works of Gyalwa Sonam Gyatso, *Selected Works of the Dalai Lama III: Essence of Refined Gold,* Snow Lion Publications, Ithaca, N.Y., 1981. Composed in the mid-sixteenth century, Gyalwa Sonam Gyatso's treatise is regarded as one of the eight greatest Lam Rim manuals to be written in Tibet over the centuries.

The Great Commentary: A Stainless Light
'Grel-chen-tri-med-od; Skt., *Vimalaprabhā*
by Kalkin Pundarika (of Shambala)

The ninth lineage holder and second kalkin master of Shambala,

Pundarika is one of the most revered early Kalachakra adepts. His *Great Commentary,* an elucidation of Manju Yashas' *The Abbreviated Kalachakra Tantra,* is considered to be monumentally important. Dozens of commentaries to it have been written in the Tibetan language. The original Sanskrit version was discovered some years ago.

A Guide to the Bodhisattva Ways

Byang-chub-sems-pai-spyod-pa-la-'jug-pa; Skt., *Bodhisattva-caryā-avatāra*

by Acharya Shantideva

This is perhaps the greatest Mahayana scripture of classical buddhist India, and is certainly the most popular Indian work for all schools of Tibetan buddhism. More than a hundred commentaries to it exist in the Tibetan language. Several English translations of it exist, the most accurate being Stephen Batchelor's *A Guide to the Bodhisattva's Way of Life,* Library of Tibetan Works and Archives, Dharamsala, India, 1981.

A Guide to the Buddhist Tantras

rGyud-sde-rnam-gzhag

by the Thirteenth Dalai Lama, Gyalwa Tubten Gyatso (rGyal-ba-thub-bstan-brgya-mtsho)

I include a translation of this work in my study of Gyalwa Tubten Gyatso's life and teachings, *The Path of the Bodhisattva Warrior,* Snow Lion Publications, Ithaca, N.Y., 1989.

A Guide to the Structure of the Kalachakra Generation and Completion Stage Yogas

dPal-dus'khor'skyed-rdzogs-rim-gyi-sa-bcad

by Longdol Lama (kLong-rdol-blama-ngag-dbang-blo-bzang)

One of the many works of Longdol Lama, a disciple of the Seventh Dalai Lama, is his *Notes on the Lamp for the Five Stages (Rim-lnga-gsal-sgron-gyi-sa-bcad),* that contains his summary of all the important tantric systems, beginning with an analysis of the famous text by Nagarjuna entitled *A Lamp for the Five Stages,* and then treating the generation and completion stage yogas of each of the important highest yoga tantra systems. The section on Kalachakra is succinct but most insightful. Each section is titled as a separate work, though not listed as such in the catalogue of his *Collected Works.*

A Guide to the Tantric Scriptures

gSang-snags-sde-snod-ming-grangs

by Longdol Lama (kLong-rdol-blama-ngag-dbang-blo-bzang)

This work, written in verse form, provides an outline to the initiations and two tantric stages of each of the four classes of tantra.

Heart of the Enlightenment Teachings
Byang-chub-lam-gyi-nying-gu
by the Thirteenth Dalai Lama, Gyalwa Tubten Gyatso (rGyal-ba-thub-bstan-brgya-mtsho)

This work is included in the translations in my study of the life and teachings of the Great Thirteenth, *Path of the Bodhisattva Warrior*, Snow Lion Publications, Ithaca, N.Y., 1988. The text is not listed separately in the catalogue of his *Collected Works*, but rather appears in the middle of one of the sixteen "Monlam Chenmo Sungshey" (sMon-lam-chen-mo-gsung-bshad) entries in that catalogue.

The Kalachakra Root Tantra: The Primordial Buddha
dpal-dus-'khor-rtsa-rgyud-dang-poi-sangs-rgyas;   Skt.,   *Kālacakra-mūlatantrarāja-paramādibuddha-nāma*

The original tantra spoken by Buddha and transcribed by Suchandra of Shambala, this text is no longer extant, even in Tibetan translation. Only isolated passages of it have survived.

A Lamp for the Path to Enlightenment
Byang-chub-lam-sgron; Skt., *Bodhipathapradīpa*
by Atisha Dipamkara Shrijnana

Composed for the Tibetans by the Indian master Atisha in the early 1040s, this short work has provided the Tibetans with a constant inspiration over the centuries. Several English translations of it are available, the best being found in *Atisha in Tibet*, by A. Chattopadhya and Lama Chinpa, Calcutta, 1976. This latter text also contains the original Tibetan, as well as a Sanskrit reconstruction.

A Letter to a Disciple
sLob-springs; Skt., *Śiṣyalekha*
by Acharya Chandragomin

The layman Chandragomin achieved great prominence in Indian buddhist history as a poet and meditation teacher. This is his most popular text with the Tibetans. No English translation has appeared to date.

A Letter to a Friend
bShes-'phrin; Skt., *Suhṛllekha*
by Arya Nagarjuna

A Tibetan translation of the Sanskrit; several English renditions are available, though none to my knowledge even slightly approaches the beauty of the Tibetan version. Again, it is one of those Indian masterpieces that achieved a universal popularity throughout Central Asia.

Legacy of the Sun-like Masters
dPal-dus-'khor-sa-lam-mkhas-pai-nyi-od
by Lama Lobzang Tayang (bLa-ma-blo-bzang-rta-dbyang)

The Mongolian lama Lobzang Tayang is regarded as one of the foremost Kalachakra masters of Central Asia. Writing just before the close of the first half of this century, he was fascinated with the Kalachakra prophecies, and felt that many of them were on the verge of fulfillment. He identified the 'barbarians' of the Kalachakra prophecies with the communists, and saw the rise of communism as the greatest single threat to modern civilization. This view is strikingly different from that of most Kalachakra writers, who look to the Muslim world for the fanatical *la-lo* menace to world civilization.

A Lexicon of Kalachakra Terms according to the Views of Lama Tsongkhapa
rGyal-ba-tsong-kha-pa'-gzhung-dang-mthun-pa-dus-'khor-ming-grangs
by Longdol Lama (kLong-rdol-blama-ngag-dbang-blo-bzang)

Longdol Lama was an important disciple of both the Seventh Dalai Lama and the Seventh's disciple the Third Panchen Lama. His *Collected Works* contain a number of important treatises extracting the central terms and concepts of various mystical traditions; but it is his Kalachakra writings that have received the most attention from Western scholars.

Lives of the Lam Rim Teachers
Lam-rim-bla-brgyud
by Tsechokling Kachen Yeshey Gyaltsen (Tse-chog-gling-bka'-chen-ye-shes-rgyal-mtshan)

This extensive work by the Eighth Dalai Lama's guru presents concise biographies of all the major gurus in the Lam Rim transmission, beginning with the Buddha and moving down over the centuries through the various Indian lineages, and then the Kadampa and Gelukpa lineages of Tibet, to the time of Tsechokling himself. Thus it includes biographies of the early Dalai and Panchen Lamas.

A Message from Lama Norzang
bLa-ma-nor-bzang-zhal-lung
by the Buriati lama Kalzang Tenzin (bsKal-bzang-bstan-'zin)

This excellent guide to the paths and stages of the Kalachakra experience was written in 1904 by the famed Buriati lama of Mongol descent, Kalzang Tenzin. It reflects the enthusiasm held for the Kalachakra doctrines in this remote area of the eastern Soviet Union.

Mystical Verses of a Mad Dalai Lama
rGyal-ba-sku-'phreng-gnyis-pai-nyams-gur
by the Second Dalai Lama, Gyalwa Gendun Gyatso (rGyal-ba-dge-'dun-brgya-mtsho)
> The Second Dalai Lama signs most of the poems in this collection as "the mad beggar monk Gendun Gyatso." I translated the collection in 1989, although I have not yet finalized the presentation for publication. The Second Dalai Lama achieved his enlightenment by means of the Kalachakra yogas.

Notes on the Two Yogic Stages of Glorious Kalachakra
dPal-dus-kyi-'khor-lo-rim-gnyis-kyi-zin-bris
by the First Dalai Lama, Gyalwa Gendun Druppa (rGyal-ba-dge-'dun-grub-pa)
> Included as Chapter Seventeen of the present volume.

The Prerequisites of Receiving Tantric Initiation
dBang-dang-rjes-snang-sogs-blo-smin-byed-kyi-sngon-sgro
by the Seventh Dalai Lama, Gyalwa Kalzang Gyatso (rGyal-ba-bskal-bzang-brgya-mtsho)
> Included as Chapter Fifteen of this volume.

A Raft to Cross the Ocean of Indian Buddhist Thought
Grub-mtha'-brgya-mtsho'-gru-zin
by the Second Dalai Lama, Gyalwa Gendun Gyatso (rGyal-ba-dge-'dun-brgya-mtsho)
> An account of the philosophical history of buddhist India, this text is included in translation in my study of the life and works of Gyalwa Gendun Gyatso, *Selected Works of the Dalai Lama II: The Tantric Yogas of Sister Niguma*, Snow Lion Publications, Ithaca, N.Y., 1982.

The Root Tantra of Glorious Chakrasamvara
bDe-mchog-rtsa-rgyud; Skt., *Cakrasamvaramūlatantra*
> From the Tibetan translation of the Sanskrit, an original tantra spoken by the Buddha.

Selected Sayings of the Buddha
Ched-du-brjod-pa'i-tshoms; Skt., *Udānavarga*

This collection of quintessential sayings of the Buddha, transcribed in verse form, is similar to though much longer than the
Dhammapada. It has appeared in English translation under the
title *The Tibetan Dhammapada*, Gareth Sparham, Mahayana Publications, New Delhi, 1983. The translation is readable enough,
although the choice of a title is somewhat spurious.

Songs of Spiritual Change

Lam-rim-blo-sbyong-nyams-gur

by the Seventh Dalai Lama, Gyalwa Kalzang Gyatso (rGyal-ba-
bskal-bzang-brgya-mtsho)

My translation of this collection of mystical poetry by the Seventh Dalai Lama was published by Snow Lion Publications,
Ithaca, N.Y., 1981, under this same title. The Seventh is one of
the principal figures in the lineage of the Kalachakra transmission.

A Summary of the Kalachakra Tradition

dPal-dus'khor-dor-bsdus-bstan-pa

by the Thirteenth Dalai Lama, Gyalwa Tubten Gyatso (rGyal-ba-
thub-bstan-brgya-mtsho)

A translation of his guide to the Kalachakra tradition is included
as Chapter Sixteen of the present volume.

The Tantric Yogas of Sister Niguma

Ni-gu-chos-drug-rgyas-pa-khrid-yig

by the Second Dalai Lama, Gyalwa Gendun Gyatso (rGyal-ba-dgen-
'dun-brgya-mtsho)

This work forms the centerpiece of the translations in my study
of the life and works of Gyalwa Gendun Gyatso, *Selected Works
of the Dalai Lama II: Tantric Yogas of Sister Niguma*, Snow Lion
Publications, Ithaca, N.Y., 1982. It outlines the structure of the
completion stage yogas in the mainstream tantras.

Tattvasamgraha

Te-nyid-sdus-pa; Skt., *Tattvasaṃgraha*

A fundamental treatise in the yoga tantra division.

The Trilogy of the Bodhisattvas

Byang-chub-sems-dpa'i-'grel-skor-gsum

This is not one text, but three fundamental treatises read in conjunction with a Kalachakra study. The three are:

—*The Great Commentary: A Stainless Light*
 'Grel-chen-tri-med-od; Skt., *Vimalaprabhā*
—*The Vajragarbha Commentary*

rDo-rjei-snying-'grel; Skt., *Vajragarbhaṭīkā*
—*The Vajrapani Commentary*
Phyag-na-rdo-rjei-stod-pai-'grel-pa; Skt., *Vajrapāṇistotraṭīkā*

Longdol Lama's *A Lexicon of Kalachakra Terms according to the Views of Lama Tsongkhapa* (see entry of this name below) throws light on the nature of these three important works: "As for the collection known as *The Trilogy of the Bodhisattvas,* this is comprised of *The Great Commentary: A Stainless Light,* which is in twelve thousand lines [i.e., verses]; *The Vajragarbha Commentary,* which is an elucidation of the (second section of) the Hevajra Tantra known as *The Tantra of Two Forms,* explained in terms of the Kalachakra path; and *The Vajrapani Commentary,* an elucidation of the *Heruka Chakrasamvara Tantra,* also expressed in terms compatible with the Kalachakra doctrine."

The Two Yogic Stages of the Yamantaka Tantra
rDo-rje-'jigs-byed-rim-gynis-grel-ba
by Lama Lobzang Chinpa (bLa-ma-blo-bzang-spyin-pa)

This commentary to a short prayer for realization of the two yogic stages of the Yamantaka tantra by the Second Dalai Lama is included in my *Selected Works of the Dalai Lama II: The Tantric Yogas of Sister Niguma,* Snow Lion Publications, Ithaca, N.Y., 1982. There are two important lamas by the name of Lobzang Chinpa in Tibetan history: one was a guru to the Seventh Dalai Lama; the other a tutor to the Thirteenth Dalai Lama.

Treatise on the Initiations
dBang-dor-bstan-pa; Skt., *Sekoddeśa*

The only section of the *Kalachakra Root Tantra* to have survived. It exists in both the original Sanskrit, as well as in Tibetan and Mongolian translations.

Vairochana Abhisambodhi Tantra
dNgnon-byang-gyi-rgyud; Skt., *Vairocana-abhisambodhi-tantra*

A tantra in the charya classification, existing in Tibetan translation from the Sanskrit.

The Vajragarbha Commentary
rDo-rjei-snying-'grel; Skt., *Vajragarbhaṭīkā*

A Tibetan translation from the Sanskrit, this is one of the three texts constituting *The Trilogy of the Bodhisattvas.*

Vajra Shekhara Tantra
rDo-je-she-kar-gyi-rgyud; Skt., *Vajraśekharatantra*

A Tibetan translation from the Sanskrit.

The Vajra Verses
rDo-rje-tshigs-rkang; Skt., *Saddharmavajragāthānāma*

> A Tibetan translation from the Sanskrit, this is one of the fundamental Indian texts in the Chakrasamvara cycle.

The Vajrapani Commentary
Phyag-na-rdo-rjei-stod-pai-'grel-pa; Skt., *Vajrapāṇistotraṭīkā*

> A Tibetan translation from the Sanskrit, this is one of the three texts contained in *The Trilogy of the Bodhisattvas,* or three works most fundamental to a study of the Kalachakra doctrines.

SECTION TWO: TEXTS TRANSLATED IN PART TWO
Listed in the order that they appear in this volume

Prayer of the Kalachakra Path
dPal-dus-'khor-rtogs-skyes-smon-lam
by the Sixth Panchen Lama, Lobzang Tubten Chokyi Nyima (bLobzang-thub-bstan-chos-skyid-nyi-ma)

> This is one of the dozen or so Kalachakra prayers written by the Sixth Panchen Lama on the occasion of his Kalachakra initiation given near Beijing just after the first quarter of this century, and is taken from the concluding section of one of his Kalachakra guruyoga liturgies. His *Collected Works* contains more than a dozen texts on Kalachakra, either written by him or composed as transcripts of his teachings on that occasion. Amazingly, the NBC film library in New York owns some rare footage, in black and white, taken during that initiation ceremony.

Concerning the Kalachakra Initiation
dPal-dus-'khor'-dbang-skor-gyi-skor
by the Fourteenth Dalai Lama, Gyalwa Tenzin Gyatso (rGyal-ba-bstan-'dzin-bya-mtsho)

> This brief text is a revision of a work originally written by His Holiness the present Dalai Lama for his 1981 Kalachakra initiation in Madison, Wisconsin.

The Prerequisites of Receiving Tantric Initiation
dBang-dang-rjes-snang-sogs-blo-smin-byed-kyi-sngon-sgro
by the Seventh Dalai Lama, Gyalwa Kalzang Gyatso (rGyal-ba-bskal-bzang-brgya-mtsho)

> This text is commonly used today as the basis of an introductory discourse given as a preliminary to the actual initiation rite. Coincidentally, the Sixth Panchen Lama used this very manual at his

Kalachakra initiation mentioned above, and his *Collected Works* contains his restatement of it.

Summary of the Kalachakra Tradition
dPal-dus'khor-dor-bsdus-bstan-pa
by the Thirteenth Dalai Lama, Gyalwa Tubten Gyatso (rGyal-ba-thub-bstan-brgya-mtsho)

This wonderful little text is not listed separately in the Great Thirteenth's *Collected Works*. It is found as a digression in a lengthy biography that he wrote on the life of his senior tutor Jampa Gyatso (Byams-pa-brgya-mtsho). In this section of the biography, beginning on folio 279, the Great Thirteenth provides an account of the structure of the four classes of tantras, concluding with Kalachakra, and then goes on to point out that this was the tantric material mastered by his tutor and then passed on to him. However, the section makes an excellent guide to the Kalachakra system by itself, and therefore I have presented it here as such.

Notes on the Two Yogic Stages of Glorious Kalachakra
dPal-dus-kyi-'khor-lo-rim-gnyis-kyi-zin-bris
by the First Dalai Lama, Gyalwa Gendun Druppa (rGyal-ba-dge-'dun-grub-pa)

These 'notes' on the Kalachakra yogic system are contained in his standard *Collected Works* and are based on the lineage that he received from Pakpa Yonten Gyatso ('Phags-pa-yon-tan-brgya-mtsho). The text is considered to be one of the clearest of its nature in the Tibetan language.

A Kalachakra Guruyoga Method
dPal-dus-'khor-thun-drug-gi-bla-mai-rnal-'byor
by Kyabjey Kangsar Dorjey Chang (sKyabs-rje-khang-sar-rdo-rje-'chang)

This short six-session prayer was composed by the great Khangsar Dorjey Chang, one of the most esteemed Kalachakra masters of the first half of this century. Both tutors of the present Dalai Lama received their Kalachakra lineages from him. His *Collected Works* have not been published in India. I received a copy of this text at the Dalai Lama's 1976 initiation in Ladakh, where 10,000 were distributed to the audience.

The Best of Jewels: A Sadhana Focusing on Glorious Kalachakra
dPal-dus-'khor-sgrub-thabs-sdor-bsdus
by Buton Rinchen Druppa (Bu-ston-rin-chen-grub-pa)

This illustrious master was one of the most influential Kalachakra teachers of the thirteenth century. At the time the complex Kalachakra teaching is said to have been in danger of extinction; he gathered together the diverse fragments of the tradition and thus saved it from this fate. Buton's lineage spread into all sects of Tibetan Buddhism, though today is mostly practiced in the Gelukpa school.

An Aspiration to Fulfill the Stages of the Glorious Kalachakra Path
dPal-dus-'khor-rim-rdzogs-smon-lam
by the First Panchen Lama, Panchen Chokyi Gyaltsen (Pan-chen-chos-kyi-rgyal-mtshan)

> The First Panchen, the tutor of the Great Fifth Dalai Lama, widely propagated the Kalachakra lineage. He composed a number of important liturgical works related to the tradition; but of them all, this is the one to have retained the greatest popularity over the centuries.

SECTION THREE:
TEXTS QUOTED BY THE AUTHORS IN PART TWO

The Abbreviated Kalachakra Tantra
dPal-dus-'khor-bsdus-rgyud; Skt., *Kālacakralaghutantrarāja*
—by Kalkin Manju Yashas

Advice Given by Vajrapani to the Mahasiddha Karmavajra
dPal-bsang-bai-bdag-pos-grub-chen-las-kyi-rdo-rje-la-gdams-pa
—by Lama Chakna Dorjey (bLa-ma-phyag-na-rdo-rje)

The Arali Tantra
A-ra-lii-rgyud; Skt., *Āralitantrarāja*
—a fundamental tantric treatise

The Aspirational Prayer in Seventy Verses
sMon-lam-bdun-bcu-ma
—by Acharya Ashvaghosha

The Commentary to the Praise of Chakrasamvara
bDe-mchog-gi-bstod-pai-grel-pa; Skt., *Cakrasamvarastotratīkā*

A Commentary to the Treatise on the Initiations
dBang-dor-bstan-pai-grel-pa; Skt., *Sekoddeśaṭīkā*
—by Naropada

The Elimination of Suffering
Mya-ngan-bsal-ba; Skt., *Śokavinodana*

346 The Practice of Kalachakra

—from the *Jowo Chochung (Joi-bo-chos-chung)* compiled by Atisha

Expressing the Experience of Seven Youthful Maidens
gZhun-nu-ma-bdun-gyi-rtogs-par-rjod-pa
—from the *Jowo Chochung (Joi-bo-chos-chung)* compiled by Atisha

Fifty Verses on the Guru
bLa-ma-lnga-bcu-pa; Skt., *Gurupancāśikā*
—by Acharya Vira

The Four Hundred Verses
bZhi-brgya-pa; Skt., *Catuhśatakaśāstrakārikā*
—by Acharya Aryadeva

Great Exposition of the Stages on the Tantric Path
sNags-rim-chen-mo
—by Lama Tsongkhapa (bLa-ma-tsong-kha-pa)

The Gandhavyuha Sutra
sDong-po-bkod-pai-mdo; Skt. *Gandhavyūhasūtra*
—a sutra spoken by the Buddha

The Great Commentary: A Stainless Light
'Grel-chen-tri-med-od; Skt., *Vimalaprabhā*
—by Kalkin Pundarika

A Guide to the Bodhisattva Ways
Byang-chub-sems-pai-spyod-pa-la-'jug-pa; Skt., *Bodhisattvacaryā-avatāra*
—by Acharya Shantideva

The Guhyasamaja Tantra
bSang-bai-'dus-pai-rtsa-rgyud-gi-rgyal-po; Skt., *Guhyasamājatantrarāja*
—a tantra spoken by the Buddha

The Kalachakra Root Tantra: The Primordial Buddha
dpal-dus-'khor-rtsa-rgyud-dang-poi-sangs-rgyas; Skt., *Kalacakra-mūlatantrarāja-paramādibuddha-nāma*
—a original tantra spoken by the Buddha

A Letter to a Disciple
sLob-springs; Skt., *Śiṣyalekha*
—by Acharya Chandragomin

A Letter to King Kanishka
Ka-ni-kai-spring-yig; Skt., *Kaniṣkalekha*
—by Matricheta

Removing the Veils of the Mind
Sems-kyi-sgrib-sbyongs
—by Acharya Aryadeva

The Root Tantra of Glorious Chakrasamvara
bDe-mchog-rtsa-rgyud; Skt., *Tantrarāja-śrī-laghu-samvaranāma*
—an original tantra spoken by the Buddha

The Rosary of Complete Yoga
(See *The Three Rosaries*)

The Rosary of Sunbeams
(See *The Three Rosaries*)

Selected Sayings of the Buddha
Ched-du-brjod-pa'i-tshoms; Skt., *Udānavarga*
—a collection of verses spoken by the Buddha

Stages on the Enlightenment Path
Byang-chub-lam-rim
—by Lama Tsongkhapa (bLa-ma-tsong-kha-pa)

The Subsequent Tantra of Guhyasamaja
bSang-bsdus-phyi-mai-rgyud
—an original tantra spoken by the Buddha

Tantra of the Vajrapani Empowerment
Lag-na-rdo-rje-dbang-bskor-pai-rgyud; Skt., *Vajrapāni-abhiṣeka-tantra*
—an original tantra spoken by the Buddha

The Tantra of Susiddhi
Legs-sgrub-gyi-rgyud; Skt., *Susiddhitantranāma*
—an original tantra spoken by the Buddha

The Tantra of Two Forms
rTags-gnyis-gyi-rgyud; Skt., *Sambhūtatantrarāja*
—an original tantra spoken by the Buddha

The Tantra Requested by Subahu
dPung-bzang-gis-zhus-pai-rgyud; Skt., *Subāhupariprcchātantra*
—an original tantra spoken by the Buddha

The Three Rosaries
—by Acharya Abhyakaragupta. Comprised of three texts:
 The Rosary of Complete Yoga
 rDzogs-rnal-'byor-gyi-'phreng-pa; Skt., *Niṣpannayogāvalī-nāma*
 The Rosary of Sunbeams

Nyid-od-gyi-'phreng-ba
The Vajra Rosary
rDo-rje-'phreng-ba; Skt., *Vajrāvali-nāma*

A Treatise on the Root Downfalls
rTsa-ltung-rnam-gzhag
—by Lama Tsongkhapa (bLa-ma-tsong-kha-pa)

The Treatise on the Initiations
dBang-dor-bstan-pa; Skt., *Sekoddeśa*
—an original tantra spoken by the Buddha

Treatise on Severing the Connections
'Brel-pa-gcod-pa

The Trilogy of the Bodhisattvas
(See entry in Section One above)

The Vajra Rosary
(See *The Three Rosaries*)

The Vajra Rosary of Initiation Rites
dKyil-chog-rdo-rjei-phreng-ba; Skt., *Vajrāvalīnāmamamandalopāyikā*
—by Acharya Abhyakaragupta

The Vajra Rosary Tantra
rGyud-rdo-rjei-preng-ba; Skt., *Vajramālātantra*
—an original tantra spoken by the Buddha

The Vajra Song
rDo-rje-gur; Skt., *Vajrapañjaratantrarāja*
—an original tantra spoken by the Buddha

The Vajragarbha Commentary
rDo-rjei-snying-'grel; Skt., *Vajragarbhaṭīkā*
—by Bodhisattva Vajragarbha

The Vajrapani Commentary
Phyag-na-rdo-rjei-stod-pai-'grel-pa; Skt., *Vajrapānistotratīkā*
—by Bodhisattva Vajrapani